ACCESS GUIDES TO YOUTH MINISTRY

Early Adolescent Ministry

Edited by
John Roberto

New Rochelle, NY

Access Guides to Youth Ministry: Early Adolescent Ministry is published as a service for adults who love the young and want to share the Gospel with them.

It is a guide to understanding the young and a resource book for helping them. As such, it is addressed to parents, parish youth ministers, clergy who work with the young, and teachers.

Forthcoming *Access Guides*:
Spirituality
Leadership

Prepared in conjunction with
The Center for Youth Ministry Development

Access Guides to Youth Ministry: Early Adolescent Ministry

475 North Ave., P. O. Box T, New Rochelle, NY 10802

Library of Congress Cataloging-in-Publication Data
Early Adolescent Ministry / edited by John Roberto.
p. cm. — (Access guides to youth ministry)
Includes bibliographical references.
1. Early Adolescence 2. Youth—Religious life.
I. Roberto, John. II. Title: Early Adolescent Ministry. III. Series.

ISBN 0-89944-207-2 $14.95

Printed in the United States of America

09/91 9 8 7 6 5 4 3 2 1

Table of Contents

PART ONE
FOUNDATIONAL UNDERSTANDINGS

PART TWO
PRACTICAL APPROACHES

Typist: Alicia Carey

PREFACE TO THE ACCESS GUIDES

A NEW CONCEPT

Welcome to the *Access Guides to Youth Ministry* series. The Center for Youth Ministry Development and Don Bosco Multimedia have created the *Access Guides* series to provide leaders in ministry with youth with both the foundational understandings and the practical tools they need to create youth ministry programming for each component outlined in *A Vision of Youth Ministry*. *Access Guides* have been developed for pop culture, evangelization, liturgy & worship, justice and retreats. Upcoming *Access Guides* will address leadership, family life, prayer, and spirituality. Each of the *Access Guides* provides foundational essays, processes for developing that particular component of youth ministry, and approaches and program models to use in your setting. The blend of theory and practice makes each of the *Access Guides* a unique resource in youth ministry. To help you understand the context of the *Access Guides* series, we would like to provide you with a brief overview of the goals and components of a comprehensive approach to ministry with youth.

A RENEWED MINISTRY

Over a decade ago, Catholic youth ministry engaged in a process of self-reflection and analysis that resulted in a re-visioning of youth ministry — establishing the goals, principles, and components of a comprehensive, contemporary ministry with youth. *A Vision of Youth Ministry* outlined this comprehensive approach to ministry with youth and became the foundation for a national vision of Catholic youth ministry. In the years since the publishing of *A Vision of Youth Ministry*, Catholic youth ministry across the United States has experienced tremendous growth.

From the outset, the *Vision* paper made clear its ecclesial focus: "As one among many ministries of the Church, youth ministry must be understood in terms of the mission and ministry of the whole Church" (*Vision* 3). The focus is clearly ministerial. "The Church's mission is threefold: to proclaim the good news of salvation, offer itself as a group of people transformed by the Spirit into a community of faith, hope, and love; and to bring God's justice and love to others through service in its individual, social, and political dimensions" (*Vision* 3). This threefold mission formed the basis of the framework or components of youth ministry: Word (evangelization and catechesis), worship, community, justice and service, guidance and healing, enablement, and advocacy.

This threefold mission also gives youth ministry a dual focus. Youth ministry is a ministry within the community of faith — ministering to believing youth *and* to the wider society — reaching out to serve youth in our society. While the experience of the past decade has emphasized ministry *within* the community, youth ministry must also address the social situation and needs of all youth in society. A comprehensive approach demands a balance between ministry *within* the Christian community and ministry *by* the Christian community *to* young people within our society and world.

The *Vision* paper described a broad concept of ministry with youth using four dimensions. Youth ministry is...

To youth — responding to youth's varied needs;

With youth — working with adults to fulfill their common responsibility for the Church's mission;

By youth — exercising their own ministry to others: peers, community, world;

For youth — interpreting the needs of youth, especially in areas of injustice and acting on behalf of or with youth for a change in the systems which create injustice.

Two goals were initially developed for the Church's ministry with youth:

Goal #1: Youth ministry works to the total personal and spiritual growth of each young person.

Goal #2: Youth ministry seeks to draw young people to responsible participation in the life, mission, and work of the faith community. (*Vision* 7)

The first goal emphasizes *becoming* — focusing on the *personal* dimension of human existence. Our understanding of the unique life tasks and social-cultural context of adolescence provides directions for fostering their growth in discipleship and Catholic identity. The second goal emphasizes *belonging* — focusing on the *interpersonal* or *communal* dimension of human existence. Active engagement of youth in the Christian community's life and mission provides an important context for growth and overcomes the danger of marginalizing youth in the Church, segregating them from the real centers of power, responsibility, and commitment in community life.

In light of the Church's priority upon justice and peace, the mission of the Church to transform society (*The Challenge of Peace* and *Economic Justice for All*), and the need to engage in a critical assessment of our culture and society, it is necessary to add a third goal to the two goals from 1976. This third goal emphasizes *transforming* — focusing on the public or *social structural* dimension of human existence. This third goal could be framed in the following manner:

Goal #3: Youth ministry empowers young people to transform the world as disciples of Jesus Christ by living and working for justice and peace.

This third goal seeks to help young people realize that living and working for justice and peace is grounded in the Gospel and Catholic social vision and is essential for being a Christian. Youth ministry needs to empower young people with the knowledge and skills to transform the unjust structures of society (locally and globally) so that these structures promote justice, respect human dignity, promote human rights, and build peace.

An underdeveloped, but increasingly important section of the *Vision* paper is the context of youth ministry. "In all places, youth ministry occurs within a given social, cultural, and religious context which shapes the specific form of the ministry" (*Vision* 10). This contextual approach seeks to view young people as part of a number of social systems which impact on their growth, values, and faith, rather than as isolated individuals. Among these systems are the family, society, the dominant culture, youth culture, ethnic culture, school, and local church community. In the last several years, youth ministry has become much more aware of the impact of these systems.

A COMPREHENSIVE APPROACH

The framework (or components) describes distinct aspects for developing a comprehensive, integrated ministry with youth. Briefly, these components include:

Evangelization — reaching out to young people who are uninvolved in the life of the community and inviting them into a relationship with Jesus and the Christian community. Evangelization involves proclaiming the Good News of Jesus through programs and relationships.

Catechesis — promoting a young person's growth in Christian faith through the kind of teaching and learning that emphasizes understanding, reflection, and transformation. This is accomplished through systematic, planned, and intentional programming (curriculum). (See *The Challenge of Adolescent Catechesis*).

Prayer and Worship — assisting young people in deepening their relationship with Jesus through the development of a personal prayer life; and providing a variety of prayer and worship experiences with youth to deepen and celebrate their relationship with Jesus in a caring Christian community; involving young people in the sacramental life of the Church.

Community Life — building Christian community with youth through programs and relationships which promote openness, trust, valuing the person, cooperation, honesty, taking responsibility, and willingness to serve; creating a climate where young people can grow and share their struggles, questions, and joys with other youth and adults; helping young people feel like a valued part of the Church.

Guidance and Healing — providing youth with sources of support and counsel as they face personal problems and pressures (for example, family problems, peer pressure, substance abuse, suicide) and decide on careers and important life decisions; providing appropriate support and guidance for youth during times of stress and crisis; helping young people deal with the problems they face and the pressures people place on them; developing a better understanding of their parents and learning how to communicate with them.

Justice, Peace, and Service — guiding young people in developing a Christian social consciousness and a commitment to a life of justice and peace through educational programs and service/action involvement; infusing the concepts of justice and peace into all youth ministry relationships and programming.

Enablement — developing, supporting, and utilizing the leadership abilities and personal gifts of youth and adults in youth ministry, empowering youth for ministry with their peers; developing a leadership team to organize and coordinate the ministry with youth.

Advocacy — interpreting the needs of youth: personal, family, and social especially in areas of injustices towards or oppression of youth, and acting with or on behalf of youth for a change in the systems which create injustice; giving young people a voice and empowering them to address the social problems that they face.

This is the vision and scope that the *Access Guides* series seeks to promote through foundational understandings and practical, pastoral approaches. We, at the Center, hope that this series will empower you with the knowledge and skills to become more effective in your ministry with youth.

WORKS CITED

The Challenge of Adolescent Catechesis. Washington DC: NFCYM Publications, 1986.

A Vision of Youth Ministry. Washington DC: USCC, Department of Education, 1976.

ABOUT THE AUTHORS

Mary Lee Becker is working as a consultant in youth ministry and as a Center for Youth Ministry Development adjunct staff member. She has served as a parish coordinator of early adolescent ministry in Seattle and is co-author of *On the Move: Activities for a Year of Early Adolescent Ministry* (DBM).

Bruce Baumgarten is Consultant for Adolescent Catechesis in the Archdiocese of Louisville and an adjunct staff member in early adolescent ministry for the Center for Youth Ministry Development. He is co-author of *On the Move: Activities for a Year of Early Adolescent Ministry* (DBM).

Joanne Cahoon is Consultant for Adolescent Catechesis and Early Adolescent Ministry for the Archdiocese of Baltimore and an adjunct faculty member and specialist in early adolescent ministry for the Center for Youth Ministry Development. She is co-author of *On the Move: Activities for a Year of Early Adolescent Ministry* (DBM).

John Hill was Professor and Chairman, Department of Psychology, Virginia Commonwealth University. He was a pioneer in research on early adolescents, authoring numerous studies and publications

Francis A.J. Ianni is Professor of Education at Teacher's College, Columbia University, and is the director of the Institute of Social Analysis. He is a board-certified psychoanalyst and a consultant in medical psychology at St. Luke's Hospital in New York City. He is author of *The Search for Structure — A Report on American Youth Today.*

Leif Kehrwald is Director of Family Ministry for the Archdiocese of Portland. He has served on several national projects to enhance the quality of family life, and chaired a task force on Family Perspective Implementation sponsored by the National Association of Catholic Diocesan Family Life Ministers. He is the author of *Caring That Enables: A Project for Developing Parish Family Ministry* (Paulist Press) and co-author of *Families and Youth* (DBM).

John Nelson teaches in Fordham University's Graduate School of Religion and Religious Education. He heads its concentration "Adolescent Religious Development." Recently, he wrote Network Paper #35, *Sexuality and Adolescents: Models and Questions*. For the past 20 years, Jack and his wife Cathy have been authoring and editing textbooks for early and middle adolescents. They live in the Bronx, NY with their early-adolescent daughter Meg.

David Ng is Professor of Christian Education at San Francisco Theological Seminary. He has been involved with youth ministry for much of his career, doing many workshops on confirmation, multicultural youth ministry, and leadership development. He has authored *Youth in the Community of Disciples*, *Developing Leaders in Youth Ministry*, and written many articles.

Brian Reynolds is currently the Director of Agency Planning for the Archdiocese of Louisville. He is the co-founder of the Center for Youth Ministry Development where he worked from 1978 to August 1990. He has authored *A Chance to Serve* and co-authored *Leadership for Youth Ministry*. He has given workshops and institutes on early adolescent ministry across the United State and Canada, and has served as a consultant to numerous dioceses in the area of early adolescent ministry.

G. Wade Rowatt is the Associate Dean of the School of Theology and Professor of Psychology of Religion at The Southern Baptist Theological Seminary in Louisville, Kentucky. He is the author of *Pastoral Care with Adolescents in Crisis* (Westminster Press), *Ministry with Youth and Their Parents* (Convention Press), and with Mary Jo Rowatt of *A Two Career Marriage* (Westminister Press).

John Roberto is Director and co-founder of the Center for Youth Ministry Development. He is the managing editor of the CYMD-Don Bosco Multimedia publishing project, and has served as editor for several *Access Guides to Youth Ministry*, including ones on *Evangelization*, *Liturgy and Worship*, *Justice*, and for *Growing in Faith: A Catholic Families Sourcebook*.

ACKNOWLEDGEMENTS

"Early Adolescent Development" by John Hill first appeared as *Understanding Early Adolescence: A Framework* (1980) by John Hill. Used by permission of the Center for Early Adolescence.

"The Social Context of Early Adolescent Development" by the Carnegie Council on Adolescent Development is excerpted from *Turning Points* by the Carnegie Council on Adolescent Development (1989). Used by permission of the Carnegie Council on Adolescent Development.

"Providing a Structure for Adolescent Development" by Francis A.J. Ianni is reprinted from *Phi Delta Kappan*, volume 70, number 9 (May 1989). Used by permission.

Part One

Overview

UNDERSTANDING EARLY ADOLESCENCE

This *Access Guide* explores the critical years from 10/11 to 14/15 known as early adolescence. Over the past 20 years there has been a growing concern about early adolescents, witnessed by the amount of research on early adolescents and by the new approaches and programming being developed for early adolescents. This *Access Guide* seeks to make available to you the best research on early adolescent development combined with practical approaches that will help you re-think your current ministry and discover new strategies for better responding to the needs of early adolescents.

In this book, we look at early adolescence from a multidisciplinary perspective — a perspective that draws on a variety of disciplines. Each provides a view of early adolescence that helps, in its own way, to further our understanding of this period of the life cycle. We will examine the fundamental changes of early adolescence, the contexts of early adolescence (family, peer, community), and the psychosocial and faith development of early adolescence. The challenge in Part One is to find ways in which to integrate contributions from different disciplines into a coherent and comprehensive viewpoint on the nature of early adolescent development in contemporary society that can assist us in ministry.

John Hill offers the introductory essay in Part One by developing a framework which integrates the primary changes, secondary changes, and settings of early adolescence. In Chapter 2, **John Nelson** explores the process of faith development in early adolescence by drawing upon social research, developmental theory, psychology, and his years of experience in teaching early adolescents. In Chapter 3, excerpts from *Turning Points — Preparing American Youth for the 21st Century* by the **Carnegie Council on Adolescent Development** provide an overview of the social forces at work in our society and the impact they are having on early adolescent development. In Chapter 4, **Francis A. J. Ianni** uses the results of his 10 year research project to suggest ways in which communities can provide the structure for healthy adolescent development.

John Roberto concludes Part One by offering specific directions for ministry with early adolescents grounded in the research foundation of the preceding essays.

Chapter 1

Early Adolescent Development

John Hill

The following is an excerpt from John P. Hill's Understanding Early Adolescence: A Framework *which is considered a "classic," and with good reason. Hill was a seminal thinker in the emerging field of early adolescence, influencing policymakers and practitioners alike from the early 1970s until his death in 1988. The literature of the field today is dominated by scholars and youthworkers whose understanding of young adolescents was profoundly shaped by John Hill. Written in 1980,* Understanding Early Adolescence: A Framework *retains an accuracy, relevance, and vitality that is rare in either acedemic or popular writing about young people.It remains an eloquent expression of the core principles that the Center for Early Adolescence believes all those who care for young adolescents need to understand.*

Center for Early Adolescence

The purpose of this essay is threefold: to define the classic issues of adolescent development further; to summarize briefly and selectively what we do and do not know about development in adolescence; and, most important, to put the issues in a framework that helps make sense out of adolescence as a whole. The framework should help connect bits and pieces of information about adolescence — whether from what you read or from what you experience yourself — with a broader view of that period. The framework is intended to be a map of what is known and what might be known. It is not the only possible map nor will it continue to be useful forever. As our knowledge grows, our understanding of key issues and their relative importance may well change. But the map already has been a guide to many different groups of practitioners in in-service training sessions; as a means of organizing adolescent development courses for graduate and undergraduate students; in the organization of review papers for policymakers, practitioners, and scientists on what we know and what we need to know about adolescence. The map is most likely to be helpful if you consult it often, considering it a tool that will become familiar through frequent use — as you probably once approached road maps.

I will first present an overview of the framework as a whole. In order to establish the framework, I will then define and clarify six psychosocial issues in adolescent development: attachment, autonomy, intimacy, sexuality, achievement, and identity. I call these issues the *secondary changes of early adolescence.* Next, the *primary changes of early adolescence* — biological change, changes in reasoning, and changes in social definition — and their connections with secondary changes will be discussed. I will then describe the relationship between the primary and secondary changes and the adolescent's position in the family, the peer group, and the school. After considering selected issues dealing with adolescents in families, peers, and schools, I shall return, in conclusion, to a discussion of the framework itself and how it can be used.

THE FRAMEWORK OF EARLY ADOLESCENCE

The framework I am working with is offered graphically in Figure 1 (p.7). The figure highlights the primary and secondary changes we will be considering. Thus, in early adolescence the primary changes play the major role in bringing about the secondary changes. Biological changes raise new issues for autonomy, achievement, identity, and the like. And so do changes in thinking ability. However, the impact of the primary changes on these psychosocial issues does not occur in a vacuum. It occurs in family, peer, school, community, media, church — and, for some, work-settings. The variations in how the issues are resolved stem not only from individuals' past histories but also from their current social relationships. The others who are important in adolescents' lives — whom they encounter in family, peer, school, and community settings — react to the primary changes with modified expectations and norms. Puberty, for example, does not directly dictate the initiation of sexual activity. How others respond to puberty is critical in determining who becomes sexually active. Changes in self-concept do not emerge only from looking at one's changing body in the mirror; they emerge also because of the reactions of parents and peers to the bodily changes. (Stating it in another way, Glen Elder has observed that adolescents do not experience society and its values directly but as it is presented to them through their actual social participations in familial, peer, school, and other settings.)

Look at Figure 1 and consider the arrows in the diagram of the framework. In this presentation of the framework the arrows are placed so that they emphasize the impact of primary changes upon the others who are important in family, peer, and school settings and the consequences of these impacts for secondary changes in psychosocial development. The direction of the arrows is a matter of emphasis rather than an absolute statement of the direction of effects. Events in families, peer groups, and schools can influence the primary changes. Nutrition and health care (generally delivered through the family) can influence the timing of the onset of puberty, for example. Some experiences in school might influence the appearance of formal operational skills or the realms in which they are displayed. Similarly, changes in identity or intimacy with peers clearly affect the roles young adolescents play in family, peer, and school settings. And we might add an arrow between primary changes and secondary changes suggesting the direct influence of biological change, for example, upon sexuality or identity.

The direction and placement of the arrows in Figure 1 are designed to emphasize two points. First, the most important effects of the primary changes appear to occur through the reactions of others rather than independent of them. Second, the figure illustrates the nature of early adolescence and the transition from childhood. The primary changes appear to raise the new issues in the development of identity, achievement, sexuality, intimacy, autonomy, and attachment. Once these secondary changes begin to occur, the interplay between them and the roles people play in families, peer groups, and schools might better be represented by arrows running in both directions. And, finally, when it comes to the transition from adolescence to adulthood, the framework would need considerable revision, perhaps emphasizing the primary nature of the movement into new work and family roles and the impact of these for secondary change in psychosocial characteristics.

The framework can be related to early adolescence in many ways. First, it may be used to assess your own knowledge of the period. What two or three things can you say about biological change? About cognitive change? About changes in reasoning? How does each affect the family? Peer relations? Schools? Boys? Girls? Do Hispanic and white families handle change differently? Does social class make a difference? What is the role of family relations in bringing about changes in sexuality? In achievement? In identity?

Second, the framework can be used in assessing the problems or the adjustment of a given adolescent. Where is the person in the pubertal cycle of growth? Is there evidence of formal operations? How have others important to the adolescent's environment responded to these changes? What has been the result in relation to the emergence of sexual activity? To the adolescent's conception of self? To disengagement from parents? Or, working backwards, if the person lacks the ability to initiate the follow-through with confidence, why? How are others in the family responding to the primary changes? Have their expectations been modified so that they give more responsibility?

Third, the framework can be used in thinking through the implications of a program of prevention or intervention. Is the program responsive to individual differences in biological and cognitive status? Does the program depend, intentionally or not, upon what goes on in family, peer, or school settings? What is the program supposed to accomplish in relation to the various areas of psychosocial development? If one area, such as self-esteem, is the target, what are the implications for other areas? Is the setting chosen for intervention — family, peer group, or school — the most appropriate, given what we know about the targeted area of psychosocial development?

The framework can be used flexibly to deal with these matters and others — reviewing research literature and evaluation reports, organizing in-service training or educational programs, designing evaluation research. In each case, it is particularly important to bear in mind a fourth set of categories not presented formally in the diagram of the framework: the gender, the social class, and the ethnic background of the adolescent of group of adolescents in question. In most cases, the framework must be used separately for boys and girls. It is also important to remember that, although we lack good information about possible ethnic differences and social class variations, these may be critical to the resolution of psychosocial issues. We might want to use the framework to generate comparative questions. Do the families of middle-class black girls react different to biological change than the families of lower-class black girls? If so, what are the implications for disengagement? For sexuality and intimacy?

Do frameworks such as the one advanced here put too much emphasis on analyzing individual aspects of behavioral development and not enough on the adolescent as a whole? In most matters, the issues of behavioral development have to be separated if the whole is to be understood. For example, the psychosocial aspects of development are integrated differently for boys than for girls. In addition, few of us apprehend a young adolescent as a whole. We see the young person from the perspective of our school, our practice, our family, or our research project. A framework of adolescent development can contribute to our broader perception of the individual as well as the age group by focusing not only upon psychosocial issues but also upon the primary changes and the important people and settings that modify their impact. Only in this broader context can we hope to achieve the sensitivity and understanding we need to work effectively with adolescents.

FIGURE 1
The Framework for Understanding Early Adolescence

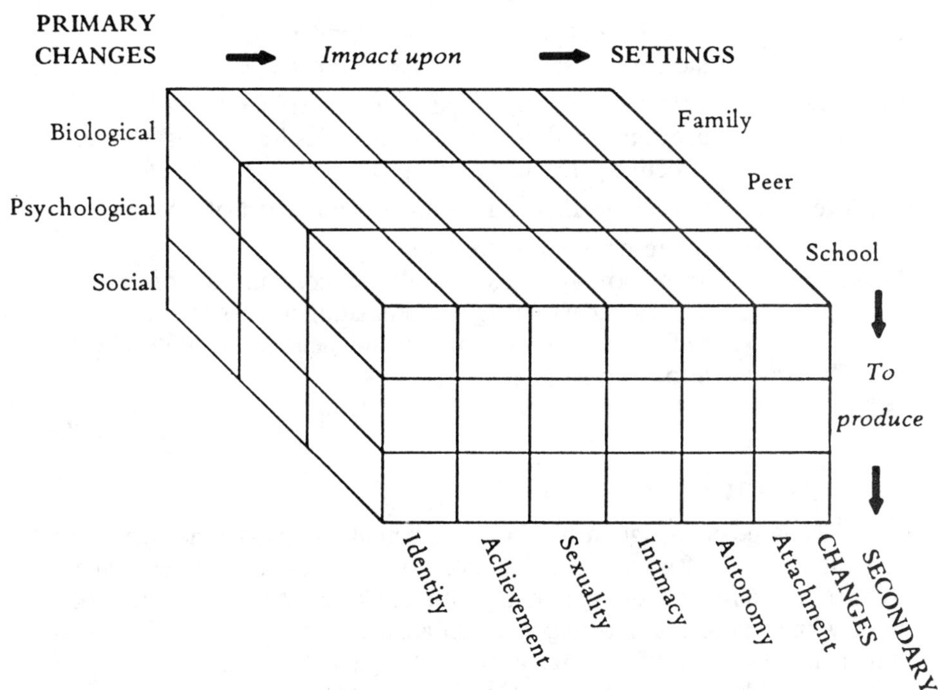

PART I: SECONDARY CHANGES OF EARLY ADOLESCENCE

To understand the significance of the biological, psychological, and social phenomena of early adolescence, the reader must be familiar with the secondary issues that arise from these primary changes. In Table 1, a brief definition of each of the psychological issues is presented.

Table 1
Psychosocial Issues in Adolescent Development

Issue	Adolescent Change
Attachment	Transforming childhood social bonds to parents to acceptable bonds between parents and their adult children.
Autonomy	Extending self-initiated activity and confidence in it to wider behavioral realms.
Sexuality	Transforming social roles and gender identity to incorporate sexual activity with others.
Intimacy	Transforming acquaintanceships into friendships; deepening and broadening capacities for self-disclosure, affective perspective-taking, altruism.
Achievement	Focusing industry and ambition into channels that are future-oriented and realistic.
Identity	Transforming images of self to accommodate primary and secondary change; coordinating images to attain a self-theory that incorporates uniqueness and continuity through time.

ATTACHMENT

The issue of change in attachment to parents is raised in its clearest form in the work of Anna Freud. Her point of view has been and continues to be reflected in the training of many different kinds of professionals who work with adolescents. The major task of adolescence, from the psychoanalytic point of view, is "disengagement," a change in the passionate attachments of children to their parents. Children are said to see their parents as all-providing and all-powerful. These fantasies of parental omnipotence and unending support and the child's intense feelings of love and anger towards parents must be modified. Perceptions must become more realistic and passions less heated if the child eventually is to form satisfactory heterosexual relationships with peers. In order for the ties of childhood to be loosened, the early adolescent must and (according to the analysts) generally does relive them in order to disengage. From this point of view, many of the phenomena of early adolescence are to be understood in terms of regression, a reworking of those powerful young-child-like feelings, fantasies, thoughts, and ideas, positive and negative, that one has about one's parents.

Consider the young adolescent's room, full of posters of pop stars or sports figures. The posters may represent idealized versions of the positive attributes children attach to parents. When the adolescent has mature investments in other people, the posters come down. As Peter Blos interprets this experience, the posters are removed when the adolescent is able to deal with real people as they are, rather than assuming that others are all-powerful, all-loving, or all-knowing like Mommy or Daddy. That so many adolescents are preoccupied for long periods of time with ideals and abstractions — of fidelity, of beauty, of equality, and the like — the analysts suggest is also a temporary refuge, a way of working through the idealistic and idolizing perceptions children have about their parents. The analysts also suggest that rebelliousness is normal during adolescence; it too is a way of bringing about disengagement. They say that storm and stress in the individual adolescent and in the adolescent's family are to be expected.

Despite the widespread acceptance of psychoanalytic theory and watered-down versions of it, few researchers have actually studied changes in attachment during early adolescence. It seems obvious from informal observation that some kind of disengagement does occur. There are noticeable changes in the expression of affection, for example. The hugs, pats, and kisses that were all right before seem less acceptable now. (Perhaps this occurs because of the emerging sexual maturity of the adolescent and the new sexual meaning that such behaviors begin to take on — even with parents.) However, we do not know enough to describe the process or its outcomes very well. What we do know from existing research is that there is not as much storm and stress involved in disengagement from parents in typical families as some psychoanalysts would lead us to believe. In middle-class families at least, many young people continue to report strong affection and respect for parents throughout the second decade of life. Even as they become more and more oriented to the world of peers and attached to others their own age, younger and older adolescents maintain strong ties to their parents. Continued integration into the world of peers is not associated with a breakdown in the parent-child relationship.

AUTONOMY

From the point of view of psychoanalytical theorists, changes in autonomy are akin to changes in attachment. Increased emotional independence from parents (disengagement) is seen as a precondition for increased behavioral independence (autonomy). Other scholars have speculated that it is increased self-reliance, initiative, and responsibility for follow-through on the adolescent's part that makes emotional independence possible. No matter how research resolves this question, it is important not to muddle disengagement and autonomy into one mix. They have to be separated conceptually so that their relationship can be studied rather than assumed.

There is a widespread impression that autonomy is a brand new issue at adolescence. Considerable empirical evidence suggests that independence training for children begins far earlier, especially in middle-class families. Parents typically expect and value increasing signs of independence with increasing age, beginning about when the child first becomes able to tie his own shoes, if not before. Behavioral independence is neither as new nor as hot an issue in typical families at early adolescence as is commonly assumed. For these reasons, the autonomy issue for young adolescents is described in Table 1 in terms of extending self-initiated activity and confidence to wider behavioral realms. Handling an increased allowance, meeting family obligations on time without being told, caring responsibly for younger brothers and sisters, remembering one's own track shoes or the day the garbage gets picked up, being expected to make one's own judgments about whether or when to take a drink — all these are examples of new choices or initiatives that may be expected, demanded, and made.

Psychoanalytic formulations have led to the assumption that rebelliousness is a natural part of the process of disengagement, implying that autonomy is produced through rebelliousness. The available data suggest quite another picture. Not only do most parents increase their demands for independence during early adolescence, but those adolescents who feel and are most independent report the most positive relationships with parents. Autonomy in adolescence, however measured, is more related to respect for parents and continued affection for them than to rebellious and oppositional behavior.

Traditionally, autonomous behavior has been more important for males than for females in our society. Thus, theories based upon rebelliousness as a means of attaining autonomy seem to be based upon clinical and field studies of boys rather than girls. Autonomy has rarely been studied longitudinally, following the same young people over a long period of time. As a result, we know relatively little about the pattern of changes in autonomy during the transition from childhood to adolescence and during adolescence itself. We do know that on a great many indices that are presumed to measure autonomy at any given point during this period, boys appear to be more autonomous than girls. And the role of autonomy in the overall personality organization of boys appears to be more central during early adolescence than it is for girls. As Elizabeth Douvan and Joseph Adelson have interpreted their data:

> For the boy....the integrated capacity for erotic ties and the solution of the identity challenge demand separation and autonomy. What the girl achieves through intimate connection with others, the boy must manage by disconnecting, by separating himself and asserting his right to be distinct.... (Douvan and Adelson 348)

SEXUALITY

Prior to Freud, sexuality was viewed as a phenomenon beginning at puberty. For Freud, however, puberty merely brought about a new phase in the development of sexual motivation. After a lengthy period of latency following early childhood, sexuality emerged *again* as an important issue defined at puberty as a matter of changing the objects of sexual expression from parents to peers. More recent views differ. Harry Stack Sullivan discounted the Freudian view of infantile sexuality. He regarded the manipulation of the genitals and "sex play" in childhood as manifestations of curiosity which were not fundamentally sexual in nature at all. More recently, William Simon and John Gagnon have argued that for the vast majority of young people, "movement into sexual experience which the actor defines and accepts as such begins with the passage into adolescence." (Simon and Gagnon 741) This is not to say that continuities are absent; rather, adolescent and adult sexuality *are* influenced by earlier developments that are not usefully thought of as *sexual*. The child learns some information (and frequently misinformation) about sex. The child certainly is exposed to and comes to internalize a set of values about bodies and physical attractiveness. Most importantly, the child learns what are called *sex roles*. (Since little if any of the content of childhood sex roles has to do with reproductive behavior — "sex" in a narrow sense — and since the word "role" is not properly used in this expression either, the term *gender identity* is preferred.) From this point of view, the psychosocial issue in adolescence has to do with the transformation of gender identity and social roles to include sexual activity. We know relatively little about the course of initiation into sexual activity with others, having found it easier to study the frequency of sexual behaviors rather than the processes by means of which adolescents typically become sexually active.

Simon and Gagnon and others have pointed out that childhood and early adolescent socialization provide an interpersonal competence for girls that is not provided for boys. The onset of sexual activity for girls involves incorporating it into social roles and identity wherein capacities for tenderness, self-disclosure, and intimacy are already present. For the boy, on the other hand, the pathway to mature heterosexual behavior is far more likely to involve sexuality first and, only secondarily, the capacity for loving relationships.

Females appear to be socialized in precisely that area for which males during adolescence are least trained and for which they are least expected to display a capacity — intense, emotion-laden relationships and the rhetoric of romantic love. When sexual arousal is reported by females during this period, it is more often reported as a response to affectional than to erotic stimuli. Girls' first intense sexual experiences appear to occur in the context of dating; those of boys appear to occur when they are alone. For both boys and girls, sexual behavior comes to be incorporated into gender identity during adolescence, but the experiences each brings are quite different: "Dating and courtship may well be considered processes in which persons train members of the opposite sex in the meaning and content of their respective commitments." (Simon and Gagnon 46)

INTIMACY

Friendships between children are common from early childhood forward. After puberty, they come to include members of the opposite sex and to be integrated with sexual activity. They also are transformed, at least among girls, to include mutual disclosure of personal experiences, feelings and attitudes, and advanced levels of empathy. The research of Elizabeth Douvan and Joseph Adelson has been especially informative in our understanding of these changes. Before puberty, young girls' friendships focus on common shared activities, on "doing things" with another person. After the physical and sexual changes are brought about by puberty and the growth spurt, friendships become more emotion-laden and involve the mutual sharing of secrets — about boys, about dating experiences, and about sex. Girls develop the skills that make later intimate relationships possible by mutual sharing and mutual resolution with other girls of initially anxiety-arousing experiences. In later adolescence, friendships appear to be less emotional, less an instrument for the reduction of anxiety, and more an equitable sharing of individual personalities, talents, and interests. The skills learned in the middle period can be transferred to relationships with males.

Boys are less likely to form intimate relationships with one another than are girls. As for the youngest groups of girls, friendship for boys through adolescence involves a tie to a congenial companion with whom one shares common activities. More often than for girls, boys' friendships tend to occur in the context of cliques and gangs which — rather than providing socialization for one-to-one intimate relationships — provide validation of and support for the autonomy that is so highly valued for males in our society.

ACHIEVEMENT

Studies of the development of vocational choice have suggested that it is not until the beginning of the second decade of life that vocational choices come to be characterized by young people's taking into account their own personal characteristics (interests, abilities, and interpersonal styles) in relation to jobs. Thus, in early adolescence, vocational choices start to become more "realistic"; that is, more and more they reflect a process of matching personal characteristics to what are thought to be the characteristics of jobs. Similarly, adolescents now have a concept of a personal future that they did not have as children. This makes it possible for them to link up their present achievements and their evaluations of those achievements with their future possible achievements in ways that were not possible for them in childhood. This new realism and their newfound ability to imagine a future must be considered in relation to the fact that, increasingly, choices made have more far-reaching consequences. For example, the girl who opts out of science and mathematics as early as possible in secondary school is closing doors that may prove difficult to reopen. Gender identity is very much linked to future ambitions.

After reviewing what is known about the socialization of achievement orientation in girls, Aletha Stein and Margaret Bailey concluded that the childrearing practices that lead to the development of feminine gender identity often are antagonistic to those that lead to achievement-oriented behavior. Moderate levels of affection and control, encouragement of individual autonomy, and high standards for accomplishment lead to a variety of achievement-oriented behaviors for *both* boys and girls. (Among such behaviors are attribution of successes and failures to the self instead of to "luck" or to others; intrinsic satisfaction from doing better on a given task; approach to, rather than avoidance of, situations where competence is to be evaluated; persistence at a task instead of withdrawal in the face of frustration, temporary setback, or failure; and high educational and vocational aspirations.) However, in the conventional socialization of girls, encouragement of and support for competence in interpersonal situations often takes the place of socialization for achievement.

There is some evidence for the notion that differential socialization by gender may be accelerated during early adolescence. Gender differences in performance on mathematics and verbal abilities tests do not emerge until adolescence. Girls also begin to opt out of "boys' subjects" in school and may even begin to underachieve in relation to their ability, apparently reacting to the common norm that "good girls get good grades" but "not too good." As Judith Bardwick and Elizabeth Douvan have put it, "[S]ome time in adolescence the message becomes clear that one had better not do too well, that competition is aggressive and unfeminine, that deviation threatens the heterosexual relationship." (Bardwick and Douvan 152)

IDENTITY

Few formulations of adolescence are as widely known as that of Erik Erikson. According to Erikson, identity formation becomes the central issue in adolescence because bodily change and new social roles demand new conceptions of self, not only from the young adolescent, but from others as well. This "identity crisis" can be resolved only through new identification with peers and with leader figures outside the family. Erikson says that identity includes a conscious sense of uniqueness, an unconscious striving for a continuity of experience, and solidarity with a group's ideals. The continuity builds two bridges: between what the person has come to be prior to adolescence (largely through partial identifications with parents) and what the person promises to become as an adult; and between what one conceives one's self to be and what others see and expect. A new sense of self is achieved neither by denying one's past nor by ignoring one's current social relationships. Adolescents' social relations influence the process of identity formation because it takes others to confirm their new biological and social status and because their attempts to try out new ways of behaving require feedback. The peer group is the primary arena used by adolescents to test new identities. Early adolescent romances, Erikson notes, may have less to do with sex than with using a close relationship to "try on" new behaviors and obtain feedback about how they "fit." "Am I really this way?" "Does she think I'm faking it or is it really me?"

Some adolescents do not take advantage of the opportunities that the peer group provides for self-exploration and feedback. They slip into conventional social pockets with their accompanying ready-made identities. Superjock, brain, and prom queen roles are good examples. Erikson refers to this as *identity foreclosure*. Some adolescents come to define themselves almost totally in terms of what parents are not and value least. The daughter of the fundamentalist minister expounds free love. The son of the liberal politician asserts his newfound preference for espionage as a career. This kind of *negative identity* appears to occur among adolescents who live in conflict-filled family settings. The adolescents involved seem not to realize that by defining themselves exclusively in terms of what parents are not, they remain just as tied to them as if their identities were based on what their parents are or profess to be. No real exploration of the self is involved.

Erikson claims that identity, as its optimum, is experienced as a sense of well-being. People feel at home with themselves, have a sense of knowing where they are going, and are confident that those who matter will recognize them as they are and as they hope to be. Changes in self-concept and in the integration of various images of self during early adolescence have been studied very little. Research on self-esteem comes closest to getting at what Erikson calls a sense of well-being. Morris Rosenberg's comprehensive research shows that adolescents with low self-esteem suffer from anxiety and have dismal interpersonal relationships.

According to Rosenberg, low self-esteem is associated with internal distress for several reasons. The strain of "putting on a front" produces anxiety. Persons with low self-esteem have a less stable fix on who they are. They lack a consistent frame of reference to which they can relate their experience of self and others. This too is anxiety provoking. Persons of low self-esteem are lonely and vulnerable. They are apt to be sensitive to criticism; to be bothered if others have a poor opinion of them; to be disturbed if they do poorly at some task; to be upset when they become aware of some fault or inadequacy; and often are described by others as touchy and easily hurt.

Rosenberg also allows that persons with low self-regard are awkward with others; they assume that others do not like them; they have little faith in human nature; and they are submissive, non-assertive, and not respected by or popular with others. They rarely participate in extracurricular activities, class discussions, and informal conversations.

Adolescents low in self-esteem are locked in a circular trap. Their isolation from others precludes the development of a more positive view of self, and their anxiety and vulnerability preclude entry into social interactions that might help. The interdependence of attitudes toward self and others so much featured in Erikson's theory is well-illustrated by Rosenberg's work and by the work of others whose findings Rosenberg has confirmed and extended.

THE SECONDARY CHANGES REVISITED

None of the six issues that have been discussed above is an issue only during adolescence. Each has a history and a future in the life cycle. For example, autonomy typically becomes an issue for children and families when children begin to walk and talk. It will be an issue again, for many children, when decisions may have to be made about the care of aging parents. The strong attachments of young children to their parents are modified not only during adolescence but later on, too, as career and lifestyle changes may mean geographical, social, or psychological separation. What is of particular interest at adolescence is not attachment but certain changes in attachment; not the presence of self-concepts but changes in their organization; not sexuality but changes in its expression. Another look at Table 1 from this perspective is helpful. Note that the emphasis is upon changes in the issues rather than upon absolute definitions of the issues themselves.

Why this particular emphasis on change? Primarily because we are accustomed to thinking about adolescence as the sore thumb of developmental periods, sticking out, hurting, somehow dramatically different from the others. While there *are* changes in adolescence, the sore-thumb view is far from accurate. The typical changes of adolescence tend to be gradual, building on what is already there and preparing the young person for the next period in life. The continuities between childhood and adolescence and between adolescence and adulthood are more impressive than the discontinuities.

Having said that there are important changes in adolescence and that they are typically not so dramatic or discontinuous as most people seem to think, let us consider how the changes come about. What causes us to make the transition from childhood to adolescence? The answers seem to lie in another set of changes, even more fundamental than the secondary changes already mentioned. These other, *primary* changes, are of three kinds — biological, psychological, and social.

PART II: THE PRIMARY CHANGES OF EARLY ADOLESCENCE

BIOLOGICAL CHANGE — THE ADVENT OF PUBERTY

The first half of the second decade of life brings with it a major transformation of the body and its functions. Outwardly the child before us begins to assume the bodily proportions and the physical characteristics of an adult. Height, for example, begins to increase at a faster rate than in childhood (see Figures 2 and 3), the rate of growth peaking for girls at about age 12; for boys, peaking at age 14, on the average. Facial features and body shape change markedly. Pubic and axilliary (underarm) hair appears; facial hair begins to sprout for boys. Female breast development begins. Males' shoulders become wide, as do females' hips. Voices deepen, although more so for boys than for girls. Strength and stamina increase, leading to an increased capacity for both work and play. The reproductive organs begin to change as well. It is not our purpose here to describe the course of these changes in detail but to comment upon their significance for behavioral development, especially of the secondary changes mentioned in Part I.

Figure 2: The Sequence of Development in Boys

Characteristic	Age Range
Growth of testes and scrotum begins	10 - 13 1/2
Pubic hair appears	10 - 15
Growth spurt starts	10 1/2 - 16
Growth of penis begins	11 - 14 1/2
Change in voice begins	11 - 14 1/2
Growth of penis and testes complete	12 1/2 - 17
Facial and underarm hair appear	12 - 17

Figure 3: The Sequence of Development in Girls

Characteristic	Age Range
Breast development begins	8 - 13
Pubic hair appears	11 - 14
Growth spurt starts	9 1/2 - 14 1/2
Menstruation begins	10 - 16 1/2
Underarm hair appears	13 - 16
Breast development complete	13 - 18

Among the most important — and most often ignored — characteristics of puberty are normal but immense variations from individual to individual in the time of its onset, its duration, and its termination. In boys, for example (see Figure 2), the pubertal sequence may begin between 10 and 13 1/2 years with an acceleration of growth in the testes and scrotum. If this sequence is considered to terminate at the time of the first ejaculation, the average age at termination is 13 1/2 to 14. However, ejaculation may also occur much earlier or later depending upon when the process began. Among the remarkable normal variations is that, given two boys of the same chronological age, one may complete the sequence before the other has begun it. Similarly, in girls (see Figure 3) the first menstrual period, or *menarche*, may occur at 10 or may not occur until about 16 1/2.

As physical characteristics change and events associated with reproductive maturity begin to occur, peers, parents, and other people important to the adolescent begin to form new assumptions about the young person. They make new inferences about overall maturity, interests, and attitudes;

and about the desirability of the person as a friend, as someone possibly no longer deserving of "little kid" treatment, as someone who might be a possible sexual partner, or as someone who can no longer be kissed or cuddled at bedtime. Given the variation in the timing of biological change, this means that adolescents of the same chronological age but of differing biological age may be living in environments with quite different social expectations. Thus, especially during the junior high school years, there is a wider range of individual differences in both biological and psychosocial characteristics than before or after.

Attachment. According to the psychoanalytic accounts of changes in attachments to parents, puberty is very much implicated in the disengagement process. It is puberty that is presumed to reawaken infantile ties to parents. While there is little empirical data bearing on this issue outside of therapeutic situations, common observation suggests a number of changes in outward shows of affection between parents and their early adolescent children. Shortly after puberty, kissing and cuddling of sons and daughters are perceived differently. Who may comfortably lie in the same bed watching television together changes. Long-existing affectional behaviors appear to acquire new connotations that were nonexistent prior to pubertal onset.

Autonomy. Physically mature adolescent children are likely to be seen as more "responsible" than their less physically mature age-mates. More initiative and follow-through in work and play are likely to be expected of those who resemble adults than of those who do not. Early-maturing boys, for example, more often occupy positions of leadership in the peer culture. On the other hand, late maturers, perhaps owing to their being on the outside so often in adolescence, as adults appear to be less conventional, more likely to engage in exploration, and less often to react to stress in rigid ways.

Sexuality. At one level, the linkage of puberty and sexuality seems so obvious as to require little comment. Sexual maturation should mean "increased sex drive." However, as Clellan Ford and Frank Beach have documented, "sexual" activity with others of both sexes is common before puberty. William Simon and John Gagnon have argued that genital activities cannot be understood as *sexual* until past puberty. Adult-like meanings are not attached to genital activities until around or after puberty. Empirically, as noted above, we know relatively little about the processes of initiation of adolescent sexual activity.

Intimacy. We have labelled certain modifications in interpersonal skills and behaviors in adolescence as changes in intimacy. The role of biological change in bringing about the new interpersonal characteristics is uncertain. We do know that much of the content of early attempts at intimacy, at least between girls, concerns dating and sex.

Achievement. We have already noted that gender differences in achievement test scores do not emerge until early adolescence. Some argue that such differences are genetically determined and are genetically linked to puberty. On the other hand, some researchers claim that signs of impending biological maturity lead the people who are important to adolescents to treat them differently by expecting and rewarding more conventional gender role behavior than before. Thus, girls may more often be expected to perform tasks well but not *too* well and especially not in "boys'" subjects. Both points of view implicate pubertal events in achievement behavior; however, we lack definite knowledge.

Identity. Erikson has argued that the onset of puberty is a major determinant of an adolescent identity crisis. While a dramatic crisis does not have to occur, it appears inevitable that the adolescent's concept of self will change to incorporate both the new physical characteristics that appear in the mirror from day to day and the new expectations that these changes arouse in others. Again, studies of early- *versus* late-maturers provide the best data we have in this regard. The former tend to think more highly of themselves than do the latter. On the other hand, early-maturing boys conform particularly well in personality and social characteristics to what Erikson labels *identity foreclosure*. Because their early maturity brings them substantial social reward, they are less likely to explore what they might be. Not surprisingly, they turn out to be more conventional as adults too.

PSYCHOLOGICAL CHANGE — THE ADVENT OF FORMAL OPERATIONS

The conception of possibilities outside the immediate environment is the central "new" feature of adolescent thinking. It is the feature that best distinguishes the kind of thinking found in adolescents from that encountered in younger children. Adolescents go beyond the information given in a situation to think about what might be true. They reason by taking what is possible as well as what is actually given as a point of departure for their thought processes. Other words for "possibility" are "hypothesis," "principle," or even "ideal." Adolescents are able to reason about physical and social events in terms of the unobserved and the unobservable. They can for the first time reason about justice, for example, and get quite worked up emotionally about other ideals, too. They are also able to come up with possibilities in a systematic way.

Children given four plastic chips of different colors and asked to put them together in as many different ways as possible, for example, manage at best to combine only two of the pieces of plastic together at a time. Beyond this, they seem bewildered and do not move ahead in any systematic way. Adolescents, on the other hand, come up with a system of ordered combinations (Elkind 142):

(1) None	(2) Red (R)	(6) RG	(12) RGB	(16) RGBY 8
	(3) Green (G)	(7) RB	(13) RGY	
	(4) Blue (B)	(8) RY	(14) RBY	
	(5) Yellow (Y)	(9) GB	(15) GBY	
			(10) GY	
			(11) BY	

Adolescents are not only able to come up with all of the possibilities, they think of more complex combinations as possibilities. And, increasingly with age, they produce the combinations systematically.

To summarize, then, adolescents can reason on the basis of possibilities instead of being restricted to what they are experiencing or have experienced in the past. And they can generate possibilities exhaustively and, gradually, in a systematic way. To do this requires a monitoring of one's own mental activities. And this ability to think about one's own thought, or *reflective thinking*, also emerges in adolescence. In the social realm, this same ability is reflected, for example, in describing a friend to a third party. The adolescent, unlike the child, is able to take into account the possible inferences the third party might make and to shape his description accordingly: "He is shy — but not anxious." "She is proud of her accomplishment — but not a show-off."

The study of the distinctive features of adolescent thinking has been most influenced by the work of Jean Piaget and his colleague, Barbel Inhelder. While much research remains to be done, the description of adolescent thinking presented by Piaget and Inhelder seems to have held up (although the logical model that Piaget believes underlies the apparent changes in reasoning recently has been challenged). Piaget refers to the mental activities of adolescents as "formal operations" in contrast to the "concrete operations" of children.

In early adolescence, there is little question that young people continue to improve their performance in the tasks that call upon concrete operations. They gradually also come to be able to reason in the more formal ways described above. Formal operations are not found at all in some non-Western societies. In Western societies, they are rarely found in much more than two-thirds of the population at any age beyond 13 or 14. Given present knowledge, it is difficult to say whether environmental influences preclude their development in some societies or whether we lack appropriate ways of probing for their presence. We have a lot to learn about formal operations, but their power to change the individual's concepts of himself and his world at adolescence is impressive.

Attachment and Autonomy. How might formal operational skills play a role in disengaging children from infantile parental ties and in expanding autonomy? Formal operational skills permit adolescents to "read" other people, including parents, in more differentiated and complex ways. They can compare their family situations to notions of what they might be. They can apply principles and ideals to their own behavior and that of their parents. They now have the cognitive equipment to think about family issues and situations independent of their own immersion in them. They are in a better position to understand rules as embodiments of principles. This new skill can be irritating to parents when young adolescents point to inconsistencies between the adults' stated principles and their behavior. With formal operational skills, adolescents are able to consider their own needs and wants, those of their parents, and those of their peers simultaneously. This equips them to manage their social interactions more than one or two moves ahead. Thus, they can be both more persuasive ("If I say this, she'll say that and that'll be the end of it; so I'd better try it another way") and more effective in managing the impressions of themselves that they create in others. While they do not always use their new abilities to reason about family situations — and often are not expected to — during adolescence young people come to appreciate social situations as adults do.

Intimacy and Sexuality. As described by theorists like Sullivan and Erikson, the more mature forms of intimacy and their integration with sexuality seem to require formal-operational interpersonal skills. Taking the self and an intimate's point of view into account in relation to some principle such as fidelity, honesty, or openness, requires the sophisticated thinking skills involved in simultaneously considering multiple perspectives on a given issue. Advanced reasoning skills need not always lead to positive interpersonal outcomes, however. Impressions can be managed to create relationships not based upon the kind of emotional empathy and caring that the notion of intimacy carries. Although we imply that the effects of changes in reasoning on "ideal" psychosocial development are "good," it is important to bear in mind that new cognitive skills can be used in the service of defense, distortion, and isolation, too.

Achievement. Because adolescents can think effectively about what is *possible* rather than being tied in their reasoning to what *is*, they have a personal future in a sense that younger children do not. The consequences of present achievements for future accomplishments are better appreciated.

Because they have more differentiated and better organized views of themselves, their personalities, abilities, and possibilities for future achievement, they are in a better position to consider the match between their interests and abilities and vocational requirements. Indeed, the matching that characterizes adolescents' career choices appears to require formal-operational skills.

Identity. Identity has to do with concepts of self and putting together these concepts into a stable picture of self. Owing to their new cognitive skills during early adolescence, young people come to have both more differentiated and more integrated self-concepts. Pre-adolescent children's impressions of self (and others) are like beads strung on a string. The elements of the description emerge, one by one, without much attention to how they fit together, to underlying qualities, or to the impression that the total might create in others. Adolescents, on the other hand, organize impressions so that the elements are not just strung together but are integrated through the use of qualifying terms, distinctions between real and apparent qualities, and a new ability to put together what may seem to be inconsistent or contradictory. Adolescents' descriptions also become increasingly *psychological*, focusing upon internal states, intentions, and traits instead of upon physical appearance and outward behavior alone.

Formal operations not only are reflected in these more organized self-concepts but also are critical to the very process of identity formation. As Erikson has defined it, the process requires simultaneous reflection on the observed behavior of both self and others. The process requires taking a number of perspectives into account simultaneously, a feat possible only when formal-operational skills are in place. "The individual judges himself in light of what he perceives to be the way in which others judge him in comparison to themselves and to a typology significant to them." (Erikson 22) And, at the same time, "...he judges their way of judging him in the light of how he perceives himself in comparison to them and to types that have become relevant to him." (Erikson 22) Judgments of self are dependent upon others' judgments of us and upon the framework we use for making judgements. But we also have to consider at another level the quality of the other persons' judgments and, Erikson is saying, we can do that only in relation to our own self-perceptions and the framework we use to make such judgments. Thus, formal operations contribute to the origins of the "identity crisis" in early adolescence because there is now a future into which one can extend one's self and because the self is now much more differentiated. And, in later adolescence, formal operations are essential to the resolution of the crisis because this requires multiple perspective-taking of the complex sort described above.

CHANGES IN SOCIAL DEFINITION

In their studies of the transition from childhood to adolescence and from adolescence to adulthood in non-industrial societies, anthropologists have brought to our attention the special set of circumstances that exists when there is universal agreement within a society about the norms for the behavior of a given age group. In such societies, the norms for what constitutes acceptable social behavior may change dramatically at or around puberty. There is not only consensus among the older generation about what the behavior of the younger group should be but support from peers during the transition as well. Important public rituals, *rites of passage*, may well make the transition from one period to another in such societies.

Implications for the Secondary Changes. In societies of the sort described, appropriate relations between adolescents and elders after puberty are likely to be highly specified. Permissible ways of showing affection may be carefully limited. Spheres in which autonomy may be exercised are clearly prescribed, if present. (It has been argued that autonomy as we understand it in more complex societies does not exist at all in non-industrial societies.) Whether such societies are more permissive or as restrictive as our own in relation to the norms that regulate intimacy and sexuality, the norms are likely to be clearly specified and more universal in application. In addition, few choices of vocation are available. Since "work" roles often are not separate from family roles, and since the family status into which one is born constrains what one will do, the need to match individual, personal characteristics to myriad "work" opportunities does not often arise. Identity is specified: one can be a man or a woman in one way, or only a few ways.

In American society, there is no such fundamental change in social definition. Minimal ages for leaving school, for adopting work roles, for serving in the military, for driving a car, or for getting married, often mean sudden and formal redefinitions of rights and obligations for individuals. However, our society does not invest these ages with universal meaning. Neither do they all occur at the same time, nor do they apply to so many realms of behavior that a socially-shared new identity is defined for individuals. It is to the absence of such consensus and role definition in complex industrial societies that problem behavior in adolescence is often attributed. Young adolescents face diversity of expectations regarding present conduct and a variety of future adult role possibilities. While there appears to be increasing age segregation in industrial societies — reflected, in adolescence, by the fact that secondary education is becoming increasingly universal — there is not a clearly defined, *responsible* role for youth. Indeed, adolescence is more likely to be seen as a period of preparation for life than as a form of life itself.

THE PRIMARY CHANGES REVISITED

In what ways are biological, psychological, and social changes *primary*? First, there is the matter of timing. The primary changes occur before the secondary changes. Second, there is the matter of causality. The assertion is that puberty and formal operations (and universal change in social definition, when it occurs) play a major role in bringing about the secondary changes. Third, there is universality in the form the biological and cognitive changes take. Primary changes are more similar from society to society than are secondary changes. While the primary changes must inevitably lead to some secondary change, what that change is will vary from society to society.

PART III: THE SETTINGS OF EARLY ADOLESCENCE

How the psychosocial issues of adolescence are resolved depends upon the sociocultural context. Consider the business of modifying attachments to parents, for example. In their studies of working-class people in East London, Michael Young and Peter Willmott noted that children, even after marriage, were expected to spend time with their parents on a weekly basis. In contrast, Herbert Gans, in his study of an Italian-American working-class neighborhood in Boston, described normative adult social relations in terms of continuing contact not nearly so much with parents as with siblings and cousins. While some disengagement always occurs, the form it is likely to take during adolescence must reflect social norms for the behavior of adult children toward their parents. Given the sources of our theories about adolescence and the populations scientists have studied, there is real danger in identifying white, middle-class, male outcomes as "normal" and "healthy."

Through considering the various values, norms, and expectations to which the adolescent is subject by virtue of the roles played in the family, with peers, and in school, the Framework of Adolescence in Figure 1 (p.7) permits sociocultural variations in outcomes to be taken into account. The intent of this discussion is to highlight the framework and not to summarize everything important that could be said about family, peer, and school roles during early adolescence.

FAMILY ROLES

The view that adolescence is by nature a stormy and stressful period, combined with the widespread talk of a generation gap that began in the late 1960s, mistakenly colors many people's views of family interaction and parental influence on children during early adolescence. Large-scale surveys of representative samples of families with adolescents in the

United States and other industrialized societies have shown, and continue to show, that adolescence is a satisfying and pacific period in three-fourths of families, or even more. There is much evidence counter to the storm-and-stress perspective of family relations. Studies where family interaction is directly observed suggest that there may be a period of temporary disequilibrium in early adolescence while the family adjusts to having a "new person" in the household — "new" in stature, "new" in approaching reproductive capability, "new" in cognitive competence — but this disequilibrium in no way approaches the shoot-out that many parents are led to expect from media reports. Instead, in most families, there appears to be a period of adaptation to the primary changes, a period when both parents and their newly adolescent children work out — often not consciously — what these changes mean for their relationships.

Little as we know about the details of this period of adaptation, in normal families that have been studied (intact families from non-delinquent, non-clinical populations) family relations appear to become more equal. Children not only are the recipients of affection and support from parents; they begin to initiate such behaviors. Nurturance comes, for the first time, to be mutual. Similarly, early adolescent males (females have not been studied as often) become more assertive in interactions with parents. They more often suggest sources of action on their own. They interrupt family dialogues not only more often but more successfully (in the sense that parents are more likely to yield to their interruptions and to listen to what they have to say). Young adolescents' opinions are more frequently reflected in final family decisions than was the case prior to puberty. It is in delinquent or otherwise deviant populations of adolescents and their families (e.g., runaway and youth abuse situations) that such changes do not seem to occur. In these families interaction does not become more equal whether we speak of supportiveness or assertiveness in exchanges with parents. Delinquent adolescents initiate less; there is less reciprocity. Our present knowledge, then, suggests that families with deviant adolescents have not been able to adjust — for whatever reasons — to the new persons in their households. Instead, as James Alexander has suggested, they develop hostility around their old patterns of interaction. Put in terms of the framework, the question for practitioners and researchers alike is how families manage the transition from childhood to adolescence, how they recognize the primary changes, how they deal with them, and what implications this has for the issues of secondary change.

We know more about parental influence on some aspects of secondary change than we do about alterations in family interaction. During early and later adolescence, parents continue to exercise sizeable influences on their children's educational and vocational aspirations. While we may only speculate that many parents respond to puberty by expecting more achievement from sons and less from daughters than before, its is clear from existing data that throughout adolescence, parental aspirations for achievement continue to play a major role in determining adolescents' goals. The aspirations of friends come to be important, too, but parental standards and encouragement continue to be influential. In addition, parental child-rearing practices continue to influence adolescents' autonomous behavior. Both authoritarian and permissive parental practices foster excessive peer conformity, lack of self confidence, and rebelliousness, driving the child out of the family and making the child more vulnerable to negative peer group influences. Most families manage to avoid these extreme parenting styles in early adolescence; they provide a secure base for young adolescents' continued movement into the world of peers. The idea that peers replace parents as agents of influence during adolescence is probably best put to rest. Rather, positive family relations before and during early adolescence lead to social competence and confidence that enable the young adolescent to be competent and confident in relationships with peers.

PEERS

I have commented often on the studies of early and late maturation that show persistent effects into late adolescence and adulthood of variations in the early or late onset of puberty and the growth spurt. Many of these effects — greater self esteem, greater social participation in the informal and formal social situations in adulthood, later initiation into the subsequent lower rates of sexual activity — depend upon the response of peers to the timing of growth, illustrating once again that the primary changes do not occur in a social vacuum. Peers respond differently to the observed biological change—or lack thereof—in early and late maturers. They view early maturers as more often having the traits they associate with prestige in the peer group (as Margaret Faust found). Early-maturing males are better equipped for athletic competition, and their peers reward athletic participation with social acceptance. Early maturers are more likely to occupy leadership positions in school-related activities. The social rewards for early-maturing males are so substantial that they may preclude self-exploration. Harvey Peskin found some support for this position in his adult-follow-up study of early and late maturers. The early maturers were more conventional in personality, life-style, and occupational achievement. The late maturers tended to be more flexible psychologically, to be able to handle ambiguous situations better, to have a greater sense of humor, and to have less conventional lifestyles and careers. There can be little doubt that how peers respond to biological change has a major impact on the implications of that change for psychosocial development and its secondary changes.

Even more important, good peer relations may well be indispensable to normal social development. We know that across the life span in general, social isolation—not being plugged into a social network — is associated with all forms of social and psychological pathology, from individual delinquency and problem drinking to child abuse and depressive disorders. Adolescent "social isolates," those youngsters who are neither accepted by their peers nor rejected by them, who are "out of the picture," are especially vulnerable as later adolescents and as adults to a plethora of problem behaviors. Why does this happen? Because they are out of the picture, they miss out on a lot of socialization that probably can occur only in the peer group. Willard Hartup has pointed to the control of sexual and aggressive impulses as strong examples of this phenomenon.

While the child may learn some (though not much) sexual information in the family, and while the child may learn some aspects of spousal relations through observation of his parents in the home, incest taboos preclude sexual exploration in the family. Thus, many learned sexual behaviors must come through experiences with peers. In considering aggression, Hartup argues that one can learn more about the consequences of striking out or holding back with others of roughly the same size and strength than one can in the family — where both the lopsided power structure and differences in physical stature make it difficult to explore the expression of aggression. Similarly, we have already noted that the new interpersonal assertiveness and autonomy of the early adolescent male in the family may reflect behaviors initially shaped in the peer group and then imported into the family. In other words, family members may respond less to the child's new physical and sexual stature than to changes in behavior that reflect peers' responses to biological change. From what we know about the development of intimacy in girls, it appears that interpersonal trust and capacities for self-disclosure are more likely to be molded in peer sharing than in familial interaction, since parents rarely disclose their intimate concerns to children.

In the absence of a universal social definition of adolescence, American communities find themselves in disagreement about the proper age for experimenting with "adult" prerogatives — sex, smoking, and drinking, for example. Such experimentation eventually does occur for most young people, however, more often in peer than in family contexts. In this connection, it is often forgotten that the peers learn a lot about control of impulses, as well as about their expression, from their peers. Admired older peers may well be important positive models for their younger peers, rather than leading them down those garden paths that adults fear their younger adolescents will tred too early.

SCHOOLS

The opening of junior high schools in their time, and now of middle schools, has been justified on grounds of the primary changes of early adolescence. The growth spurt and the onset of puberty were used as arguments for the removal of seventh- and eighth-graders from elementary schools. And, given that the age of pubertal onset has decreased over the past decades, the same rationale is appearing for the creation of middle schools that place sixth-, and sometimes fifth-graders, in separate buildings with seventh- and eighth-graders. Individual differences in the onset, duration, and termination of the pubertal growth cycle often are cited as the foundation for decisions about what grade levels belong together. Yet outcomes of such change in school arrangements have been little studied and the processes that might account for such change even less so.

Studies illustrate two different, but compatible, ways of thinking about the effects of schools. First, one may think that schools have impact on social development because school arrangements generate patterns of peer association that persist inside and outside of school. The effect on self esteem reported by Simmons and Blyth probably occurs not because of anything different in teaching and learning situations in the two kinds of schools but rather because different patterns of informal peer association are generated by the two systems. In the junior high school, informal peer networks may be more likely to contain older students than in the elementary school structure. To cite another example, tracking arrangements within schools may break up patterns of neighborhood peer association. New peer associates from outside the neighborhood, owing to their different expectations and the example they provide, may change the socialization of the child in and out of school.

The second way of considering the effects of schools lies in the examination of what happens in more formal teaching and learning situations. What are the effects of "time on task" on work habits in situations outside school? Do teacher styles and disciplinary practices affect moral reasoning and moral judgments? How can formal operational capabilities be recognized in classrooms where not all children have reached the level of formal operations? Schools may influence adolescent development, then, through the roles young adolescents play in peer groups associated with schools or through student roles played in teaching and learning situations.

WORKS CITED

Bardwick, Judith, and Elizabeth Douvan. "Ambivalence: The Socialization of Women." *Woman in Sexist Society: Studies in Power and Powerlessness*. Ed. V. Gornick and B.K. Moran. New York: Basic Books, 1971.

Douvan, Elizabeth, and Joseph Adelson. *The Adolescent Experience*. New York: John Wiley & Sons, 1966.

Elkind, David. "Cognitive Development in Adolescence." *Understanding Adolescence: Current Developments in Adolescent Psychology*. Ed. J.F. Adams. Boston: Allyn & Bacon, 1968.

Erikson, Erik. *Identity: Youth and Crisis*. New York: Norton, 1968.

Simon, William, and John Gagnon, "On Psychosexual Development," *Handbook of Socialization Theory and Research*. Ed. David A. Goslin. Chicago: Rand McNally, 1969.

Chapter 2

Faith Development in Early Adolescence

John S. Nelson

"What questions and concerns bring you here?" asks the director of a workshop on adolescents at a religious education institute. From among the more than 100 taking part in the workshop, at least 20 hands go up. Some have at-risk worries: drugs, sexual experimentation, lessened communication in family, parish, and school. Others speak of local faith-community concerns: fewer adolescents worshiping, failing youth programs, a drifting apart of youth from the expressions of faith of their parents. Several ask how-to questions: how to re-start a program which has been dropped, how to learn from others who are having some success, how to win back young people for whom celebrations, such as confirmation, seem to be rites of termination more than of initiation.

This chapter cannot answer all those practical questions from that workshop. It hopes, however, it can gather together some underlying data on faith and religion among early adolescents which can help in the discussion and perhaps point toward solutions.

With regard to faith and religion, early adolescents present a very mixed picture. They differ from group to group. They differ from one another within a group. They differ even within themselves as unique individuals. This complexity raises sets of questions about early adolescents such as these:

What is faith for early adolescents? How do they image the God in whom they believe? How important for them is religion?

From where does their religious belief and practice derive? How do they receive it? How can they share it?

How do we respect their personal freedom when we present the faith of their community? How do we respect the faith of their community when we encourage them to reflect on it critically?

How do we know where they are with regard to faith and religion? What is the value of the data which we do have?

What programs for early adolescents work? Why? How best can a faith-community go about organizing a youth program?

To answer these questions we have multiple sources. Some overlap, but we can divide them into the following categories:

1. Our own experience of adolescents in general and of early adolescents in particular as parents, as teachers, as youth ministers—and as one-time adolescents. Such experiential or anecdotal data (sometimes called soft data) have their value, especially when we reflect upon them critically.

2. Empirical studies done by social scientists (sometimes called hard data). Such studies may be treating all adolescents or they may be limited to early adolescents. Since young people change so much as they move through adolescence, it is wise to filter out what applies especially to early adolescents.

3. Stages or patterns of faith as explicated by developmental psychologists. Such data rely upon interpreting a large number of in-depth interviews which include their share of early adolescents.

4. Insights from a psychoanalytic point of view derived from the clinical experience of trained specialists.

From all these sources, hopefully, we can sketch a rough composite picture of faith and religion among early adolescents. Even with all these sources, however, we have to keep reminding ourselves that our data are limited and that people differ and are complex beyond easy summary.

FAITH, YES; RELIGION, MAYBE

A study concerned exclusively with young adolescents and their parents summarizes faith and religion for the adolescents in this way:

> The majority of young adolescents report that religion is "the most important" or "one of the most important" influences in their lives.
> Boys attach less importance to religion than do girls.
> Young adolescents are more likely to experience religion as liberating than as restricting.
> Boys are more likely than girls to experience religion as restricting.
> Most young adolescents believe that religion has both *vertical* (focus on God) and *horizontal* (focus on acts of love and justice) responsibilities. (*Young Adolescents and Their Parents* 154)

This summary can be clarified by distinguishing between two closely related realities, faith and religion. The distinction can be heard in what one 13 year old girl said in a national survey on adolescents:

> I don't think you have to go to church to find God. My parents try and make me go by saying God wants you to go. I think it's just the same praying at home as praying in church. He doesn't care where you do it. I don't think I'll be as strong for religion as my parents, but I still feel towards God as they do. (Norman and Harris 266)

In brief, "faith" is a person's response to the transcendent (whom we usually call "God") present and active in one's life. "Religion" refers more to how a person articulates this response in such observable ways as a creed of beliefs, as formalized prayer and worship, and as a recognizable way of living. Faith is more internal and personal. Religion tends to be more external and communal. Thus in the study of young adolescents and their parents, on the topic "What's Important in Life," to the item "God at center of my life" 66% of seventh-graders responded "want very much" or "at the top of my list." To the item "to be part of a church," 55% gave similar positive responses. (*Young Adolescents and Their Parents* 136) The young people in this study were for the most part church-related youth. If they had been more a cross section of the nation's early adolescents, the distance between God and church would probably have been greater.

EXPERIENCE OF GOD

Since 1987, Boys Town in Nebraska has been surveying the at-risk youth who come to their facilities. This survey occurs before the youth take part in the Boys Town religious education programs and thus its results do not represent answers learned at Boys Town. In the category of "religiosity" the survey indicates in part:

> All youth experience God most often in troubled times, alone in quiet, in church, and with family.
> Youth reported that words that best describe God are Loving, Mysterious, Patient, Gentle, and Comforting.
> Most youth are satisfied with their prayer life.
> Girls report more interest than boys in religious growth.
> Black youth report more interest than white youth in religious growth.
> Girls experienced God more than boys when in nature, and with special friends (63%).
> Boys report experiencing God more than girls when "on the streets" (61%).
> Black youth reported experiencing God more than white youth "on the streets."
> White youth reported experiencing God more than black youth "in nature" (63%/49%).
> 11% of all youth reported never experiencing God.
> 80% of new-arrived youth agreed that "God loves me as I am."
> (Carotta and Oswalt 1)

These findings support data from other studies in some important ways; they also introduce something new.

First, adolescents tend to find God (or God finds them) more in their own present experience than in their faith community's tradition. More than a quarter of a century ago Pierre Babin called this "naturation." (Babin 24-35) It seems to be true for adolescents of all ages and all backgrounds. It means that in ministering with adolescents, we should be especially alert to their personal experience for God's active presence. It does not mean that we abandon the tradition of the faith community. Rather we need to take special pains to uncover the ways in which the historical categories of the community's story correspond to the more immediate categories of the adolescent's experience, such as God as Abba or parent, Jesus as friend, the Church as supporting community, the sacraments as life, strength, nourishment, Christian morality as a positive way of life, etc.

Second, adolescents tend to image God more as warm and close than as cold and distant. The same patterns surfaced in the study *Young Catholics of the United States and Canada*, which surveyed persons aged 15 to 29. In theological language, God is for the adolescent more immanent than transcendent. This is important not only for the faith-life of the individual, but also for the loyalty and sense of affiliation to the faith community. As the *Young Catholics* study highlighted its findings:

> "Warm" images of God, Jesus, and Mary are typical of persons within a church community. "Cold" images characterize the feelings of those persons who are estranged from the church.
>
> The more that the church is seen as "mother"—warm, welcoming, comforting, affectionally strong—the more those who have left the church will want to return. (Fee, Greeley, McCready, Sullivan 31, 69)

Third, there is something new in these Boys Town findings: the differences between boys and girls and between black youth and white youth in their experiencing of God. It long has been known that adolescents find God in nature and in friendship. What is new is that this is true for girls more than for boys and for white youth more than for black youth. What is new is the experience of God "on the streets" as characteristic for boys more than for girls and for black youth more than for white youth. These data may call for a shift of focus in our ministry with boys and black youth.

STAGES OF FAITH

How does an early adolescent believe? For developmentalists like James Fowler and his colleagues, the question is not so much what does the young person believe, but how. How is he or she structured within to explain his or her pattern of believing? Does the early adolescent believe somewhat differently from his or her younger brother, still in middle childhood, or older sister, now in middle adolescence? According to developmentalists, the answer is yes. Even though there is continuity in how a person believes, there are discreet stages which can be detected through guided interviews.

The stage most commonly found among early adolescents is the third in Fowler's schema, called "synthetic-conventional." Its distinctiveness can be seen especially in these seven dimensions: form of logic, perspective taking, form of moral judgment, bounds of social awareness, locus of authority, form of world coherence, and symbolic function. (Fowler 151-173)

FORM OF LOGIC

In early adolescence young persons become capable of early formal operations. That means they are able not only to think, but also to know, reflectively and critically, that they are thinking. They begin to be more critical of what authority tells them, but they are only beginning. Full critical reflection on one's faith and religion comes a few years later.

It is sometimes said that early adolescents today are going through a crisis of faith that in prior generations did not happen until late adolescence. Perhaps some are. It seems more likely, however, that the crisis for the early adolescent has not so much to do with a foundational faith in God as it has to do with loyalty and allegiance to the religious community of their childhood.

PERSPECTIVE TAKING

Perspective taking is the ability to walk in someone else's shoes. Early adolescents can appreciate the perspective of their friends, of individuals in cultures similar to their own, and of individuals in strange cultures insofar as those individuals are seen to be like themselves. They have difficulty taking the perspective of other groups as groups or of alien groups insofar as they are alien.

This ability, with its limitations, has great bearing upon the faith of the adolescent insofar as it is horizontal as well as vertical. A mature faith tries to appreciate not only the other as an individual person like oneself, but also as a member of a different group or culture. It is good for early adolescents to reach out in that direction, but success may be difficult at their stage of development.

FORM OF MORAL JUDGMENT

Early adolescents, to a large extent, make their moral judgments in keeping with what is expected of them by family, peers, and other significant others in their lives. To a degree this is good, because it is more mature than a reward-punishment orientation. On the other hand, the early adolescent can be tyrannized by others, by the "they." A mature moral judgment is more internal, more personal, more free to do what one judges to be right moral behavior.

Although faith and moral development are not identical, they are interrelated. It seems that maturity in moral judgment is usually a condition for mature faith development. In practice, parents, teachers, and youth ministers do well when they understand where early adolescents are and where they may be going with regard both to moral and faith development.

BOUNDS OF SOCIAL AWARENESS

Bounds of social awareness are similar to degrees of perspective taking. They stake out the limits of those people who we are aware of as persons in their own right. For early adolescents this seems to be the group in which they have interpersonal relationships. If they are members of more than one such group, their bounds are a composite of these groups.

Again, we can apply this dimension of early adolescence to faith insofar as it is both horizontal and vertical, with the emphasis this time on the vertical. They experience God in terms of how they experience other human persons. Where their bounds are wide, so their imaging of God will be more encompassing. Where their bounds are narrow, so their God may be only a limited tribal god.

LOCUS OF AUTHORITY

It is important to understand this dimension of faith for Fowler and his colleagues. Other statements in this chapter may lead one to believe that in early adolescence young people are beginning to make their faith their own, freely and on their own authority. Not so, says Fowler, or at least not yet. The authority for their faith is still outside themselves, in valued groups and in those who represent the beliefs and values of one's traditions. The youngsters are more aware and more critical, but they are not yet on their own.

The implications for youth catechesis are also important. If Fowler and his colleagues be right, then early adolescence is a time for encouraging affiliation and allegiance to one's faith community though knowledge of its tradition and through participation in its present life and vitality. It is a time for heroes and heroines, for models and mentors.

FORM OF WORLD COHERENCE

Form of world coherence means what holds things together so that life makes sense. With regard to world coherence for early adolescents, three claims are made. First, the system is tacit, that is, it is accepted without critical examination of its parts. Second, its meaning is communicated through concrete symbols rather than by abstract concepts. Third, its pieces are not accepted or rejected one by one; the entire system fits together as a whole.

Several practical applications derive from this position. Early adolescence is not yet the time for critical examination of each element of one's belief system. It is more a time for active participation in the life of the faith community, with its symbols, rituals, history, and traditions. It is a time for affiliation and allegiance.

SYMBOLIC FUNCTION

A symbol functions in several ways. In early childhood it may be magical. In middle childhood it becomes literal or one-dimensional. In late adolescence it can become separated from its meaning so that the meaning becomes more important than the symbol which conveys it. In early adolescence a symbol has many dimensions. It connotes more than it denotes. It is opaque rather than transparent. The symbol and its meaning cannot be separated. The symbol has power to express God's active presence precisely because it is a symbol.

The implications here are similar to those made for other aspects of the synthetic-conventional stage three of Fowler's developmental schema. The task is to incorporate the young into the life of a tradition-bearing community, with the signs and symbols through which this tradition is expressed and shared. It is not yet the time for critical analysis of them, even though that time may very quickly be at hand.

PATTERNS OF FAITH

An Australian sociologist, Marcellin Flynn, has borrowed upon the developmental stages of Fowler and their catechetical transposition by John Westerhoff III, but has changed the basic understanding of what a stage means. (Flynn 245-262) Flynn finds in adolescents not so much discreet stages which displace one another, but rather identifiable patterns which coexist with one another. One or more patterns may be rising in importance and dominance, another or others may be declining, still another may be perduring with continued strength. Flynn speaks of the following patterns for 12th graders in Catholic high schools in Australia. Some of his findings can apply to adolescents in the United States and some of his vocabulary can help describe the faith of early adolescents. These patterns are:

Experienced faith: begun in childhood, especially within the family, and continuing strong throughout adolescence.

Conventional faith: the beliefs of the faith-community, now on the decline because of increasing criticism from the adolescent.

Searching faith: looking for a style of belief which is more one's own; this pattern becomes particularly strong in middle and late adolescence.

Rejection of church-related faith: this pattern may have its beginnings in early adolescence, but it is more typical in middle and late adolescence.

Owned faith: similarly, this pattern may have its beginnings in early adolescence, but it seems to be achieved only in late adolescence / young adulthood.

Personal faith in Jesus: though this may be the goal in much of Christian ministry with adolescents, it is the dominant form of faith only for a minority; yet it is often also a dimension of one or more of the other patterns of faith.

FAITH AND IDENTITY

There is a rich but indirect source for understanding faith and religion among early adolescents: the psychosocial tasks which come into ascendancy during that period of life. Here we are on ground that is both firm and shaky. It is firm insofar as the human epigenetic cycle as articulated by Erik Erikson has withstood testing and criticism and has been widely accepted as a working model for describing adolescence. It is shaky insofar as the religious dimensions of this cycle have not been much expressed or agreed upon. In brief, in this section to make applications to the faith of early adolescents we shall be stretching our imaginations a bit.

Identity formation is a complex process. It may help to break it into its more important dimensions. They are: autonomy, sexuality, relationships, occupation, and ideology.

AUTONOMY

The study on young adolescents and their parents reports that among 24 value statements, "to make my own decisions" increased between fifth and ninth grades more than any other value statement. The study says:

> In other words, "To make my own decisions" grows in importance quite rapidly across the five years of early adolescence, and it grows more dramatically than any other value area. There is a noticeable rise with each advance in grade from 5th to 8th, and no significant rise occurs after 8th grade. By the 8th grade, 6 out of 10 young adolescents (62%) place high importance on autonomy. At each grade, girls report as much interest in autonomy as boys. (*Young Adolescents and Their Parents* 12)

This reaching out for greater autonomy is also called separation-individuation. Although usually it is not completed until late in adolescence or early in adulthood, it is particularly strong in early adolescence. In some ways the terrible two's of early childhood are recapitulated in the terrible 12's of early adolescence. Some youngsters separate from the world of their childhood more noisily and painfully (*Sturm und Drang*); others make the transition more quietly and gracefully. Yet all have to make the transition or they risk being frozen in their childhood immaturity.

What bearing does separation-individuation have upon faith and religion among early adolescents? It begins the process of shifting from inherited authority (especially the family) to self-chosen authority (eventually oneself). This does not necessarily imply conversion to another religion or to no religion at all, although it does include that possibility, especially in a pluralistic society like the United States. Yet it does mean that if the young person does not begin the process to make his or her faith his or her own through free choice, to that extent the person lacks full religious maturity.

This presents a certain amount of tension for parents, teachers, youth ministers. They would like adolescents *freely* to choose what they, *the adults*, personally value. But isn't that what parenting and teaching and ministering are all about?

SEXUALITY

In *Dear God*, George Burns as God confesses to some mistakes in creating, such as the ostrich's putting its head in the ground and the size of the avocado's pit. Sometimes we may wonder whether joining sexual puberty with early adolescence was such a great idea. Yet, as we read in Genesis, God looked at all God had made and found it very good—including ostriches, avocados, and adolescent puberty.

There is a vast literature on adolescent sexuality. Here we will consider a few aspects of it which seem to have some bearing on the faith and religion of adolescents.

Authors usually distinguish between sexuality and sex (or genitality). Sexuality refers to oneself as this female person or this male person. It is how we experience ourselves as embodied. It is the unitive and procreative energy of the whole person. Sex is the ordinary word we use for the various kinds of genital expression of our sexual selves.

Between sexuality and genitality it may help to introduce sensuality. Sensuality refers to experiencing oneself or the other through our senses: as seeing, hearing, smelling, tasting, touching, etc. We live in a sensual culture, and in it boys and girls often miscommunicate with one another. Girls tend to read sensuality as an expression of overall sexuality, something diffused throughout one's whole person. Boys incline to interpret sensual expression as an invitation to sex, to an experience more focused on genital stimulation and satisfaction. Girls may contend: "Boys want just one thing"; boys may counter: "Girls are looking for it."

Sexuality/genitality may offer one reason why during early adolescence girls remain relatively constant in religious practice, while boys decline significantly. We have to confess that we do not know for sure why this happens. The reasons may be more sociological than developmental, such as the presumption in many cultures and subcultures that church-going is for women and children. A developmental factor, however, may be that boys feel ill at ease in churches and congregations where the genital expression of their sexuality is judged to be sinful. Adolescent boys may feel that they no longer belong and that it would be hypocritical on their part to pretend that they do.

RELATIONSHIPS

Books in the "young adult" section of a bookstore tell us something. First, many are written for early adolescents, not young adults. Second, they are more for and about girls than for and about boys. Third, though they still offer mystery, sports, science fiction, and stars of film, music, and television, they show increasing concern for membership in a group, for close friendships, and for budding romance. Relationships—or the lack of them—are enormously important for adolescents. The relational identity of an adolescent may shift dramatically in character from 12 to 22, especially moving from a larger group to a smaller circle to a one-to-one pairing, yet the need and concern for friendship remains constant.

This quest for relational identity affects the faith of early adolescents at its roots, that is, in the way they experience and image God. As already stated above, most (but not all) early adolescents experience and image God as warm more than as cold, as close more than as distant, as friend and confidant more than as lord and lawgiver. Granted, this kind of faith may reflect a childhood relationship with parents more than adolescent friendships with peers. Yet peer influence rises steadily throughout adolescence, especially with regard to significant relationships.

The relationship between faith and friendship calls for some commentary and qualification. First, with varying emphases, religions tend to see God as both near (immanent) and beyond (transcendent). Augustine of Hippo wrote that God is "higher than my topmost part, closer than my inmost part." Our response to such a God should be not only ease but also awe, not only relaxation but also reverence. Near and beyond, God remains mystery.

Second, commonly today religious educators present Jesus to adolescents predominantly as a friend. Yes, this is good, but... The analogy of friendship does help us appreciate what faith in Jesus can mean for us, but it remains an analogy with differences as well as similarities. Jesus is a friend like, but not the same as, other friends in our lives. To experience Jesus as friend is totally a faith experience.

Third, adolescents seem to be striking a good balance between the vertical and horizontal dimensions of faith. The two great commandments interrelate as one. In a way, this has been a triumph for churches and congregations. They seem to have deprivatized themselves and have raised the social and relational consciousness of their members.

OCCUPATION

Among identity's components, occupation, career, or profession would seem to have least impact on the faith of early adolescents. Although adults ask children from their earliest years what they want to be when they grow up, the issue does not usually become critical in western society until late adolescence/young adulthood (18-22 years of age). Up till then adolescents enjoy a psychosocial moratorium, that is, they are encouraged to keep their options open and explore possibilities before making a commitment to one specific occupation for their adulthood.

Yet something is already at stake here even in early adolescence. It is not so much what precise occupation one will make one's own. It is the wider question which can be called "vocation." It is a response to a call. It is the beginning of a style of life that may express itself in many different occupations, careers, or professions. Such a response actually begins earlier in childhood, within family, school, and community. With adolescence the response becomes more personal, more reflective, more self-chosen.

How does this call come to an early adolescent? The most operative factor seems to be one or more significant persons who model a way of life. Young persons tend to identify with those who are significant to them. They try on for size their life styles. They imitate and they grow into what they imitate. All this happens without their hardly averting to it.

The process of identification is not something determined or fatalistic. Young persons internalize with what they identify, and they integrate within their larger self what they internalize. They do so, to some extent, freely and selectively. Others may have parented them into infancy and childhood, but they should be parenting themselves into adolescence and adulthood.

With regard to this vocational-identity of early adolescents there are implications for the faith development of adolescents. Parents, teachers, and youth ministers should try to provide for them the best possible people-environments within which they may identify. They can help the young reflect critically on what they may be internalizing. They can enable them to own as part of themselves what they may be integrating into their own selves.

IDEOLOGY

Perhaps the most profound dimension of identity is ideology. Ideology has a wide and a narrow meaning. The narrow meaning may be technically more precise, but our concern is mainly its wide meaning.

In its wide meaning, ideology is the way in which we organize our world. It is how we construe reality and how we make sense of our lives. It is the values we stand for and the truths we believe in. It is who and what we love and for what we are willing to sacrifice, even at great cost. In this sense, ideology is a fervent faith.

It its narrow meaning, ideology is a cause which elicits a dedicated response. Ideology derives power from its direct simplicity. It reduces complexity by posing either-or alternatives. It proposes radical solutions and inspires radical actions. It favors rhetoric over rational discourse. It relies more upon charismatic than democratic leadership. In this sense, ideology allies itself with movements which enlist and unleash powerful forces in society.

Like occupational identity, ideological identity usually comes into its ascendancy during late adolescence/young adulthood. Studies done on occupational and ideological identities have been remarkably successful with college-age youth and notably unsuccessful with high-school-age middle adolescents.

Yet the process is at work throughout life. In early adolescence, ideology recapitulates, anticipates, and has a meaning of its own. It recapitulates the earliest of all life's crises, that of trust vs. mistrust. The early adolescent begins to wonder: Does this life of mine make sense? What kind of a mixed-up world am I living in? Can I trust and build upon the view of life which I have received from my family, school, church?

Early adolescence anticipates the final of life's crises, that of integrity vs. despair. Questions such as these arise: How free am I to believe what I think is true? Is it enough to accept what I have been taught, or should I open myself to new ideas? What meaning do I really live by in my everyday life?

Early adolescence has some ideological questions of its own. Implicitly or explicitly, some may be: As I move from childhood to adolescence, what do I take with me and what do I leave behind? Are my church, my school, my community always right? From the values of my family, of my friends, of my wider world, which do I want to own as truly my own?

CONCLUSION

Perhaps we may conclude this chapter on a positive and a practical note by referring to two recent studies which offer their own bits of advice.

Effective Christian Education: A National Study of Protestant Congregations is a refreshing study on the importance and effectiveness of Christian education programs for adolescents in local congregations. The study isolates the following five areas of congregational life which help youth and adults to mature in faith and grow in loyalty:

a thinking climate (challenging and questioning);
a warm climate (welcoming);
a caring church (among church members);
service to others (beyond church members);
worship (uplifting worship services). (Benson and Eklin 49)

A second study, *The Troubled Journey: A Portrait of 6th-12th Grade Youth*, concludes with a chapter entitled "Strategies for Change." It suggests the following strategies to staff and volunteers in congregations and other youth-serving organizations:

reinvent programming for high school-aged youth
connect youth to adult mentors
provide and/or advocate for quality day care and after school care
place a premium on the development of positive values
equip parents with parenting skills, particularly in the areas of support-giving, control, and values formation
involve youth in helping projects
program directly to multiple at-risk behavior domains
build social competencies (Benson 82)

WORKS CITED

Babin, P. *Faith and the Adolescent*. New York: Herder and Herder, 1965.

Benson, P. *The Troubled Journey: A Portrait of 6th-12th Grade Youth*. Minneapolis MN: Lutheran Brotherhood, 1990.

Benson, P, and C. Eklin. *Effective Christian Education: A National Study of Protestant Congregations*. Minneapolis MN: Search Institute, 1990.

Benson, P., D. Williams, and A. Johnson. *The Quicksilver Years: The Hopes and Fears of Early Adolescence*. San Francisco: Harper & Row, 198 (A republishing of *Young Adolescence and Their Parents*)

Carotta, M., and G. Oswalt. *The Boys Town Profile of At-Risk Youth*. Boys Town NE: Unpublished Study, 1991.

Fee, J., A. Greeley, W. McCready, and T. Sullivan. *Young Catholics in the United States and Canada*. New York: William H. Sadlier, 1981.

Flynn, M. *The Effectiveness of Catholic Schools: A Ten-Year Study of Year 12 Students in Catholic High Schools*. Sydney Australia: St Paul Publications, 1985.

Fowler, J. *Stages of Faith: The Psychology of Human Development and the Quest for Meaning*. San Francisco: Harper & Row, 1981.

Norman, J., and M. Harris. *The Private Life of the American Teenager*. New York: Rawson, Wade Publishers, Inc., 1981.

Young Adolescents and Their Parents. Minneapolis, MN: Search Institute, 1984. (Republished as *The Quicksilver Years: The Hopes and Fears of Early Adolescence*)

BIBLIOGRAPHY

Bibby, P., and D. Posterski. *The Emerging Generation: An Inside Look at Canada's Teenagers*. Toronto: Irwin, 1985.

Coles, R. *The Spiritual Life of Children*. Boston: Houghton Mifflin Company, 1990.

Hyde, K. *Religion in Childhood and Adolescence: A Comprehensive Review of the Research*. Birmingham AL: Religious Education Press, 1990.

McCauley, E., and M. Mathieson. *Faith Without Form: Beliefs of Catholic Youth*. Kansas City MO: Sheed and Ward, 1986.

Shelton, C. *Adolescent Spirituality*. Chicago: Loyola University Press, 1983.

Chapter 3

The Social Context of Early Adolescent Development

The Report on the Task Force on Education of Young Adolescents

Carnegie Council on Adolescent Development

Young adolescents today make fateful choices, fateful for them and for our nation. The period of life from ages 10 to 15 represents for many young people their last best chance to choose a path toward productive and fulfilling lives.

Depending on family circumstances, household income, language, neighborhood, or the color of their skin, some of these young adolescents receive the education and support they need to develop self respect, an active mind, and a healthy body. They will emerge from their teens as the promising youth who will become the scientists and entrepreneurs, the educators and health care professionals, and the parents who will renew the nation. These are the thoughtful, responsible, caring, ethical, and robust young people the Task Force envisions. To them, society can entrust the future of the country with confidence.

Under current conditions, however, far too many young people will not make the passage through early adolescence successfully. Their basic human needs — caring relationships with adults, guidance in facing sometimes overwhelming biological and psychological changes, the security of belonging to constructive peer groups, and the perception of future opportunity — go unmet at this critical stage of life. Millions of these young adolescents will never reach their full potential.

Early adolescence for these youth is a turning point towards a diminished future. Many will live outside or on the fringes of those communities that produce the achievers and the leaders in their society. A substantial number will grow into adults who are alienated from other people, who have low expectations for themselves and for whom society has low expectations, and who are likely to produce a disproporionate share of the unhealthy, the addicted, the criminal, the violent, and the chronically poor. These are the youth left behind.

In even the most affluent communities, young adolescents display the attitudes and behavior that portend difficulty. Such young people often drop out of school or participate at such a low level of effort that, even if they graduate, they have few marketable skills. They may abuse alcohol or drugs, or engage in other antisocial or criminal conduct. For many of us who ought to be concerned, however, daily life is too demanding, change comes too rapidly, money is too plentiful for us to care about troubled teenagers, school dropouts, juvenile offenders, or adolescents who can neither read nor write nor choose to participate fully in school.

Apart from our moral responsibility, we also face an economic imperative to ensure that these young people are properly educated. With the number of elderly rising rapidly, the economy cannot support both swelling ranks of the retired and the endless addictions to the unemployed and the underemployed. Response to drug addiction, crime, violence, and teenage pregnancy continues to consume substantial national resources. With the need for literate and skilled workers increasing, and the pool of such people decreasing, business and industry cannot idly watch a new generation of potential workers slide into chronically unproductive lives.

Who are these young people left behind? How do they differ from their counterparts who enter the later teen years so ready for the demands of life? Why are some youth so well and others so ill prepared for their future? Answers to these questions begin with an understanding of what it means to be a young adolescent in America as the 21st century approaches.

EARLY ADOLESCENCE BRINGS NEW CHALLENGES

By age 15, millions of American youth are at risk of reaching adulthood unable to meet adequately the requirements of the workplace, the commitments of relationships in families and with peers, and the responsibilities of participation in a multicultural society and of citizenship in a democracy. These young people often suffer from underdeveloped intellectual abilities, indifference to good health, and cynicism about the values that American society embodies.

These characteristics of a critical mass of young people in this country are apparent to any observer. What is less clear, because this period has until recently been the least understood of any stage of life, are the causes of this alienation.

During early adolescence, many youth enter a period of trial and error, of vulnerability to emotional hurt of humiliation, of anxiety and uncertainty that are sources of unevenness of emotions and behavior associated with the age. Yet the turmoil can herald the emergence of a new individual with the potential to learn, to think critically and independently, and to act responsibly according to principles and a code of ethics.

This time is of immense importance in the development of the young person. Biologically, young adolescents experience puberty, a period of growth and development more rapid than in any other phase of life except infancy. Over four or five years, dramatic changes occur in height, weight, and body composition, and young people acquire the capacity to reproduce. Youth enter puberty at a significantly younger age today than in previous generations. In the United States 150 years ago, the average age of a girl's first menstrual period was 16 years; today it is 12.5 years. The change for boys is less pronounced but follows a similar trend. While they become biologically mature at earlier ages, many young adolescents remain intellectually and emotionally immature. Thus, young people at 10, 11, and 12 years old are able to, and do, make fateful choices involving their own sexuality that can affect their entire life course.

YOUNG ADOLESCENTS FACE NEW CONDITIONS

Young adolescents increasingly look outward from the home to gain an understanding of themselves and their circumstances. It is here, as they come face-to-face with realities of life in America: The terms and conditions of early adolescence have changed dramatically.

These young people enter a world in which they will likely be tempted, if not pressured, to experiment with drugs and alcohol. They may live in neighborhoods so dangerous that they fear walking to school. They date earlier in life than their parents did. They are at once admonished to control their sexual urges and bombarded through the media with the allure of sex. They are challenged to make the ideals and values of a just society their own, yet made painfully aware that money and power are the keys to success. They begin to assess their prospects and to decide how much to invest in their future by staying in school and keeping out of trouble. They begin to perceive their own future either as promising or as hard, bleak, and empty of opportunity.

In our changed America, the sense of community that once existed in urban neighborhoods and in some rural towns has eroded. Stable, close-knit communities where people know and look out for each other are far less common than they were a generation or two ago. Although the economy continues to expand and jobs are plentiful, the unskilled can find only low-paying work. Many families struggle to maintain their standard of living and often sacrifice time with each other. Family structures have changed dramatically, as both divorce and single-parent households are far more common than a decade ago. Families and individuals move frequently to find jobs, affordable housing, or other opportunities. The workplace has changed, as more women work outside the home and people switch jobs more often. Whole industries have disappeared in recent years.

In these times of rapid change, when young people face unprecedented choices and pressures, adult guidance is all too often withdrawn. Many parents, seeing that their child is developing in profound ways, mistake the stirring of independent thinking for the capacity to make adult decisions. They do not realize that their child's needs for autonomy require not rejection of filial bonds, but a realignment of roles and relationships within the family.

The young adolescent is moving from dependency to interdependency with parents, as well as with friends, relatives, and other persons outside the home. While renegotiating relationships with parents and other care-givers, often in outwardly stormy ways, the young person simultaneously seeks to maintain strong ties with exactly those people.

Freed from the dependency of childhood, but not yet able to find their own path to adulthood, many young people feel a desperate sense of isolation. Surrounded only by their equally confused peers, too many make poor decisions with harmful or lethal consequences.

YOUNG ADOLESCENTS TODAY FACE GREATER RISKS

During early adolescence, all youth are caught in a vortex of new risks. They face risks that were almost unknown to their parents or grandparents, and face those risks at an early age. Many youth today first experiment with tobacco, alcohol, and illicit drugs during early adolescence. For example, 92 % of the high school class of 1987 had begun drinking before graduating; of those 56 % had begun drinking in the 6th to 9th grades and 36 % in the 10th to 12th grades. (Johnston, O'Malley, and Bachman) These data do not include those youth who dropped out before graduating high school, a population even more prone to early use of alcohol and drugs. In the short term, drug use may interfere with physical development, motivation, and ability to concentrate in school, and may impair judgment about risky behaviors. The fact that so many youth are involved with drugs and alcohol at such young ages is alarming because of compelling evidence that drug use in early adolescence is a critical factor in long-term substance abuse. (Kandel)

More and more teenagers below the age of 16 are becoming sexually active. (Hofferth, Kahn, and Baldwin 46-53) Partners face extremely high risks of the young woman becoming pregnant. These pregnancies lead disproportionately to the birth of low-weight babies who are vulnerable to a variety of poor outcomes. Moreover, these young mothers tend to drop out of school early. This fact, along with economic disadvantage, often limits future opportunities for many of these women. (Hayes; Furstenberg)

Besides the risk of pregnancy, young people are in serious jeopardy of contracting sexually transmitted diseases. Fully one-fourth of all sexually active adolescents will become infected with a sexually transmitted disease before graduating from high school, a grave situation that makes AIDS a potential timebomb for millions of American youth. (National Institutes on Allergies and Infectious Disease Study Group)

Motor vehicle and other accidents, taken together, are the leading causes of death among young people 10 to 14 years of age. (*Chartbook on Adolescent Health*) Substance abuse and risk-taking behavior account for many of these accidents, so does association with other adolescents involved in such behavior, especially while driving. Between 1980 and 1985, the suicide rate more than doubled for 10 to 14year olds, although suicide remains one of the least likely causes of death for early adolescents. (Waller, Baker, and Szocka 310-315) Seriously delinquent activities rise during early adolescence and peak at age 15. (Dusek)

Many problem behaviors of young adolescents appear to be interrelated. Young people who smoke and drink often experiment with illegal drugs and early, unprotected sex as well. These same young people are also prone to school failure. (Dryfoos) They are not merely exploring new behaviors, in short, but trying out lifestyles that become more entrenched as they grow older. (Jessor 69-90)

POVERTY AND DISCRIMINATION ADD TO RISK

Although all young people face significant stress in early adolescence, many reach late adolescence relatively unscathed. (Peterson) But many others fail to develop the intellectual capacities and coping skills that they will need to meet the demands of adult life.

The risk that all young people face are compounded for those who are poor, members of racial or ethnic minorities, or recent immigrants. These youth generally attend the weakest schools, have access to the least adequate health services, and have the fewest clearly visible paths to opportunities in the mainstream.

Rates of retention in grade (being kept back a year) — a school practice directly related to students' dropping out — are far higher among minority youth in the middle grades. (Bachman, Green, and Wirtanen) For many of these young people, the decision to drop out is clearly made before they begin high school. An estimated 59% of Hispanic dropouts leave school before completing the 10th grade. (Hirano-Nakanishi) Data from one school system, Washington, D.C., which is seeking to understand its dropout problems through careful research, show that more than half of all dropouts leave before completing the 10th grade. Ninety-two percent of all students in the Washington, D.C. school system are Black. (Jenkins)

It is not acceptable that minority youth are chronically the worst educated in our society. By the year 2020, because of higher birth rates among minority populations and patterns of immigration, nearly half of all school-aged children will be non-white. (Natriello, McDill, and Pallas) Continuing to allow minority youth to face extraordinary risks of failure is a direct threat to our national standard of living and democratic foundations.

UNPREPARED MILLIONS COST SOCIETY

No definitive statistics exist on the numbers of youth at risk of unhealthy and unproductive lives. Recent first attempts at estimating these numbers indicate, however, that of the 28 million girls and boys ages 10 to 17 in the United States, about 7 million may be extremely vulnerable to the negative consequences of multiple high-risk behaviors such as school failure, substance abuse, and early unprotected intercourse. Thus it is estimated that the future of about 7 million youth — one in four adolescents — is in serious jeopardy.

Another 7 million may be at moderate risk, because of occasional substance use and early but more often protected intercourse. About half of the nation's youth are at low risk of engaging in seriously damaging behaviors. They may, however, require strong and consistent support to avoid becoming involved in these problems. (Dryfoos)

That half of our nation's youth is at serious or moderate risk is cause enough for alarm. But even among those at little or no risk of damaging behaviors, the pervasiveness of intellectual underdevelopment strikes at the heart of our nation's future prosperity. American 13 year olds, for example, are now on average far behind their counterparts in other industrialized nations in mathematics and science achievement. (Lapointe, Mead, and Phillips)

Most distressing is the fact that the critical reasoning skills of many American young adolescents are extremely deficient. A recent National Assessment of Educational Progress (NAEP) found that only 11 % of 13 year olds were "adept" readers, that is, able to understand relatively complicated written information. In NAEP tests requiring analytic or persuasive writing, fewer than one in five 8th graders wrote adequate or better essays. The study concluded, "...students at all grade levels are deficient in higher order thinking skills." (Applebee, Langer, and Mullis)

The economy will increasingly have little use for youth who are impaired by high-risk behaviors or who are intellectually unprepared for the challenges of a changing economy. Job growth is concentrated in occupations that require much more than basic literacy. Three million of the 27 million new jobs created between 1972 and 1986 required only a basic level of literacy. More than 10 million of the new jobs were in professional, technical, administrative and managerial occupations, and the remaining 14 million were in sales, clerical, and crafts. (Mark 26-29; Bailey)

The domestic job market today reflects the intense international competition in which the Untied States finds itself. This nation needs a workforce capable of critical thinking and creative problem solving. Yet we continue to educate youth for the smokestack economy of generations past.

As a nation, therefore, we face a paradox of our own making. We have created an economy that seeks literate, technically trained, and committed workers, while simultaneously we produce many young men and women who are semi-literate or functionally illiterate, unable to think critically and untrained in technical skills, hampered by high-risk lifestyles, and alienated from the social mainstream. Unemployment rates for high school dropouts are more than twice those for high school graduates. (*The Forgotten Half*) The few jobs for which these people qualify often pay too little to support a family. For many of these young people, the American dream ends with the recognition that they are not wanted and are of little value in this society.

What is left for these young men and women is a life on the edge of society. Those with minimal competencies will barely get by. The most poorly prepared will move in and out of crime, drug abuse, or alcoholism. Some will be forced to depend on government assistance in one form or another — income maintenance, health care, and housing. Many will pay little in taxes and will be able to contribute little to Social Security or to caring for themselves in their later years.

The specter of a divided society — one affluent, the other poor — looms ominously on the American horizon. Inherent in this scenario is the potential for serious conflict between generations, among races and ethnic groups, and between the economically disfranchised and middle- and upper-income groups. It is a disturbing scenario that must not occur.

TRANSFORMING THE EDUCATION OF YOUNG ADOLESCENTS

Middle grade schools have been virtually ignored in discussions of educational reform in the past decade. Yet, they are central not only to channeling every young adolescent into the mainstream of life in American communities, but also to making vast improvements in academic and personal outcomes for all youth.

Middle grade schools — junior high, intermediate, or middle schools — are potentially society's most powerful force to recapture millions of youth adrift. Yet all too often they exacerbate the problems youth face.

A volatile mismatch exists between the organization and curriculum of middle grade schools, and the intellectual, emotional, and interpersonal needs of young adolescents. (Eccles and Midgley) For most young adolescents, the shift from elementary to junior high or middle schools means moving from a small, neighborhood school and the stability of one primary classroom to a much larger, more impersonal institution, typically at a greater distance from home. In this new setting, teachers and classmates will change as many as six or seven times a day. This constant shifting creates formidable barriers to the formation of stable peer groups and close, supportive relationships with caring adults. (Simmons, Rosenberg, and Rosenberg; Blyth, Simmons, and Carlton-Ford) The chances that young people will feel lost are enormous. Today, as young adolescents move from elementary to middle or junior high schools, their involvement with learning diminishes and their rates of alienation, drug abuse, absenteeism, and dropping out begin to rise. The warning signals are there to see.

The ability of young adolescents to cope is often further jeopardized by a middle grade curriculum that assumes a need for an intellectual moratorium during early adolescence. Some educators consider the young adolescent incapable of critical, complex thought during rapid physical and emotional development. Minimal effort, they argue, should be spent to stimulate higher levels of thought and decision-making until the youth reaches high school and becomes teachable again. Existing knowledge seriously challenges these assumptions. (Keating) Yet many middle grade schools fail to recognize or to act on this knowledge.

Furthermore, many middle grade schools pay little attention to the emotional, physical, and social development of their students. Young adolescents need proper nutrition, health, and social services to maintain good physical and mental health and fitness. Students who are hungry, sick, troubled, or depressed cannot function well in the classroom, no matter how good the school. Moreover, young adolescents need adult guidance to help them cope with one of life's more confusing periods.

Middle grade schools cannot meet all these needs alone. To fulfill their vital functions, they will need to operate at the center of a network of community resources that includes local government, health services, youth-serving organizations, private businesses, and the philanthropic sector. In many localities today, that network does not exist, and the middle grade schools are unable to meet their responsibilities to their students or to the community.

Caring is crucial to the development of young adolescents into healthy adults. Young adolescents need to see themselves as valued members of a group that offers mutual support and trusting relationships. They need to be able to succeed at something, and to be praised and rewarded for that success. They need to become socially competent individuals who have the skills to cope successfully with the exigencies of everyday life. They need to believe that they have a promising future, and they need the competence to take advantage of real opportunities in a society in which they have a stake. We need to create for every young person a community that engages those for whom life already holds high promise, and welcomes into the mainstream of society those who might otherwise be left behind.

WORKS CITED

Applebee, A., J. Langer, and I. Mullis. *The Writing Report Card, Writing Achievement in American Schools.* Princeton, NJ: National Assessment of Educational Progress, Educational Testing Service, 1986.

Bachman, J.G., S. Green, and I.D. Wirtanen. "Dropping Out — Problem or Symptom. *Youth in Transition,* Volume III. Ann Arbor, MI: Institute for Social Research, University of Michigan, 1971.

Bailey, T. "The New Economy, New Skills, and the Limits of Education Reform." Paper presented at the American Educational Research Association, New Orleans LA, April 1988.

Blyth, D.A., R.G. Simmons, and S. Carlton-Ford. "The Adjustment of Early Adolescents to Schools Transitions." *Journal of Early Adolescence* 3.1&2 (1983): 105-120.

Chartbook on Adolescent Health. Rockville, MD: Public Health Service, Health Resources and Services Administration, Bureau of Health Care Delivery and Assistance, Division of Maternal and Child Health, 1990.

Dryfoos, J.G. *Adolescents at Risk.* New York: Oxford University Press, 1990.

Dusek, J.B. *Adolescent Development and Behavior.* Englewood Cliffs NJ: Prentice-Hall, 1987.

Eccles, J.S. and C. Midgley. "Stage/Environment Fit: Developmentally Appropriate Classrooms for Early Adolescents." *Research on Motivation in Education* (Volume 3). New York: Academic Press, 1990.

The Forgotten Half: Pathways to Success for America's Youth and Young Families. Washington DC: Youth and America's Future: The William T. Grant Commission on Work, Family and Citizenship, 1988.

Furstenberg, F.F., J. Brooks-Gunn, and S.P. Morgan. *Adolescent Mothers in Later Life*. New York: Cambridge University Press, 1987.

Harwood, H.J., D.M. Napolitano, P.L. Kristiansen, and J.J. Collins. *Economic Costs to Society of Alcohol and Drug Abuse and Mental Illness: 1980*. (Publication No. RTI/2734/00-01FR, June 1984). Research Triangle Park NC: Research Triangle Institute, 1980.

Hayes, C.D., editor. *Risking the Future: Adolescent Sexuality, Pregnancy, and Childbearing*. Washington, DC: National Academy Press, 1987.

Hirano-Nakanishi, M. *Hispanic School Dropouts: The Extent and Relevance of Pre-High School Attrition and Delayed Education*. Los Alamitos CA: National Center for Bilingual Research, 1984.

Hofferth, S.L., J.R. Kahn, and W. Baldwin. "Premarital Sexual Activity Among U.S. Teenage Women Over the Past Three Decades." *Family Planning Perpsectives* 19.2 (1987): 46-53

Jenkins, A.E., III. *A Study of Students Who Left: D.C. Public School Dropouts*. Washington DC: District of Columbia Public Schools, Division of Quality Assurance and Management Planning, October 1988.

Jessor, R. "Adolescent Development and Behavioral Health." *Behavioral Health: A Handbook of Health Enhancement and Disease Prevention*. Ed. D. Matarazzo, S.M. Weiss, J.A. Herd, and N.E. Miller. New York: John Wiley and Sons 1984.

Johnston, L.D., P.M. O'Malley, and J.G. Bachman. *Illicit Drug Use, Smoking and Drinking by America's High School Students, College Students, and Young Adults: 1975-1987*. (DHHS Publication No. (ADM) 89-1062). Washington DC: U.S. Government Printing Office, 1985.

Kandel, D.B. "Effects of Drug Use from Adolescence to Young Adulthood on Participation in Family and Work Roles. *Longitudinal Research on Substance Use in Adolescence*. R. Jessor (Chair). Symposium conducted at the meeting of the International Society of the Study of Behavioral Development, Tours, France.

Keating, D.P. "Adolescent Thinking." *At the Threshold: The Developing Adolescent*. Ed. S. Shirley Feldman and Glen R. Elliot. Cambridge MA: Harvard University Press, 1990.

Lapointe, A.E., N.A. Mead, and G.W. Phillips. *A World of Difference: An International Assessment of Mathematics and Science*. Princeton NJ: Educational Testing Service, January 1989.

Mark, J.A. "Technological Change and Employment: Some Results from BLS Research." *Monthly Labor Review* 110 (April 1987): 26-29.

National Assessment of Educational Progress (NAEP). The Reading Report Card, Progress Toward Excellence in Our Schools, Trends in Reading Over Four National Assessments, 1971-1984. Princeton NJ: Educational Testing Service, 1985.

National Institutes on Allergies and Infectious Disease Study Group. *Sexually Transmitted Diseases — Summary and Recommendations*. Washington DC: U.S. Department of Health, Education, and Welfare, National Institutes of Health, 1980.

Natriello, G., E.L. McDill, and A.M. Pallas. *In Our Lifetime: Schooling and the Disadvantaged.* Unpublished Manuscript 1987.

Petersen, A.C. "Adolescent Development." *Annual Review of Psychology* 39 (1988): 583-607.

Simmons, R.G. and D.A. Blyth. *Moving into Adolescence: The Impact of Pubertal Change and School Context.* Hawthorne NY: Aldine, 1987.

Simmons, R.G., M. Rosenberg, and F. Rosenberg. "Disturbance in the Self-Image of Adolescence." *American Sociological Review* 39. (1973): 553-568.

Waller, A.E., S.P. Baker, and A. Szocka. "Childhood Injury Deaths: National Analysis and Geographic Variations." *American Journal of Public Health* 79. (1989): 310-315.

Chapter 4

Providing a Structure for Adolescent Development

Francis A. J. Ianni

There is significant congruence between the world views of teenagers and those of the adults in their lives. However, such congruence means that the problems of adolescence are our problems, too.

In March of 1987 two boys, ages 18 and 19, and two sisters, ages 16 and 17, brought national attention to the northern New Jersey community of Bergenfield when they committed suicide in a pact that bound them in death as they had been in their short but troubled lives. All four teenagers had experienced problems with their families. One of the boys had seen his father kill himself a few years earlier. The two girls were having difficulty adjusting to their mother's remarriage and to their stepfather and his children, who had become part of their household. Both boys and the older of the sisters had already dropped out of school, while the younger sister, who had recently been suspended, showed little inclination to return to school.

All four had also been "burnouts," members of a troubled and troublesome peer group addicted to punk fashions and heavymetal music. Since leaving school, the two young men had been employed only intermittently, and there were indications of frequent drug and alcohol use by these four teens and their friends. According to the local police chief, these were "pain-in-the-ass-type kids" who were "going nowhere fast" ("Copycat Suicides").

Who was responsible for the uneasy lives and easy deaths of these young people? No one seemed to agree. Some blamed uncaring families that had neglected their children and had not heeded their calls for help; others faulted an insensitive school system that had failed these adolescents at risk. However, many saw the tragedy as yet another example of the excesses of a media-hyped national "youth culture" and of the power of the peer group to pressure its members to conform. Even the experts on teenage suicide could not agree on whether media exposure of teenage suicide only exacerbates the problem by planting the idea of suicide in young minds throughout the country.

Suicide is only one of a variety of social problems, such as pregnancy, drug and alcohol abuse, crime and delinquency, and dropping out of school, that mark adolescence in America as a troubled period of transition to adulthood. The drama associated with these social problems also supplies the forms, the symbols, and the colors with which the popular culture produces its portrait of what most American adolescents are supposed to be like.

Since World War II American teenagers have been portrayed in a number of different ways. In the 1950s, a period of relative peace and prosperity, most were portrayed as clean-cut, materialistic conformists, indifferent to political and social issues. To liven things up there were a few greasers, beatniks, and "rebels without a cause." In the 1960s, a decade scarred by the Vietnam War, urban riots, and political assassinations, the media portrayed teenagers as angry, assertive, hedonistic, idealistic, and anti-materialistic.

Then, in the 1970s, teenagers were shown to be disillusioned by the failure of the activism and reforms of the 1960s and by an oversupply of would-be professionals. In the public mind, at least, young people once again became grade-grubbing, apathetic, and conservative. Still another picture began to emerge in the 1980s. As concern deepened over problems of physical and mental health, sexual and social conduct, and various forms of abuse of self and others among young people, we began to see and hear adolescents described as the "New Lost Generation."

Are such collective characterizations accurate portrayals of what most American adolescents are like? Are teenagers and their peer groups pretty much the same in urban, suburban, or rural areas? Are parents and other adults really so powerless? Are communities, their schools, and other social institutions helpless in the face of some compelling youth culture that seems to shape their peer group no matter where teenagers live?

THE IDEA OF A "NATIONAL" YOUTH CULTURE

The idea that adolescent society or youth culture is unique emerged most clearly with James Coleman's study of peer behavior in high schools during the late 1950s. Coleman identified the peer group as the major source of socialization for adolescents because "adolescents are looking to each other rather than to the adult community for their social rewards." What Coleman dubbed the "adolescent society" was a separate social system, with a psychosocial unity of its own, that was capable of resisting and even countering the adult society's authority and demands for integration into the general community. Other voices, both before and after Coleman's, have reinforced the idea of a unique "adolescent society."

By the 1960s we were coming to view adolescence less as one of many stages in a continuous path through life and more as a distinct and disruptive sub-society with values, norms, and a culture of its own. Widely publicized notions of a "generation gap" and a "counterculture" linked the local peer group to a national youth culture — in the popular perception as well as in much of the sociological literature on teenagers. Adolescents supposedly looked to this collective cultural consciousness — broadcast nationally through the lyrics and beat of rock-and-roll music and made increasingly visible as television spread throughout the country — rather than to parents or to local community norms for support and guidance.

The creation of the notion of a youth culture did more than supply an explanation for the mounting social problems of teenagers. *It took both the source of the crises and the hope of their resolution out of the hands of local communities and out of the hands of parents and other adults who were close to the daily lives of teenagers.* The idea that a youth culture was the source of the problems of adolescence moved those problems to a distant national arena. And if the problems were national, then national strategies and resources were required to combat them; local options and the community authority structure were powerless. Lost in this nationalization was the fact that just as communities differ, so do the families, the schools, the workplaces, and other social institutions within them. Moreover, these differences have important and lasting effects on teenagers and the groups they form.

THE DIVERSITY OF THE ADOLESCENT EXPERIENCE

For more than a decade, spanning the 1970s and 1980s, my associates and I observed and interviewed adolescents in 10 communities throughout the U.S. We found that the diversity among communities and the effects of local differences on adolescents and on the groups they formed persisted over time. The teenagers in the 10 communities we studied were as different from one another as they were from the adults in their own communities. Teenagers live in poverty, in affluence, or someplace in between. They come from broken or intact families, attend good or bad schools, and encounter very different role models in their communities. Adolescent development takes place within a specific community, as the individual teenager's internal resources are nurtured or stifled by what is available.

Just as teenagers differ, depending on where and how they live, so do the peer groups they form. Our comparative data from the communities we studied led us to question whether a "national" youth culture could homogenize all this diversity and come between the social institutions of local communities and the youngsters they teach and enculturate. Indeed, our data convinced us that the local peer groups were not parts of any distinctive and enduring subsociety that isolates adolescents from the adult world while escorting them out of childhood. Peer groups are necessary and effective arenas of social reference that do exert powerful influence, often coupled with considerable anxiety and stress, on their teenage members. But local peer groups grow out of and continue to be related to the adult institutions that sanction them, and they are usually short-lived and dedicated to specific purposes. Although peer groups do provide occasions for interaction among peers and for questioning adult values, few teens ever do completely reject those values.

We tend to talk about adolescence as if it were a single, unified period of life. But teenagers more often experience adolescence at a number of more or less coterminous periods, each structured by such socializing environments as the family, the peer group, the work place, the media, or the criminal justice system. In some of the communities we studied, we found that different rules and roles for adolescents emerge from each of several institutions and that differentiating among them is a difficult process that requires an understanding of societal and personal agendas.

Unfortunately, the adolescent is often left to rationalize these competing and sometimes conflicting ideologies for himself or herself. This is particularly true in those communities in which the family and the school are in opposition, in which the criminal justice system is antagonistic to both institutions, and in which employers berate both institutions for turning out unmotivated and nonliterate youngsters. Conflict and confusion are inevitable when such social institutions as the home, the school, and the workplace present different standards of adulthood. For example, proclaiming 21 as the minimum age for the legal use of alcohol means that, in some states, young people cannot drink legally until three years after they have been given the right to vote and the young men have been required to register for the military draft. While we are raising the legal age of adulthood for some activities, we are lowering it for others. And despite all we know about individual differences in maturation and development, we continue to think of and treat adolescents as members of a distinctive and age-defined caste.

The sense of identity and the social role of a teenager can change radically with the surrounding social environment, as any parent can attest who has watched a son or daughter who is quiet, withdrawn, and perhaps even surly at home suddenly become expansive and outgoing with peers. Consolidating the real and fantasied roles and self-images that adolescents adopt in various social contexts into a more or less integrated representation of self is part of growing up. This conception of self is then internalized and becomes a characteristic style of relating to social environments. However, what adolescents internalize is a function of experience, and different communities offer very different environments to developing youngsters.

COMMUNITY PROFILE: SOUTHSIDE

Southside, one of the 10 communities we studied, has all the ingredients to create the serious social problems and personal tragedies that tend to be associated with adolescence. It is one of a number of inner-city neighborhoods in a major eastern city. It is multiethnic, poor, and made up of massive public housing projects and squalid, aging tenements. And it seems to have always been that way. Generations of European immigrants in pursuit of the American dream have lived in Southside and struggled to leave, only to be replaced by new immigrant groups in a seemingly unending process of ethnic succession. Recently, this process seems to be accelerating, and more than a quarter of a million people live out their lives huddled within this two-square mile area, as Chinese and Hispanic immigrants crowd in next to the few remaining European families. Josie is one of the teenagers we observed and interviewed in Southside.

Josie is 16 and has lived in Southside ever since her family came to the U.S. from the Dominican Republic when she was 7. She is the youngest of 10 children and the only one who lives at home — though several married siblings live in the same building or nearby in the neighborhood. For Josie, a combination of language, residence, and perhaps even preference makes her peer group and her close friends — male and female — mostly Hispanic and usually Dominican. She attends what is for all intents and purposes a segregated high school, one in which students choose their friends from among those to whom they are bound by language, culture, and ethnicity.

Up before 7 a.m. on school days, Josie dresses, applies some makeup, and eats breakfast in time to meet a girlfriend or two (usually Dominican) for the walk to school. Arriving at school a few minutes before the 8:30 bell, she smokes a cigarette with her friends outside the school in a place frequented by other Dominican students.

Nobody has ever said that Josie or that other Dominicans must congregate in that particular place. Yet the students in Josie's school always group themselves in the same way: blacks congregate on the north side of the school, Hispanics on the west side, and the white and Chinese students on the south side. Such segregation is certainly not school policy, and most of the teachers and administrators try to combat it. But it happens anyway.

The bonding of ethnicity follows the students into the school, where they sit together in similar patterns. In classes Josie sits with her fellow Hispanic students, just as most Chinese and black students sit with their ethnic peers.

The members of Josie's family are not greatly involved with what happens in the school — not only because they feel incompetent to deal with education in a new country, but also because they are content, as teachers and administrators put it, to "leave the driving to us." These same teachers and administrators will tell you that the families of Chinese students are very much involved with the school and try to give their children "a positive learning environment." Chinese students and their families, say these educators, are like the Jewish students and their families back in the 1930s and 1940s.

Now the examples begin. The principal recalls the father of a Chinese student who complained that there was too much class discussion in his son's advanced math course. "My son is here to learn from teachers," he said, "not from other students who don't know any more than he does." The principal was so pleased to have a parent come and say that he respected what the school and the teachers were trying to do that he thanked the father for his complaint. One of the older teachers remembers a Jewish student who came to class one day without his reader — because his father had fallen asleep trying to learn to read it late at night, after his son had gone to bed. Then the comparisons go the other way, and the teachers compare today's Hispanics and blacks with the Italians of past generations, who always believed that you should not educate your children beyond your own level, lest they forget the family.

In our talks with educators, we found similar perceptions of the lack of parent involvement in each of the inner-city areas and depressed rural areas that we studied. Such perceptions stood out in sharp contrast to the descriptions of community involvement and the complaints of parental interference that we heard about in the suburbs.

COMMUNITY PROFILE: SHEFFIELD

The town of Sheffield, another of the communities we studied, is a small, affluent suburb near the city in which Southside is located. In fact, many heads of Sheffield households commute daily into the business district that lies close to the slums of Southside. Sheffield is not a newly developed suburb; it is actually an old town by American standards, dating to the days before the Revolutionary War. Not only did George Washington sleep there, but he had his headquarters in the town for some time. Today, Sheffield retains its small-town flavor; its streets are lined with arching trees, its houses are painted in subdued shades, and its broad lawns are trimmed with abundant, well-manicured shrubbery. Like Southside, Sheffield is a little more than two square miles in area, but fewer than 10,000 people live there.

If the ethnic diversity of Southside is tangible, in Sheffield one immediately feels the homogeneity of the people and of their lifestyles. Differences of religious and politics do exist, of course, but these distinctions have nowhere near the visibility or power of the ethnic differences that divide Southside. There are virtually no black or Hispanic families in Sheffield. And despite a few affluent Japanese families that have settled in Sheffield in recent years, visible ethnic differences are unknown there.

Families are just as important in the enculturation of children in Sheffield as they are in Southside. But similarity rather than diversity characterizes child-rearing practices and family organizations in Sheffield, because parents have such similar social and cultural backgrounds. Bruce, a high school senior whom we observed and interviewed, moved to Sheffield at age 11, when his father was transferred to the area by the multinational corporation for which he works as a mid-level executive. Bruce's mother, who taught school when the family lived in Michigan, chose not to seek a teaching position in Sheffield, for fear that doing so might detract from the time she could spend overseeing the education and development of Bruce and his two younger sisters. Bruce remembers that both his mother and father — but especially his mother — encouraged him to make friends as soon as possible, so that the family's integration into the community could be facilitated by social contacts with other families. "It wasn't so much that she was a joiner," Bruce recalls. "It's just that we learned in Michigan that families are important for feeling part of what is going on."

In Sheffield, peer association and socialization are organized and directed by the parents, who play active roles on school committees and in the organization of sports and other extracurricular activities at the school. The churches and the schools offer a variety of family activities, ranging from family outings to youth clubs with parents advisors. These family-centered groups not only share a common culture and values, but they also have similar goals for their children and similar standards for measuring progress toward those goals. Both the present lifestyles and the orientation of Sheffield families toward the future focus on preparing youngsters for college and careers. Peer groups tend to be quite small, and the most common form of interaction is within a small and noncompetitive group of "best friends." Students are also differentiated by a complex system of ability grouping in the schools, and teachers and administrators complain that some parents threaten to send their children to private schools if they are not placed in honor courses. The schools, which reflect community and family expectations, are structured to encourage a competitive spirit, not only in sports but also in academic and social life. People in Sheffield will tell you that the two things you never ask at a cocktail party are a family's income and the Scholastic Aptitude Test scores of the children.

A WORLD STRUCTURED BY RELATIONSHIPS

Differences between growing up in Southside and growing up in Sheffield entail more than the contrast between urban poverty and suburban affluence. These differences grow out of the many ways in which the daily world of the adolescent is structured by relationships that begin in the family and spread out from there into other social environments in the community. The peer group, though often described as emancipating adolescents from the adult community, is subject to the same constraints.

Peer groups, which are important influences in the lives of all children, are particularly important for teenagers. As adolescence proceeds over the course of the teen years, peer groups become social environments in themselves. They are institutional settings for adolescent social development (just as much as families, schools, and churches are), and their influence on adolescents is considerable. However, unlike the more traditional and recognized institutions, peer groups do not have their own physical structures. Lacking a territory of their own, adolescents as groups must either stake out space belonging to one of the traditional institutions, such as the home or the school, or they must find some neutral and usually temporary space in which to meet, outside the scrutiny of adults. Nor do peer groups have the legal status and protection enjoyed by these other institutions. They tend to form and interact, particularly in the early teen years, at the sufferance of one or more of the adult institutions.

Both Bruce and Josie belong to peer groups whose members live in the same neighborhood, come from the same kinds of families, go to the same school, and share other kinds of involvement in their respective communities. Their peer associations are not random choices but are influenced by the families in which they grew up, by the communities in which they live, by the schools they attend, and by the ways in which these institutions relate to one another.

However, the influence of these institutions can work in two different ways: 1) by leading one to accept the attitudes, beliefs, and opinions espoused by members of the institution as one's own; or 2) by leading one to seek social approval from — and avoid rejection by — members of the institution, without necessarily internalizing its values. In the communities we studied, adult influence on teenagers tended to be longstanding, reaching back into childhood. While the teenagers might challenge that influence, it nonetheless continued to shape their basic values.

The peer influence that we observed tended to be of the second type, leading teenagers to seek approval of the group through conformity to its norms. Moreover, peer influence was usually transitory, lasting only as long as the teenager was a member of or continued to accept the norms of the peer group. Teenagers did not internalize the norms of peer groups to the same degree as they did adult-mediated norms, and usually the norms of the peer group did not cause conflict with adults.

Peer groups were influential without really meaning to be. The individual teenager's willingness — and perhaps even need — to conform, particularly in the early years, rather than any consciously articulated group pressure, had the greatest impact in the groups that we observed. While there were differences among the adolescent peer groups we saw and talked with in each of the communities, there were certain characteristics and feelings that they shared. For example, the most important reason virtually all the teenagers gave for wanting to spend time with their peers was "just to be together." Most of them said that peer association provided them with "understanding." Many said that such understanding was the result of "being the same age," of "wanting the same things," or of "wanting to help each other"; some said that the important thing was "going through the same changes" or "facing the same problems."

Through seemingly random interchanges, adolescents can test their developing abilities and craft socially competent behavior. They learn from their own mistakes and from those of their agemates. They also learn to evaluate what people outside their families say, as they move into the wider and more socially diverse world of the community.

However, for most adolescent peer groups in the communities we studied, we found that association with agemates was not the sole reason that the groups first formed. Instead, a variety of inter-personal relationships with significant adults and even with adult ideological or religious systems first brought the groups together. In most cases, these relationships provided both a setting and a rationale for continuing association. Peer groups are important social settings in adolescent life, but focusing only on teenagers paints a distorted picture of adolescent life and overlooks the significant role of adult guidance in shaping a secure and successful transition from childhood to adulthood. It also masks the vital role that the social institutions of the community — the family, the school, the workplace, religious institution, and other social agencies — play in determining both adolescent development and the emergence of peer groups.

The vast majority of the teenagers we met, observed, and interviewed were well aware of both adult and peer influences in their lives. There was no question in their minds (or ours) that both kinds of influences helped to resolve doubts about present and future and that the teenagers distinguished between the two kinds of influences. The real question, however, is how near to or far from the local community such sources of influence can be and still have a developmental effect on the norms and attitudes of teenagers.

We did not find any indications of strong, active resistance — on the part of individuals or groups of teenagers — to the preferred norms of communities, as long as the institutions representing the adult authority structure agreed on what teenagers were supposed to be and do, not just on what they were not to be and do. As teenagers mature, they seek to move away from the normative pressures of the adult community. But we found far more congruence than conflict between the world views of parents and their adolescent children.

Children are certainly socialized by their parents, but, as they become teenagers and gain more experience in the world outside the family, they bring what they have learned back to the family and share that knowledge with parents and siblings. While we found some parent-child conflict within families and some teacher-student conflict within schools, most adolescents in the communities that we studied became integrated into the social fabric of their communities — and, indeed, into the mainstream of American society — under the guidance of parents and other adults. In fact, in peer-structured support groups; in adult-developed and adult-mediated peer support networks in drug rehabilitation programs, mental health programs, and programs for runaways; and in scout troops, church youth groups, and schools, we found that teenagers seeking to influence the beliefs and behaviors of their peers quoted the values proclaimed by adults. We much more frequently heard teenagers preface comments or observations to peers with "my mom says" than with any attribution to heroes or pundits of the youth culture.

Reasserting the continuing importance of parents and other significant adults in adolescent development does not negate the crucial role of peer groups in shaping adolescents' relationships with a community's social environments. Peer groups allow adolescents to explore relationships outside the boundaries of kinship, to test and further develop self-knowledge and self-esteem, and to resolve self-doubts. They also provide an informal support group that provides opportunities for peer counseling and peer tutoring in which both the helper and the helped benefit from the exchange. A variety of programs involving youngsters helping youngsters are already in place in various communities; most are school-based and involve small groups or one-to-one tutoring.

In each of the communities we studied, youths and adults expressed and exhibited a common culture of the community. The notion of a compelling and separatist teenager subculture perpetuates the myth that all adolescents are alike. In doing so, it masks the considerable diversity among adolescents and overlooks their attachments to the cultural, ethnic, and social class lifestyles of their parents.

For example, family and community combine to provide the dominant influences of socioeconomic status in childhood and adolescence. Backgrounds of poverty impose major developmental hardships on adolescents by restricting their participation in the social and cultural functions of institutions. Youngsters from low-income backgrounds are more likely to have learning disabilities and to record lower educational achievement. They are also more likely to drop out of school, to experience teenage pregnancy and early parenthood, to become involved in criminal and delinquent acts, to be arrested and incarcerated, to be unemployed, and to continue their working lives on the lowest rungs of the work force.

The lives of more affluent adolescents are quite different, but these young people have some problems as well. The pressures to excel are strong in suburbia. (Elkind; Elkind and Brooks) We witnessed the stressful effects of such parents and community pressure in many of the suburban schools we studied. We also saw pressure in other areas of adolescent social life, such as sports. We watched early adolescents spending four to five hours a day in an effort to fulfill their parents' dreams that their offspring become sports superstars and bring home Olympic gold medals.

Yet family income alone does not completely determine the character and outcome of the adolescent years for all individuals. Differing parental and community strategies for adolescent development, chance encounters and unique experiences, and the motivation, determination, resilience, and personal belief systems of teenagers themselves make for a variety of patterns of growing up in America.

Communities also differ in the ways in which they structure the patterns of relationships among families, schools, peer groups, and other institutions. And the influence of these relationships can be more important to adolescent development than the effect of any one institution. While each can help or hinder an adolescent's preparation for adulthood, multiple deficits can combine and reinforce one another with devastating effect. It is possible for adolescents from impoverished backgrounds to succeed; it is possible for them to overcome early educational deficits or association with peers who derogate the schools. But such successes require exceptional intrinsic motivation on the part of the individual adolescent, a family that values and encourages educational attainment, a teacher or school dedicated to success, or some combination of all of these. Many teenagers told me of having met some adult, read some book, seen some film, come in contact with new ideology or lifestyle, "taken up" running or health foods, entered some program, found religion, or discovered some environment that "completely changed" their lives. Indeed, some of the most dramatic of these changes took place in surroundings that were most foreboding and where more firm and consistent interventions were necessary.

THE CONTEXT OF COMMUNITY

Adolescents do generate their own norms and rules, but this process does not and cannot develop in isolation from the institutional context of the communities in which they live and learn. The norms of adolescents can be in harmony or in conflict with the "ideal" values of the community or of particular institutions, but they can never be independent of them. To that extent, we believe it is not possible to identify some independent "youth subculture." Moreover, the value structures of ethnic groups and social classes also influence the psychological development of adolescents.

However, none of these influences, in isolation, can be said to be the determining factor in the psychological development of adolescents. Rather, we have found that a complex mix of all these factors and of the relationships among the institutions within a particular community establish the pattern. For example, minority status did not have any intrinsic effect on self-regard and was important to self esteem only to the extent that it was featured in the community's — or more frequently in some component social institution's — ideal identity for adolescents. Daniel Yankelovich has identified the two "truths" that we all know about the self: "one is that the self is private and alone and wholly encased in one's body. The other is that one is a real self only to the extent that caring and reaching beyond the self continue." (Yankelovich 240) And communities can and should care about and try to help with the self-development of their younger members as well.

Every community can and should shape the relationships among its various socializing institutions into a network that fosters the learning of its values. Moreover, the messages that each of the institutions send to individual adolescents should be mutually reinforcing, rather than disharmonious or even working at cross purposes. In addition, the opportunity to internalize those values should be available to all children and not just to a fortunate few. The importance of integrating the socializing institutions to provide such a caring structure and the interdependence of the adult and adolescent social worlds in producing and interpreting it were visible in the social and behavioral standards set by each of the communities we studied for its young.

These standards and the expectations they described were not so much a set of rules sanctioned by the community as they were a loose collection of shared understandings that limited the variability of permissible behavior. For example, if we asked a teenager why he or she did or did not become involved in some activity, seek some goal, avoid some risk, or behave in one way rather than another, the reason was seldom said to be because of any specific rule or authority system, such as family or peers. Rather, we heard much more generalized reasons, such as, "I don't know why, but it seemed to be the right thing to do" or "That's the way it is here in Sheffield."

Parents and teachers were equally vague in describing the origins of their expectations of teenagers. In explaining what time they expected a teenager to be home at night, parents would usually cite the general perception of neighbors or community residents that youngsters of a particular age should be home "at about" such and such a time, and we seldom found great discrepancies among families. Teenagers, though they might protest that the times were too early, would usually mention the same general time limits as parents. Teenagers also agreed with parents and with one another on how much leeway they would be granted and what extenuating circumstances their parents would accept. Asking teachers about homework assignments or school administrators about discipline almost always elicited similar references to "what this community expects."

We came to call this unwritten, "sensed" set of expectations and standards the community's "youth charter." While it is nowhere codified, both youngsters and adults usually know the limits set by the youth charter for various kinds of behavior, and the daily lives of the teenagers are governed largely by the conventions that emerge from the shared understandings of the charter.

Like so much else in life, the development of these tacit understandings begins in the family, when the growing child learns from the comments and choices of parents and older siblings to value or devalue individual and group traits, as well as to evaluate the shoulds and should-nots of individual and group behavior. These influences lay a foundation for future reference, and for most youngsters the family continues to be more influential than any other social group.

Beginning in the early adolescent years, peers become increasingly important in spontaneous decision making, but their judgments and opinions are considered along with, rather than as replacements for, parental influences. As the school and other social worlds of the community become increasingly important in the teenagers life, the community establishes a comprehensive frame of reference that both integrates and transcends the influence of any particular institutional sector. Decisions about schooling, for example, involve parental and peer influences and, less directly, the worlds of work and of school. Thus adolescents perceive themselves as interacting within a social environment, and the way in which that environment structures reality becomes their charter for action. Communities can create youth charters that encourage youngsters to move from dependence to interdependence, from the ethnocentrism of early adolescence to the social competence of young adulthood, and from definitions of self provided by surrounding social contexts to those arising from within.

Schools can be instrumental in providing the community and its constituent institutions with a structure for transmitting the expectations and standards that we found most teenagers are desperately seeking. Schools are central to the lives of adolescents — not only because so much of their waking time is spent in them, but also because schools have been assigned a role at least commensurate with that of families in the preparation of adolescents for later life. The schools are expected to teach occupational preparation, information about health, a measure of self-discipline, and good citizenship.

Indeed, we have come to see schools — particularly high schools — as the principal remediators of social ills. We include new courses in the curriculum in the belief that this offers our best chance for prevention as well as for cure. Wide spread drug abuse led to drug education courses, alcohol abuse led to alcohol education courses, and teen pregnancy led to sex education courses. Even so, the specter of Acquired Immune Deficiency Syndrome will inevitably lead to AIDS education courses, however controversial that may be. But the introduction and continuation of such courses is much more a matter of local community sentiment and sensitivity than of any education policy at the state or national level.

The influence of the community on the culture of the schools is so strong that it calls into question the notion of a "school culture" independent of community culture. As part of that interaction, the school establishes networks among adolescents that reinforces the connections between the social organization of the community and the growth and development of individual adolescents. To the extent that the school relies on social, racial, and ethnic identification to sort students' access to educational resources, it confuses and confounds the consolidation of identity. Ethnographers Signithia Fordham and John Ogbu have argued that one reason that black students do poorly in school is the ambivalence and dissonance they experience from "the burden of acting white." (176-206) Fordham and Ogbu found that many academically able black students do not put forth the necessary effort, because they are caught between a school system that fails to acknowledge that black students are capable of academic achievement and a black community that considers academic striving as "acting white."

Once we accept the ability of local peer groups to mediate a variety of external influences and to help youngsters become members of the community of adults, it may even be possible to help teenagers develop peer-group structures that enhance their cognitive and social development. Benjamin Bloom underscored the feasibility of such an approach through the formation of peer groups; he proposed establishing student support groups of two or three students working together to raise the level of learning of the group members. (Bloom) Peer groups provide the informal support that can give adolescents access to a vast new set of opportunities for peer counseling and peer tutoring in which both the helper and the helped benefit. As I have already noted, a variety of programs involving youngsters helping youngsters are already in place in various communities; most are school-based and involve small groups or one-on-one tutoring.

In response to suicide pacts, such as the one in Bergenfield, some schools are setting up peer networks that work with adult counselors to watch for signs of potential suicide and to offer help and care. Similar networks have been tried as ways of dealing with alcohol and drug abuse. Other approaches, such as the Primary Prevention School Program of the Yale Child Study Center, are more broadly based and stress academic competence and help as well.

Adult-mediated peer groups offer a creative means of bringing adult concerns to groups of youngsters who have daily access to one another. But they are largely dependent on adults and on their continuing concern. The more spontaneous and less formal groups that youngsters negotiate for themselves lack the continuity of adult social institutions and tend to respond to changes in adult agendas rather than to their own agendas or to forces from outside the community. For example, peer groups are one of the social contexts most affected by changes in the structure and functioning of the family. As more mothers have entered the labor market, adolescents have tended to have less adult supervision and have spent more time with peers, becoming more dependent on peer-defined cultural, social, and behavioral norms. This has meant less time for the loving support of parents, which all children need, even when they do not seem to be asking for it. But none of these changes were initiated by any intentional activity of the adolescent peer group.

A COMMUNITY YOUTH CHARTER

When we first undertook our research program, the development of an officially endorsed youth charter was but a dream. We even included a caution in our early proposals and reports, citing Sigmund Freud's *Civilization and Its Discontents*, in which he asks, "What would be the use of the most acute analysis of social neurosis since no one possesses the power to compel the community to adopt the therapy?"

Now, more than a decade later, at least one community is developing precisely such a charter. Sparked both by research and by a number of program initiatives, the city of Seattle has adopted and made explicit a Policy Plan for Children and Youth, which was developed 1) to gain a better understanding of the status of children and youth in Seattle and of current efforts to address their needs; and 2) to promote community agreement on goals and priorities in order to establish a clearer understanding of the roles to be played by various jurisdictions and organizations in the service system for children and youth.

This plan, which looks to young people as a community resource rather than as a liability, makes the community's youth charter (what Seattle calls a community youth agenda) clear and available to all. It is designed to 1) help parents better fulfill their responsibilities to their children; 2) improve the health and well-being of children and youth and protect them from harm; 3) prepare young people for a successful transition to adulthood; 4) help young people better understand cultural differences and value the ethnic diversity of the community; 5) project to all young people a vision of high expectations and hope for their futures and a sense of the responsibilities they bear; and 6) involve children and youth as active participants in the community. The plan, which goes on to describe the responsibilities and the rights of all the constituent social institutions (including those of children), has now become the "official" policy of Seattle and is overseen by a committee of city officials and citizens, including two youths elected by their peers.

The next step that Seattle is taking will convert what is essentially a plan into a charter. Groups of 30 teenagers meet frequently to develop the plan, item by item, into a series of expectations and standards. They have conducted youth surveys to determine how best to disseminate these standards to all youngsters in the city. [1] Of course, it is too soon to call Seattle's plan a success and to assume that this or any other such formalization of a community's adolescent charter will or can be made to work as a new or expanded chance for a smoother and more productive transition to adulthood. However, the experience in Seattle does offer the hope that communities are beginning to accept their local responsibility to treat adolescence as a period in which young people requires a stable and consistent environment in which to grow and develop.

Despite continuing assumptions — both professionals and popular — that adolescents look toward peers and away from the adult community, we found significant congruence between the world views of teenagers and those of the adults in their lives. However, such congruence means that the problems of adolescence are our problems, too, and cannot be explained away by referring to a "youth culture" that we claim adolescents invented. I believe that we have made the adolescent peer group the scapegoat for our own sins, both those that we commit ourselves and those that adolescents learn from us. The use and abuse of drugs, alcohol, and tobacco began as adult problems and became teenage problems only when we introduced young people to them as signs of having reached adult status. Other adult-proclaimed youth problems, such as unemployment and delinquent behavior, follow similar demographic and cyclical patterns among young people as they do among adults. And some, such as poor nutritional and other health habits, are first learned in the family. While we seldom hear about the social benefits of peer groups, they do exist. As we observed the style and the spirit of interaction in peer groups, we found them to offer important ways of allowing youngsters to experiment with and learn about egalitarian relationships and about new and different patterns of representing themselves. The lessons learned in peer groups are sometimes painful, but they are necessary preparation for adult social relations.

The popular picture of a deeply troubled and rebellious generation of young Americans is not the picture we saw emerging during the decade of our research. By the second half of the 1980s, adolescent pregnancy was down to 51 per 1,000 teenage girls from the 68.3 per 1,000 in 1970 and the 89 per 1,000 in 1960. While there is some cause for concern in the fact that well over half of these young mothers-to-be were unmarried in the second half of the 1980s, whereas only one-third were unmarried in 1970, it could well be that as a society we are becoming more accepting of the choice to be a single mother. Educational attainment, particularly among blacks, has increased steadily, and the dropout rate has been declining. Eighty-six percent of all 25 to 29 year olds have earned high school diplomas (twice the percentage of 1940), and 22% are college graduates (four times the 1940 rate). Drug use among young people has decreased significantly, the rate of alcohol abuse among young people has decreased somewhat, and some leveling off has occurred in crime, homicide, and suicide rates.[2]

Teenagers do have time to make choices about their present and future lifestyles, and the adolescents whom we met and interviewed expressed considerable confidence that they could make such decisions, given the time and the adult guidance that they know they need. It was the adults we observed and interviewed who seemed to be in a hurry for teenagers to "settle down" into adulthood — often ignoring or forgetting that developmental tasks and the achievement of a mature identity proceed as much from what the community can provide for guidance and encouragement as from teenagers' own resources and motivation.

With a firm but sensitive set of expectations and standards, undergirded by a youth charter, and with our acceptance of the fact that time is abundant, adolescent crises can become less urgent and can even provide opportunities for learning and progress. This suggests less concern about the prolongation of adolescence and more concern about how we can integrate adolescence into the life course as a time in which teenagers seek identity rather than interdependence. We can provide an explicit guidance structure within which they can work rather than offer only benign neglect or outraged moralizing. The transitional role of adults and adult-mediated institutions should be one of patient, guided tutoring. The youth charter seems to be an ideal place to map out the roles of adults and adolescents, since it is more accessible than teenage fantasy for discussion and negotiation — and at the same time has less immediate and less critical consequences than the reality we so often insist that teenagers face. Youth charters and the structure of expectations and standards experienced through adolescent life in the community interact with individual personalities in a variety of social worlds to produce behaviors, motivations, and attitudes that shape the movement to adult status. It is in the harmony of these social contexts that adolescence can — and usually does — become a period of joy and challenge as well as a sentimental journey from what must be left behind in the migration to the new adult world.

END NOTES

[1] Personal communication from Robert Aldrich. For an excellent description of the type of data gathering and organization required to move a community in this direction, see Robert A. Aldrich, "Children and Youth in Cities: Seattle's Kidsplace," in Rick Carlson and Brooke Newman, eds., *Issues and Trends in Health* (St. Louis: C. V. Mosby, 1987), 63-69.

[2] See *The Forgotten Half: Non-College Youth in America* (Washington, D.C.: William T. Grant Foundation Commission on Work, Family and Citizenship, January 1988).

WORKS CITED

Bloom, Benjamin S. "The Search for Methods of Group Instruction as Effective as One-to-One Tutoring." Educational Leadership 40 (May 1984): 4-17.

Coleman, James. Youth: *Transition to Adulthood.* Chicago: University of Chicago Press, 1974.

——. *The Adolescent Society.* Glencoe, IL: Free Press, 1960.

"The Copycat Suicides." *Newsweek* 109 (March 23 1987), 28.

Elkind, David. *Miseducation: Preschoolers at Risk.* New York: Knopf 1988.

Elkind, David, and Andree Aelion Brooks *Children of Fast-track Parents*. New York: Viking, 1989.

Fordham, Signithia and John U. Ogbu. "Black Students' School Success: Coping with the Burden of 'Acting White.'" *Urban Review* 18 (1986): 176-206.

Freud, Sigmund. *Civilization and Its Discontents*. Trans. Joan Riviere. Garden City NY: Doubleday, 1958.

Yankelovich, Daniel. *New Rules: Search for Self-Fulfillment in a World Turned Upside Down*. New York: Random House, 1981

Chapter 5

New Directions in Ministry with Early Adolescents

John Roberto

How do the insights on adolescent development, drawn from psychology, faith development, family systems, and social research shape our ministry? What are the implications of these insights for our current ministry efforts? How will they challenge us to move in new directions? Practically speaking, how do we integrate these insights into directions that we can use in creating or enhancing a comprehensive ministry with early adolescents? This chapter will attempt to provide practical directions for early adolescent ministry that builds on the foundations provided in the first four essays of this *Access Guide*.

First, I will examine the inadequacy of our current approach to early adolescent ministry. Second, I will report on a contemporary research study on healthy adolescent growth which provides a rationale from which to build a new approach. Third, I will propose new directions that have potential for pastorally addressing the research base developed in this book. Lastly, I will suggest practical strategies for action.

PART ONE: THE NEED FOR A NEW DIRECTION

The Church's ministry with early adolescents has been dominated by a *schooling* approach in which its efforts have been modeled on the organization of a school with courses built around a textbook series and classes organized in weekly, one-hour sessions held in classrooms. While many new and exciting approaches to early adolescent catechesis/religious education are taking place, the *inadequacy* of maintaining a schooling approach to early adolescent ministry is becoming increasingly apparent. *I strongly believe that catechesis/religious education is an essential and integral element of a comprehensive ministry with early adolescents.* Research shows that quality religious education and the family's socializing influence are the two most important ingredients promoting faith maturity in adolescents. (Search Institute) What I am calling into question is the adequacy of organizing all our ministry efforts into a schooling model.

Let me illustrate several examples of this inadequacy. The schooling approach does not address the wide range of early adolescent developmental needs; many times it only addresses doctrinal instruction, which is a need of the Church but not necessarily a need of early adolescents. It does not provide the range of programming called for by early adolescent developmental needs, nor does it provide a vehicle for meaningful involvement of early adolescents in the life of the faith community and the local community. *The limits of the schooling approach often mean that a young person's experience of church becomes another experience of school!* The schooling approach does not offer a framework to assist the Church in ministering with families of early adolescents or partnering with families in promoting the healthy faith growth of early adolescents.

At the heart of the inadequacy of a schooling approach to early adolescent ministry is the view of early adolescent development as an individual affair, separate from the socializing influence of the larger community(s) of which the early adolescent is an integral member. The framework proposed by John Hill in Chapter 1 and reinforced through Part One of the *Access Guide* gives great credence to this broader view. In Chapter 1, Hill writes,

> ...the impact of the primary changes on these psychosocial issues does not occur in a vacuum. It occurs in family, peer, school, community, media, church — and, for some, work-settings. The variations in how the issues are resolved stem not only from individuals' past histories but also from their current social relationships. The others who are important in adolescents' lives — whom they encounter in family, peer, school, and community settings — react to the primary changes with modified expectations and norms...(Stating it in another way, Glen Elder has observed that adolescents do not experience society and its values directly but as it is presented to them through their actual social participations in familial, peer, school, and other settings.)

Such a view is supported by family systems and family life cycle research, faith development research, and social research. Adolescent development must be viewed within the context of socializing community where the early adolescent is an integral member of a variety of communities: family, peers, activity groups, school, community, and church. In Chapter 4, Francis A. J. Ianni supports this approach.

> Every community can and should shape the relationships among its various socializing institutions into a network that fosters the learning of its values. Moreover, the messages that each of the institutions

> send to individual adolescents should be mutually reinforcing, rather than disharmonious or even working at cross purposes...The importance of integrating the socializing institutions to provide such a caring structure and the interdependence of the adult and adolescent social worlds in producing and interpreting it were visible in the social and behavioral standards set by each of the communities we studied for its young.

The adolescent is engaged in a *search for structure*, a set of believable and attainable expectations and standards from the community to guide their movement from child to adult status. Young people need a *caring community* — a supportive network of social institutions (family, school, church, youth organizations) which create a community-based socialization. We are challenged to view individual growth within this broader context. We now turn to the factors that promote healthy adolescent development within this broader context.

PART TWO: GROWING UP HEALTHY — INTERNAL SUPPORTS AND EXTERNAL ASSETS

In 1990, the Search Institute completed a major research study of 46,000 young Americans in grades 6 through 12 entitled *The Troubled Journey: A Profile of American Youth.* [1] The research project studied 20 indicators that placed young people at risk. The study developed a wide range of factors in the family, in the community, in the schools, and within young persons themselves that predispose youth to either healthy or unhealthy growth during their teenage years. As a result, the research is able with considerable certainty to trace a pattern of factors that promote the positive development of youth. These factors, promoted by a young person's family and community provide the structure and context for healthy adolescent development.

The Troubled Journey: A Profile of American Youth reveals two important groups of factors that promote healthy development and reduce the likelihood of adolescents' participation in behavior that puts them at risk. One group identifies *assets external to the adolescent*, but present in family and community. Another group identifies *strengths to be found within the adolescent.*

> When children are growing up, the kind of help they most need is usually supplied by a combination of the family and the surrounding community. The family provides rules, discipline, encouragement, and caring. The community makes available such things as educational experiences, community rules and expectations, friends, recreational experiences, and spiritual nurture. These are the external assets.

> These external assets, taken together, form a kind of temporary scaffold around a child in order to support and encourage while the growing child is developing an internal system of supports that will see him or her safely into adulthood. Their function is much like that of the scaffolds built around buildings during erection or repair to provide a temporary stability until the building is ready to stand on its own. They are there to do what needs to be done while young people are developing their own internal supports — until they develop *backbone.* (April 1991 *Source* 1)

Our focus in this section will be to look at how we can promote the positive through the Church's ministry with early adolescents: promoting internal strengths and strengthening external assets. [2]

In a perfect world, these internal strengths would develop gradually throughout adolescence while external supports were being removed at the same gradual rate. The research shows, however, that, while some internal strengths increase during the teen years, too often the external assets are being removed before adequate internal strength development occurs. Certain of the internal strengths, in fact, are found to diminish between sixth and twelfth grade.

PROMOTING INTERNAL STRENGTHS

The Troubled Journey: A Profile of American Youth indicates 14 elements of the essential internal supports that make positive growth possible for teenagers. Thirteen of the 14 are positive, a listing of values, attitudes, and skills that caring adults hope young people develop during their adolescent years. They are divided into three categories: commitment to education, positive values, and social competence. Only one (values sexual restraint) implies a "just say no" message.

Educational Commitment

The first essential component of internal support is enthusiasm for the educational process, now and well into the future. Four elements were identified in the study:

1. *School Performance*: working at above average performance.
2. *Achievement Motivation*: caring about their school performance and wanting to do well.
3. *Homework*: spending six or more hours each week on homework.
4. *Educational Aspiration*: hoping to go on after high school either to college or technical school.

Positive Values

The second essential component of internal support is positive values — values that center on caring about others as well as oneself. Four elements were identified in the study:

5. *Values Sexual Restraint*: postponing sexual activity as a personal goal, "just say no".
6. *Values Helping People*: being of help to others.
7. *Is Concerned About World Hunger and Poverty*: expressing a desire to better the circumstances of those who are hungry and in poverty.
8. *Cares About Other People's Feelings*: attending to the well-being of others.

Social Competence

The third essential component of internal support is social competence and social skills — success in interacting with others, in learning how to work in groups, in "holding your own" against opposition, and in anticipating what is coming. Six elements were identified in the study:

9. *Self Esteem*: having a reasonable sense of one's own value
10. *Assertiveness Skills*: standing up for what one believes — explaining your understandings and needs clearly and firmly, without being angry or abrasive in doing so.
11. *Decision-making Skills*: dealing with increasingly complex decisions and selecting the things to which one will "just say no."
12. *Friend-making Skills*: mastering the skills for making and keeping friends.
13. *Planning Skills*: being able to map out one's future over the next days, months or years and being able to delay what seems most attractive right now in order to complete the less-desirable but necessary task.
14. *Positive View of Personal Future*: feeling positive about the future and their own future.

STRENGTHENING EXTERNAL ASSETS

One of the major contributions of the *The Troubled Journey: A Profile of American Youth* is that it identifies those elements in the family and in the community that appear, in effect, to protect teenagers against the kinds of trouble most feared by parents, teachers, and others who work with adolescents. The more assets a given teenager reports being present in his or her life, the fewer the at-risk behaviors that teenager displays.

These 16 external assets provide the kind of interest, care, and structure that are essential if an adolescent is to progress through the teenage years relatively untroubled. They supply a necessary network of support while adolescents develop internal supports firm enough to carry them successfully into adult life.

Eight of these external assets lie mostly within the control of individual families. The remaining eight are community-based, requiring the cooperation or initiative of persons or groups outside the family. Thus it is evident that neither the community nor the family can assume the entire responsibility for the support of adolescents. They have to work together.

External Assets: Support

The first essential component of external assets is support, creating an atmosphere of appreciation and encouragement that provides young people with experiences of being loved, successful, and worthwhile. Thus equipped, one can survive the inevitable temporary failures and defeats of daily life. Of the seven external assets included under external assets: support, the first four assets are almost entirely family-generated and the remaining three depend largely on institutions outside the family.

1. *Family Support*: providing high levels of love and support.
2. *Parent(s) as Social Resource*: viewing parents as people one can go to for advice, comfort, and encouragement.
3. *Parent Communication*: having frequent, in-depth conversation with parents.
4. *Parent Involvement in Schooling*: continuing to show interest in the nature of their children's school work and success in school.
5. *Other Adult Communication*: having frequent, in-depth conversations with adults other than parents.
6. *Other Adult Resources*: knowing non-parent adults to go to for advice and support.
7. *Positive School Climate*: caring, encouraging school environment.

External Assets: Control

The second essential component of external assets is controls on behavior — learning how to exercise some self-discipline, to develop willpower to complete projects, to allocate time to life's demands according to carefully-thought-through priorities rather than momentary impulse. These are essential capacities that most adults absorbed by having certain controls imposed throughout adolescence. While the first four elements of this category are largely parent-controlled, the final one is related to circumstances largely beyond family control:

8. *Parental Standards*: making expectations of behavior and the penalties for inappropriate behavior known to adolescents.
9. *Parental Discipline*: disciplining adolescents for violating family rules.
10. *Parental Monitoring*: knowing where the adolescent is going

when he or she leaves the house, with whom, and for approximately how long.

11. *Time at Home*: insuring that the adolescent goes out for fun and recreation no more than three nights a week.

12. *Positive Peer Influence*: developing friends who approve of and model responsible behavior.

External Assets: Structured Use of Time

The third essential component of external assets is the development of a disciplined structure — working at a task to meet given deadlines, not at one's own convenience or whim. Four elements fit into this category of external assets. All of them, though partly dependent on family decision, largely depend on activities provided and supervised for youth by adult members of the community.

13. *Involved in Music*: spending one hour or more per week in music training or practice.

14. *Involved in School Extra-curricular Activities*: spending one hour or more each week participating in school-related sports, clubs, or organizations.

15. *Involved in Community Organizations or Activities*: spending an hour or more each week participating in organizations or clubs outside of school.

16. *Involved in Church or Synagogue Activities*: spending an hour or more per week attending worship services or participating in church activities.

The 14 internal characteristics together with the 16 external assets make up a network of interior and exterior strengths that has remarkable power to *shield* adolescents against at-risk behaviors and *promote* positive teenage development. They equip adolescents to make wise choices.[3]

Both deficits and assets, as measured in this report, strongly influence at-risk behaviors. The more assets one has, the less the at-risk behavior. Conversely, the more deficits one has, the greater the at-risk behavior. A two-pronged approach — to prevent deficits and to promote assets — is necessary to alter the frequency with which adolescents make choices which compromise their health or jeopardize their future.

Since most adolescents experience at-risk behavior in several areas, communities must offer effective prevention and intervention programs that address behavioral areas and equip young people with multiple internal and external assets. This kind of effort helps strengthen families, schools and other institutions to provide strong support and control and to nourish in young people the kinds of commitment, values and competencies that lead to healthy choices. (April 1991 *Source* 3)

PART THREE: NEW DIRECTIONS FOR EARLY ADOLESCENT MINISTRY

Exciting new directions are suggested by the research in the four chapters in this volume and by the Search Institute study. The research suggests new kinds of programming that cultivate the internal assets of early adolescents. It suggests new approaches/strategies for strengthening their external supports by developing a systems approach to ministry with early adolescents — focusing on the broader community, especially their families. Above all it refocuses the Church's ministry and locates it within a broader framework. If we take seriously this research we will more and more talk about our ministry as one of prevention of deficits, promotion of assets, and nurturance of positive, healthy adolescent faith development.

In this section, I would like to propose a way of viewing the national vision document, *A Vision of Youth Ministry*, that has the potential for provide pastoral direction for ministry with early adolescents.

A BROADER SCOPE

A Vision of Youth Ministry offers an *integrated, holistic, comprehensive vision* of ministry with youth. It transcends the narrower approaches of a schooling model or group model of ministry. It maps out a ministerial framework that attends to a wider set of early adolescent needs. The *Vision* clearly states that youth ministry is one of the ministries of the Church and therefore participates in realizing the mission of the Church with youth.

> As one among many ministries of the Church, youth ministry must be understood in terms of the mission and ministry of the whole Church. ...The Church's mission is threefold: to proclaim the good news of salvation, offer itself as a group of people transformed by the Spirit into a community of faith, hope, and love; and to bring God's justice and love to others through service in its individual, social, and political dimensions (*Vision* 3).

This grounding of youth ministry in the mission of the Church broadens the scope of our efforts. *Youth ministry means becoming Church with young people* — focusing the ministries of the Church upon this unique stage of life with its distinct life tasks and social context *and* actively engaging young people as disciples in the mission of Jesus and the Church. Such an approach addresses so many of the developmental needs of early adolescents (e.g., meaningful involvement in the life of the community).

This threefold mission, rooted in the Reign of God as proclaimed by Jesus, forms the basis for the goals and the framework (components) of youth ministry: Word (evangelization and catechesis), worship, community, justice and service, guidance and healing, enablement, and advocacy.

The threefold mission is reinforced by the broad scope of ministry embraced by *A Vision of Youth Ministry*. This scope carries us well beyond the notion that early adolescents are simply the "recipients" or "objects" of ministry or programs rather than active participants or "subjects." This broad scope includes ministry:

TO youth — responding to youth's varied needs;
WITH youth — working with adults to fulfill their common responsibility for the Church's mission;
BY youth — exercising their own ministry to others: peers, community, world;
FOR youth — interpreting the needs of youth and acting on behalf of or with youth for a change in their community/social systems.

A DUAL FOCUS

If we are going to attend to the twin concerns of promoting internal assets and enhancing external, community supports, then youth ministry must adopt a *dual* focus. The *Vision* is quite clear in this regard. Youth ministry is a ministry *within* the community of faith as we minister to the needs of young people through our ministry efforts and programming. Youth ministry is, however, more than what happens within the four walls of the church building. Youth ministry is a ministry *to* the broader community as we serve youth in our communities through outreach and as we collaborate/partner with families, youth organizations (like scouting), and schools in promoting healthy adolescent development. While many in youth ministry have emphasized ministry within the faith community, youth ministry also addresses the broader community context. In the style of Jesus' ministry *to* people by healing, preaching, teaching, forgiving, and serving, youth ministry brings a ministry to youth beyond the confines of our in-church youth programs.

A CONTEXTUAL APPROACH

Supporting this dual focus is the contextual or systems approach advocated by the *Vision*. This contextual approach is an essential ingredient in the new directions proposed in this essay. This contextual approach seeks to view young people as part of a number of social systems which influence their growth, values, and faith, rather than as isolated individuals. "In all places, youth ministry occurs within a given social, cultural, and religious context which shapes the specific form of the ministry." (*Vision* 10) Among these systems are the family, society, the dominant culture, youth culture, ethnic culture, school, and local church community. Attention to the impact, positive and negative, of each of these systems on youth and ministry to these systems are essential for effective youth ministry.

One example of a systems approach in youth ministry is an emphasis on ministry with families — encouraging and supporting the role of parents, restructuring youth programming to include families (or parents), and providing programs and services for parents (and youth) that respond to their needs. A second example is the attention youth ministry gives to the cultural impact of media upon young people (e.g., rock music, music videos, advertising, TV) by raising young people's awareness of this influence. The increasing importance of these contexts or systems points to a direction for continuing growth in youth ministry.

AN ENRICHED SET OF GOALS

Toward what ends are we working? *A Vision of Youth Ministry* articulated two goals that still guide youth ministry today.

> *Goal #1: Youth ministry works to foster the total personal and spiritual growth of each young person.*
>
> *Goal #2: Youth ministry seeks to draw young people to responsible participation in the life, mission, and work of the faith community.* (*Vision* 7)

The first goal emphasizes *becoming* — focusing on the *personal* dimension of human existence. Our understanding of the unique life tasks and social-cultural context of adolescence provides direction for fostering their growth in discipleship and Catholic identity. This goal challenges us to promote the internal assets of young people through personal guidance and specialized programming like catechesis and service.

The second goal emphasizes *belonging* — focusing on the *interpersonal* or *communal* dimension of human existence. Active engagement of youth in the Christian community's life and mission provides an important context for growth and overcomes the danger of marginalizing youth in the church, segregating them from the real centers of power, responsibility and commitment in community life. This goal challenges us to provide the meaningful participation early adolescents require, broadening our ministry to support family life and to integrate young people into the life of the faith community.

A third goal, implicit in *A Vision of Youth Ministry*, can be proposed. I would state it in the following manner:

> *Goal #3: Youth ministry empowers young people to transform the world as disciples of Jesus Christ by living and working for justice and peace.*

This third goal emphasizes *transforming* — focusing on the public or *social* dimension of human existence. This third goal seeks to help young people realize that living and working for justice and peace is grounded in the Gospels and the Catholic social vision, and is essential for being a Catholic Christian. Youth ministry empowers young people with the knowledge and skills to serve others and to learn how to transform the unjust structures of society (locally and globally) so that these structures promote justice, respect human dignity, promote human rights, and build peace.

Our challenge is to help early adolescents use their considerable energy and efforts in positive ways. *The Troubled Journey* calls this *prosocial behavior*, describing it this way:

> Prosocial behavior covers a wide range of human actions — helping people in distress, donating time or energy to voluntary service organizations, attempting to reverse political, economic and social injustice or inequality. The common thread among prosocial behaviors is the desire or intent to promote the welfare of others.
>
> When it comes to raising healthy children, promoting prosocial behavior is as important as preventing antisocial or health-compromising behavior. Acts of compassion help develop social competencies, positive values, and a sense of purpose in life. Furthermore, prosocial behavior may actually reduce risky choices. Students who engage in helping behavior on a weekly basis are shown in this study to be less likely than non-helpers to report risky behaviors. (*The Troubled Journey*)

There is nothing that can compare with the increase in sensitivity to others, sense of personal value, and compassion that adolescents develop when adults provide concrete structures to channel teenagers' energy. Combined with this involvement is reflection which brings them to new insights and a more positive view of themselves, their world, and their future

A FRAMEWORK

As we have said, the totality of a ministry with early adolescents is not captured by a youth group, or a religious education program, or a confirmation program. These are all programs within a comprehensive ministry. Youth ministry is also not limited to the programs and activities sponsored within the Church community. It is also directed outward to the needs, concerns, and issues of youth in society. The wisdom of a comprehensive approach is that a broad range of youth's concerns, needs, struggles, and hopes can be addressed since no one program must carry the burden of the entire scope of ministry.

A Vision of Youth Ministry challenges leaders to envision and plan ministry efforts around the seven components of a comprehensive approach. The framework (or components) describe distinct aspects for developing a comprehensive, integrated ministry with youth. Briefly, these components include:

Word

Evangelization: reaching out to young people who are uninvolved in the life of the community and inviting them into a relationship with Jesus and the Christian community. Evangelization involves proclaiming the Good News of Jesus through programs and relationships.

Catechesis: promoting a young person's growth in Christian faith through the kind of teaching and learning that emphasizes understanding, reflection, and transformation. This is accomplished through systematic, planned, and intentional programming (curriculum). Catechesis for younger adolescents includes the faith themes of Church, Jesus and the Gospel Message, Moral Decision-Making, Personal Growth, Relationships, Service, and Human Sexuality. (Reference: *The Challenge of Adolescent Catechesis*.)

Prayer and Worship: assisting young people in deepening their relationship with Jesus through the development of a personal prayer life; and providing a variety of prayer and worship experiences with youth to deepen and celebrate their relationship with Jesus in a caring Christian community; involving young people in the sacramental life of the Church.

Community Life: building Christian community with youth through programs and relationships which promote openness, trust, valuing the person, cooperation, honesty, taking responsibility, and willingness to serve; creating a climate where young people can grow and share their struggles, questions, and joys with other youth and adults; helping young people feel like a valued part of the church.

Guidance and Healing: providing youth with sources of support and counsel as they face personal problems and pressures (for example, family problems, peer pressure, substance abuse, suicide) and decide on careers and important life decisions; providing appropriate support and guidance for youth during times of stress and crisis; helping young people deal with the problems they face and the pressures people place on them; developing a better understanding of their parents and learning how to communicate with them.

Justice, Peace, and Service: guiding young people in developing a Christian social consciousness and a commitment to a life of justice and peace through educational programs and service/action involvement; infusing the concepts of justice and peace into all youth ministry relationships and programming.

Enablement: developing, supporting, and utilizing the leadership abilities and personal gifts of youth and adults in youth ministry, empowering youth for ministry with their peers; developing a leadership team to organize and coordinate the ministry with youth.

Advocacy: interpreting the needs of youth (personal, family, and social), especially in areas of injustices towards or oppression of youth, and acting with or on behalf of youth for a change in the systems which create injustice; giving young people a voice and empowering them to address the social problems that they face.

For *A Vision of Youth Ministry* to be realized there must be collaboration among all those who minister with youth. This is essential for the creation or enhancement of a caring community which provides support and structure for healthy adolescent development.

> No one aspect of youth ministry is independent of others; they are all interdependent elements of a unified total vision. The multifaceted nature of youth ministry requires a process of collaboration among all persons involved in it, rather than fragmentation or competition. ...Part of the vision of youth ministry is to present to youth the richness of the person of Christ, which perhaps exceeds the ability of one person to capture, but which might be effective by the collective ministry of the many persons who make up the Church.
>
> In all of these developing models (parish, school, diocesan), however, the process of dialogue, collaboration, and joint planning is the key to ending fragmentation and restoring a sense of balance to the ministry with youth (*Vision* 24).

IMPLICATIONS FOR EARLY ADOLESCENT MINISTRY

What are the implications of the research and *A Vision of Youth Ministry* for new directions early adolescent ministry. Let me offer the following nine guidelines as a way to think about our ministry with early adolescents:

#1 *Early Adolescent Ministry Views Adolescents Holistically* — viewing early adolescents as part of the social fabric of a family, community, ethnic group, and society.

#2 *Early Adolescent Ministry Promotes Healthy Adolescent Development* — focusing on the goals of becoming, belonging, and transforming and designing all programming and ministry efforts to promote the development of the early adolescent's internal assets and to strengthen their external support systems.

#3 *Early Adolescent Ministry is Comprehensive* — providing a multi-ministry involving evangelization and catechesis, community life, prayer and worship, justice and service, guidance and healing, enablement of leadership, and advocacy organized in four formats: gathering, non-gathering, family, and community.

#4 *Early Adolescent Ministry is a Ministry with Families* — integrating a family perspective into all programming and providing a distinct ministry to parents and the family through support, education, encouragement, programming, guidance, and involvement in church life and youth ministry.

#5 *Early Adolescent Ministry is Multicultural* — respecting and building upon the strengths and riches of an adolescent's ethnic culture and promoting a multicultural awareness and understanding among all youth.

#6 *Early Adolescent Ministry is Relational and Community-Based* — providing a context for the healthy development of Catholic Christian values and identity and a community of engagement for youth, and developing positive relationships between early adolescents and adult Catholic Christians role models.

#7 *Early Adolescent Ministry develops Leadership and Ministerial Abilities of Youth and Adults.*

#8 *Early Adolescent Ministry offers Variety* — creating variety in programming, scheduling, content, formats, settings, and leaders, organized around the needs of youth as surfaced from adolescent research and from the needs of youth in the community.

#9 *Early Adolescent Ministry is a Collaborative Ministry* — integrating early adolescent ministry with the other ministries of the church community, and involving the church in the life of the broader community in a coordinated attempt to develop or strengthen the external assets (social fabric of the community) which promote healthy adolescent development.

These nine guidelines have implications for the way we structure our ministry with early adolescents. I would like to reinforce and expand upon the *Contact Point Model* developed by Brian Reynolds (see Chapter 6). The strength of the *Contact Point Model* is that it serves to link all the ingredients which encompass a total early adolescent ministry program by utilizing the comprehensive approach of *A Vision of Youth Ministry*: evangelization, catechesis/religious education, worship, community, justice and service, enablement/leadership development, and guidance.

Each category of the *Contact Point Model* model includes programs developed in three formats: gathering, non-gathering, and parent/family programs. *Gathering* efforts are organized events which youth attend in groups of their peers. Through *non-gathering* methods the Church reaches out to youth without requiring attendance. *Parent and family* programs provide opportunities for youth to strengthen their family relationships.

In light of directions suggested by the research, I would add a fourth category or format: *Community Collaboration*. The Search Institute describes its importance this way,

> Each and every community, regardless of size or location, faces the immense challenge of encouraging positive youth development. Solutions do not come easily. Positive change will require extraordinary commitment to children and adolescents by multiple sectors, including government, business, schools, parents, service organizations, law enforcement, youth-serving organizations and religious institutions.
>
> One of the reasons why it is crucial for communities to develop a multi-sector commission or task force is to help ensure that community, school, family and congregational strategies for positive youth development are integrated and complementary. (1991 April *Source* 3)

This fourth category would provide for a way to plan joint activities, programs, and meetings with the different organizations in the life of a community (e.g., other churches, schools, scouting programs, athletic programs). If a coordinated approach to early adolescent ministry is essential, then an early adolescent ministry must plan for such involvement. By adding *Community Collaboration* to the *Contact Point Model* this will happen.

PART FOUR: STRATEGIES FOR ACTION

This final section will offer practical ideas and strategies for implementing some of the new directions suggested in this essay. I have focused on suggestions not found in Part Two of this volume, like family perspective. Here are several ideas to start you thinking about how to move in new directions.

DEVELOP A COMMUNITY PERSPECTIVE

First, observe and analyze the social institutions in your community and the values, expectations and standards they are sharing with young people. Where are the agreements and disagreements among institutions? How do they compare to the values and standards the church is sharing with youth? Remember that the church has a role to play, but that the family, school, peer group, and other youth-serving organizations are very powerful shapers of youth's identity. Second, begin discussions with leaders of the social institutions in your community. Hold a conference, symposium, or community meeting (town meeting) to discover areas of shared values and standards and ways that leaders and institutions can work together. Third, work with these leaders to identify and/or create a *youth charter* for your community that will serve as a basis for continuing collaboration. (See Francis A. J. Ianni's essay in Chapter 4.)

DEVELOP MENTORING OPPORTUNITIES

The presence of significant adults in the lives of young people can help facilitate their growth by offering them the security of a caring environment. The adolescent needs to be in relationship with an adult friend or mentor, a person with whom the young person can communicate and in whom he or she can see what it means to be Christian.

Five characteristics that are important in mentor relationships:

> 1. The adult takes a personal interest in the particular young person. ...The adolescent comes to feel a sense of personal worthiness just from seeing his or her particular and unique worth reflected in the eyes of an adult who is not a parent.
> 2. The adult tends to become a model for the young person. The adolescent sees in the adult the beliefs, attitudes, the values, the patterns of behavior, the accomplishments, and the style of life that, to a significant degree, the adolescent desires to emulate and adopt as his or her own. The adult's response is to become teacher, guide, counselor, sponsor, and host to the young person.
> 3. The adult acts as a guarantor for the adolescent. ...He or she lets the young person know that in experiences of struggle, doubt, and confusion or during feelings of inadequacy about the journey ahead, the young person is not alone. Others have been there before, have found resources within themselves that they did not know were there, and made it.
> 4. The adult provides an open ear to the adolescent.
> 5. The adult sometimes takes on the role of advocate. As an advocate, the adult will stand up for the adolescent when the young person comes up against destructive opposition. ...In short, the adult empowers the young person when the adolescent's own power is not enough. (Dykstra)

Potential strategies for intentionally creating mentor relationships include a matchmaker program between youth and adults who have similar interests, vocational counseling programs with a one-on-one relationship between an adult in a career and a young person exploring that career, one-on-one teaching, intergenerational and family cluster programming, apprenticeships between adult leaders in parish ministries and committees and youth who want to be leaders in these areas, and youth programs which invite adults from the community to participate.

DEVELOP A LIFE SKILLS CURRICULUM

Early adolescents need to learn how to make decisions, how to communicate with others, how to resolve conflict, how to negotiate, how to solve problems, how to think critically, how to plan, how to get things done. They need to learn responsibility and self control. They also need opportunities to deal directly with important adolescent struggles and to discuss these issues and the feelings they generate. A life skills curriculum must be skills-based and highly experiential. A youth ministry can become a laboratory where youth practice the how-to's of life as well as the how-to's of the Christian faith. We must equip youth with skills that empower them to become responsible adult followers of Christ.

ENCOURAGE POSITIVE YOUTH DEVELOPMENT

Peter Benson, in a summary report of *The Troubled Journey*, developed the following 30 recommendations for parents, educators, and community leaders based on the research findings.[4]

Recommendations for Parents

* Place high priority on giving frequent and tangible expressions of love, care, and support. Avoid the common tendency to assume high school-aged adolescents are less in need of such expressions than are younger adolescents.
* Set clear rules and limits. Negotiate with children reasonable consequences for rule-breaking; consistently follow through with consequences and consistently reward positive behavior.
* Encourage involvement in structured youth activities.
* Minimize attendance at drinking parties; band together with other parents to prevent their occurrence.
* Model responsible chemical use and vehicle safety behaviors.
* Make "family helping" projects a priority, in which parents and children together give help to others in need.
* Encourage and reward achievement motivation, post-high school educational aspirations, and homework.
* Minimize overexposure to television and other mass media forms.
* Emphasize the development of positive values, including prosocial values and values of behavioral restraint.
* Advocate for effective schools and community youth-serving organizations.

Recommendations for Educators
* Personalize schools so that each and every child feels cared for, supported, and important.
* Enhance social competencies, including friendship-making skills, caring skills, assertiveness skills, and resistance skills.
* Emphasize the development of positive values, particularly those that build a sense of personal responsibility for the welfare of others.
* Offer quality prevention programming in multiple areas of risk, including alcohol, tobacco, illicit drugs, suicide and depression, sexuality, and vehicle safety.
* Enhance academic effectiveness to ensure that students in all income levels gain in academic motivation and competence.
* Emphasize service learning programs, seeking to provide all students with helping opportunities and personal reflection on the meaning of helping.
* Provide strong support services for youth at risk.

Recommendations for Community Leaders
* Assemble a permanent child and youth task force involving leaders from all community sectors. Ideally, raise funding to permanently staff the task force.
* Create a community-wide vision for positive youth development.
* Continually assess progress toward the vision through systematic exploration of youth perceptions, behavior, values, and needs.
* Create a detailed action plan to promote positive youth development with an emphasis on increasing youth access to effective schools, families, and youth-serving organizations.
* Advocate for greater state or federal support for school effectiveness, parent education, day care and after school care, prevention programming, and other efforts crucial for promoting positive youth development.
* Ensure that one's community offers a range of support services for families and structured, adult-led activities for youth.

Recommendations for Staff and Volunteers in Youth-Serving Organizations
* Reinvent programming for high school-aged youth.
* Connect youth to adult mentors.
* Provide and/or advocate for quality day care and after school care.
* Place a premium on the development of positive values.
* Equip parents with parenting skills, particularly in the areas of support-giving, control and values formation.
* Involve youth in helping projects.
* Plan programs to address multiple at-risk behavior areas.

My hope is that this essay will provide the basis for re-thinking our ministry with early adolescents and to begin moving in new directions. Part Two of this *Access Guide* provides many of the strategies and skills needed for this movement.

ENDNOTES

[1] The study reports on more than 46,000 young Americans in grades 6 through 12 and yields information of great significance to all those who are interested in providing youth with a chance to grow up healthy. The students included in this research come mainly from the Midwest; most of them live in communities under 100,000 in population. Ninety percent of them are white. However, in spite of this sample, on key indicators for which representative national data are available (e.g., alcohol use, tobacco use, sexual abuse, involvement in extracurricular activities, and exposure to television), percentages in this study are remarkably similar to those of national data on in-school youth.

[2] Material in this section is drawn from *Source* 6.3 (December 1990) and *Source* 7.1 (April 1991) published by the Search Institute, 122 W. Franklin, Suite 525, Minneapolis, MN 55404. Additional material is drawn from *The Troubled Journey: A Profile of American Youth* developed by Peter Benson of the Search Institute and published by RESPECTEEN, Lutheran Brotherhood, Minneapolis, MN 55415.

[3] The study reports that only 10% of students in this research project meet what the study identified as minimal standards for overall well-being. The criteria used were: having 20 or more of the 30 assets, having two or less of the 10 deficits, doing at least one hour per week of prosocial behavior, having two or less of the 20 at-risk indicators.

[4] Order *The Troubled Journey* or an overview of it by calling 1-800-888-3820. Have this survey administered in your school system. It is available through RespecTeen at no charge, and will highlight important issues for community discussion and action. There is no better way to raise the community's consciousness about youth than through current information about your community's own students.

WORKS CITED

"Backbone: Essential for Survival on the Troubled Journey." *Source* 7.1 (April 1991).

Benson, Peter. *The Troubled Journey: A Profile of American Youth.* Minneapolis MN: RESPECTEEN, Lutheran Brotherhood, 1991.

Dykstra, Craig. "Agenda for Youth Ministry: Problems, Questions, and Strategies." *Readings and Resources in Youth Ministry*. Ed. Michael Warren. Winona MN: St. Mary's Press, 1987.

"The Troubled Journey: New Light on Growing Up Healthy." *Source* 6.3 (December 1990).

A Vision of Youth Ministry. Department of Education. Washington DC: USCC Office of Publishing, 1976, 1986.

Part Two

Overview

PRACTICAL APPROACHES FOR EARLY ADOLESCENT MINISTRY

Part Two is a wonderful collection of practical approaches intended to guide the development or enhancement of your ministry with early adolescents. Each essay provides you with key foundational insights and practical approaches/strategies for ministry. All too often youth ministers and religious educators working with early adolescents use programming assumptions and resources geared for older adolescents. The essays in Part Two seek to ground programming in the reality of adolescent development, suggesting ways to be more responsive to their needs. Each of the essays in Part Two includes a resource bibliography on the topic.

Brian Reynolds keynotes this section with his essay describing how to develop responsive programming with early adolescents. He offers concrete principles for early adolescent ministry, his *Contact Point Model* of ministry and practical models for more effective ministry. **Leif Kehrwald** offers ideas for developing a family perspective in early adolescent ministry. **David Ng** describes the particular dynamics of ministry with racial/ethnic minority youth, offering many practical strategies for ministry in multicultural settings. **Bruce Baumgarten,** in the first of his two essays, uses the principles from the *Challenge of Adolescent Catechesis* to outline how to develop a responsive early adolescent curriculum. In his second essay, he proposes foundational guidelines for the ministry of the catechist/teacher and guidelines for effectively teaching early adolescents. **Joanne Cahoon** offers six principles for developing prayer with early adolescents that will lead them toward an encounter with God. **Mary Lee Becker** develops four elements of effective service programming: appropriate justice education, a clear understanding of early adolescent needs, adequate planing, and diversity of activities. In her second essay, she identifies essential factors and practical strategies for building community with early adolescents. In the concluding chapter, **G. Wade Rowatt** provides an understanding of adolescent crises while offering principles and practical approaches to caring for adolescents in crisis.

Chapter 6

Developing Responsive Early Adolescent Ministry Programming

Brian Reynolds

A deeper and more comprehensive understanding of early adolescent development and the social-cultural forces which impact youth will lead parishes and schools to a reassessment of present program models and approaches for 10 to 15 year olds. The second section of this essay provides specific guidelines for designing and leading a comprehensive early adolescent ministry.

SEVEN DEVELOPMENTAL NEEDS OF EARLY ADOLESCENTS

Identifying these areas of development gives a starting point for appropriate responses to the complex needs of young adolescents. The work of William Kerewsky and Leah Lefstein in *Young Adolescents and Their Communities* suggests that there are seven developmental needs that must be considered in youth programs:

1. Physical Activity
2. Competence and Achievement
3. Self-Definition
4. Creative Expression
5. Positive Social Interaction with Peers and Adults
6. Structure and Clear Limits
7. Meaningful Participation

Physical Activity: The rapidly changing bodies of early adolescents require that they have time to stretch and exercise. We need to remember however, that each young person is developing physically at a different pace and, therefore, there is great diversity in strength and size of youth in this age group. Competitive physical activities tend to reward the early developers and punish the late developers. This competition is not only unfair but can harm the social development of these young people. Of course early adolescents also need time out to relax and be quiet. Properly spaced time for thinking, writing, reading, and other forms of reflection can bring a helpful balance to an active young person's day.

Competence and Achievement: Early adolescence is a time of extraordinary self-consciousness. Because these young people are struggling mightily with their new selves, they are preoccupied with others' attitudes toward them and with their own success or failure. They hunger for chances to prove themselves; they want to learn to do things well and to receive the respect and affirmation of those whom they admire. They need to know that what they do is valued by others.

Self-Definition: Early adolescents learn about themselves through their interactions with others. They want and need opportunities to test out their ideas of what it means to be a man or woman, a member of an ethnic group, a race. Talking about their experiences and their discoveries with friends and adults is an important vehicle for self-discovery. As they explore their world, they will begin to draw meaning for themselves and to see themselves as participants in society, not just observers.

Creative Expression: Opportunities to express their new feelings, interests, abilities, and thoughts help early adolescents to understand and accept the new people they are becoming. Art, music, drama, dance, literature, prayer and worship, all invite this freedom of expression. Through exposure to the creative expression of others, young people discover that others before them have experienced the emotions and thoughts that they may find confusing and sometimes frightening.

Positive Social Interaction with Peers and Adults: Young adolescents still look primarily to parents and family members for values, affection and direction. Peers offer needed support and companionship. Also important are adults, other than parents, who are sources of guidance and encouragement as early adolescents imagine life as an adult. Young adolescents need relationships with caring adult models who are willing to share views, values, and feelings.

Structure and Clear Limits: Early adolescents, prone to insecurity and self-criticism, need to know clearly what is expected of them in a world of conflicting demands. While too much structure smothers them, too little confuses them. They need opportunities to express preferences, to make decisions, and to work with adults in framing their own rules and limits, but they are helped by explicit boundaries that define the areas where they may legitimately explore their freedoms.

Meaningful Participation: Young adolescents need to participate in the activities that shape their lives. Successful programs are planned with, not for them. This builds ownership, teaches responsibility, and gives programs added meaning for the young adolescent participants. The Church needs to affirm the full membership of young adolescents, which involves rights as well as responsibilities.

These seven needs can be used as guidelines in designing an over-all program or a single event or class. They also can be used to evaluate a specific program to determine how well it responds to each of the developmental needs of youth. Here is an example of a program that was evaluated and improved in light of the seven needs.

Program: Thanksgiving Food Collection
Students are asked to bring in cans of food from home to be gathered in baskets by a parish committee for needy families in the community.

Evaluation: This project meets few if any of the developmental needs.

Improvements: Working in small groups have the students make up a common menu including their favorite foods from their own Thanksgiving celebrations. Combine ideas from each small group and create a single menu representing ideas from all the youth. Ask each person to contribute a small portion of money instead of food items from their home. The whole group or a few representatives should then go shopping to purchase the necessary items. Create a basket using a large box decorated with messages about the holiday. Include a copy of the menu in the basket. Ask the young people to say a quiet personal prayer for the people receiving their basket when they eat their favorite food item on Thanksgiving. In this model all seven developmental needs are considered.

MOTIVATING EARLY ADOLESCENTS

Motivation is created when a young person has a reason to want to do something. If that reason or motive comes from within the person, then it is most likely to prompt action. Ideas, needs, and emotions can all be *internal* motives. Manipulation, distinct from motivation, occurs when we get young adolescents to do what *we* want them to do by exercising our power. Typical statements include: "If you don't..." or "Because I said so...." This approach uses an *external* force for motivation. The result is apathy or outright rejection of the adult leader, the program, or the institution.

Adult leaders need to carefully examine how they attempt to motivate the young adolescents they serve. There are several important concepts that provide some direction.

OWNERSHIP

Programs should be planned with, and not just for, young adolescents. If they have some ownership of the program, they are more likely to attend, actively participate, and enjoy it. Ownership is built through consultation. Leaders must listen to their needs before designing programs. Written surveys, personal interviews, and observation are all methods of gathering information about the young adolescents in your community. In order for ownership to be developed, it is important that young adolescents know they are being listened to. It is not enough to simply distribute a survey. They need to see how their input is being used.

Program planning provides early adolescents with a great deal of motivation. They like to plan programs that allow them to accomplish something and to see the results of their work. They learn about responsibility and develop a sense of confidence. Even in more structured programs, ones with a pre-determined content, young people can be involved in decisions about everything from time schedules to furniture arrangements and the types of refreshments to be served. Ownership is developed through regular evaluations which continually invite participant input.

COLLABORATION, NOT COMPETITION

While some early adolescents may be motivated by competitive activities (sports and contests), many others are not. The wide diversity in the physical, social, and emotional development of 10 -15 year olds leads to a great deal of confusion and self-doubt. Many competitive activities provide early developers with unfair advantages and may punish late developers. Competition emphasizes comparison and winning, yet early adolescents need to feel accepted, valued, and included.

Early adolescent programming which provides opportunities for youth to collaborate with each other and with adults, receives an enthusiastic response. Group projects, non-competitive sports, discussion groups, and family and intergenerational programs are effective with young adolescents. When youth link together to complete a task, they begin to both appreciate their own giftedness and acknowledge the gifts of others. Motivation will come from experiencing themselves as valuable participants in the group.

PEER RELATIONSHIPS

Adolescent peer pressure is often viewed as a powerful negative force that controls the actions of young adolescents. While the peer group obviously plays an important role in motivating them, it is not necessarily a negative influence. They are often very self-conscious and therefore want to "be like everyone else" in order to be accepted. The task for adult leaders is to channel group influence towards positive actions.

All early adolescent ministry programs need to build healthy peer relationships. These relationships can become a primary motivation for ongoing involvement in the church. Catechetical/religious education programs should enable young adolescents to learn from each other. Worship events, planned and conducted by young people, will allow them to share and celebrate their faith together. Service programs are excellent opportunities for young adolescents to work together in helping others. Social events can build bonds of support as they recreate together. Most importantly the church must provide an environment that warmly welcomes young adolescents as full members of the community.

ADULT ENCOURAGEMENT

Young adolescents look to adults whom they like and respect as models for their behavior and attitudes. In addition, they are more likely to be actively involved in a program and follow-through on commitments when they know adults they care about expect this of them. Personal encouragement from a caring teacher or youth minister can be a powerful motivator for those who are unsure of themselves.

Programs, therefore, need adults who are willing to spend time building supportive relationships with young adolescents. When adult-youth relationships are well established and based on mutual respect, there will be little need to motivate through threats or warnings. Adult affirmation and encouragement will lead to positive responses.

PROGRAMMING PRINCIPLES FOR EARLY ADOLESCENT MINISTRY

New research on adolescent development and the impact of social-cultural trends challenges the church to re-examine the types of programs offered for early adolescents. New and exciting programs have emerged as parishes and schools pay close attention to the many developmental and social issues presented in this *Access Guide*. To guide the work of program developers in early adolescent ministry, the following principles are offered. They form the basis of a well-grounded, comprehensive approach to programming with young adolescents.

1. Early adolescent ministry is a multifaceted ministry which includes catechesis/religious education, community building, prayer and worship, justice and service, and guidance.

2. Early adolescent ministry integrates young adolescents into the parish community through involvement of young adolescents in community worship and celebrations.

3. Early adolescent ministry acknowledges young adolescents as valuable members of the church and reaches out to them through personal contact (like home visits) and personal communication (like newsletters and birthday cards) as tangible signs of the church in their lives.

4. Early adolescent ministry responds to the needs of parents and families of young adolescents. Parents should have input into program planning, and there should be programs where parents and family members can attend with each other. Special efforts must be made to assist parents in their role of parenting young adolescents.

5. Early adolescent ministry is a year-round effort and should not be based on a school year calendar.

6. Early adolescent ministry provides opportunities for young adolescents to gain a sense of confidence and competence by performing meaningful tasks in their church and in their community.

7. Early adolescent ministry promotes positive relationships: youth to youth, adult to youth, parent to child, and church to member.

8. Early adolescent ministry is concerned with the total personal growth of the young person: spiritually, intellectually, physically, morally, and emotionally.

9. Early adolescent ministry programs are planned with and not for young adolescents in order to develop a sense of ownership and insure greater support.

10. Early adolescent ministry programs occur in a variety of settings, employ a variety of formats, and allow young adolescents the freedom to choose their own level of involvement.

11. Early adolescent ministry programs reflect each of the seven developmental needs of early adolescents: physical activity, competence and achievement, self-definition, creative expression, positive social interaction with peers and adults, structure and clear limits, meaningful participation.

12. Early adolescent ministry programs are organized by a team of leaders (adults and younger adolescents) responsible for planning, implementation, and ongoing evaluation.

13. Early adolescent ministry programs are guided by mature adults who are comfortable with young adolescents and are willing to share their lives with them.

14. Early adolescent ministry programs promote a sense of security for young adolescents through clearly articulated rules that participants appreciate and accept.

15. Early adolescent ministry programs balance time for laughter, high spirits, and physical activity with time for reflection and individual work.

16. Early adolescent ministry programs encourage collaboration over competition, promoting equality and fairness among youth.

DEVELOPING PROGRAMMING USING THE CONTACT POINT MODEL

The *Contact Point Model* serves to link all the ingredients which encompasses a total early adolescent ministry program. This model broadens the scope of ministry beyond the traditional approach which often focused only on catechesis/religious education, by utilizing the comprehensive approach of *A Vision of Youth Ministry.*

Reflective of *A Vision of Youth Ministry*, the Contact Point Model includes five components or categories: catechesis/religious education; worship; community; justice and service; and guidance. Each category of the model includes programs developed in three formats: gathering; non-gathering; and parent/family programs. *Gathering* efforts are organized events which youth attend in groups of their peers. Through *non-gathering* methods the Church reaches out to youth without requiring attendance. *Parent and family* programs provide opportunities for youth to strengthen their family relationships.

Catechesis/Religious Education includes courses, classes, and materials through which the Church teaches young adolescents about the values and beliefs of the faith community. Examples:

Gathering: classes, mini-courses, speaker series.
Non-gathering: youth newsletters, books, videos.
Parent/Family: Advent/Lent family retreat, home study resources, TV recommendations, parent education.

Worship provides time for young adolescents to celebrate the sacraments as well as opportunities for prayer, Scripture study, and various forms of ritual and worship. Examples:

Gathering: youth liturgy, early adolescent Stations of the Cross, greeting youth before Sunday Liturgy, refreshments for youth at socials after Mass (not just coffee!).
Non-gathering: book of young adolescent prayers, prayers for youth concerns at Sunday liturgy, using "their" music in prayer services so that they will recall the prayer when they hear it again.
Parent/Family: family liturgy involving youth and parents, home prayer books, family or parent-youth prayer night.

Community comprises programs which help young adolescents build friendships with peers and adult members of the community. Through these efforts they can develop a sense of belonging and personal membership in the church. Examples:

Gathering: social events (like movies), sports, scouting, trips/outings, service projects.

Non-gathering: birthday cards, newsletters, bulletin board, home visits.

Parent/Family: family picnic, parent-youth dance, games night.

Justice and Service informs young adolescents about the responsibility to carry out the Gospel challenge to love and care for our neighbor and the earth which God created. Education about justice must be paired with opportunities to serve the community in meaningful ways. Service projects for early adolescents should only require short-term commitments. Long-term programs should provide optional starting and stopping points. Examples:

Gathering: course/classes/speakers on social issues, service projects, fundraising projects for those in need.

Non-gathering: international pen-pals, adopting a migrant or refugee family, newsletters.

Parent/Family: home discussion guide, Lenten fast program, family service opportunity, articles on justice issues mailed home.

Guidance programs assist young adolescents with support and counsel as they face problems and make important decisions regarding sexuality, family struggles, and pressure to use drugs and alcohol. Examples:

Gathering: education programs on drugs/alcohol, sexuality education program, babysitting training, tutoring, preparing for exams night.

Non-gathering: printing cards with emergency numbers (for example, runaway hotline), providing a counseling referral list.

Parent/Family: parent-teen workshops (for example, communication), providing resources for parents on drugs/alcohol/sexuality.

Designed using the layout of a matrix, the model arranges 15 methods of early adolescent ministry.

CONTACT POINT MODEL

	Gathering	Non-Gathering	Parent/Family
Religious Education			
Community			
Prayer & Worship			
Justice & Service			
Guidance			

The specifics of each program vary from parish to parish;however, there are four characteristics that seem to be present in most effective programs.

1. Caring adult leaders, teachers/catechists, coaches, and chaperones work to build personal relationships with the youth they serve. Through them young adolescents know that they are loved by God and feel at home in the church.

2. Parental support and ownership of the program is obtained through regular communication, parent education sessions, and numerous opportunities for parents to volunteer. Remember, most parents get involved in small ways such as assisting with publicity, transportation, or food preparation.

3. Young adolescents provide input into the planning of all programs and assist the adult leader(s) with specific tasks during each event.

4. An organized planning team has designed a comprehensive program which responds to the diversity of needs of young adolescents. The early adolescent ministry includes a variety of components using several different formats. The program is evaluated at regular intervals throughout the year.

PROGRAMMING MODELS

To assist you in thinking creatively about programming for early adolescents, the following models are proposed. They are offered as a way to stretch your thinking beyond the weekly, school year format of programming. Test out the possibility of using new models for organizing your programming. You may be pleasantly surprised by the response of the early adolescents.[1]

ACTION-LEARNING MODEL

Action-learning can take the form of study followed by action, involvement in a service project followed by reflection and study, or awareness and analysis followed by action and reflection. In each of these formats, action-learning focuses catechesis on the learning which is a by-product of action or a means to increase the effectiveness of action. Involvement in a soup kitchen, nursing home for the elderly, food center, hunger walk, advocacy work on human rights or hunger can all lead to reflection and further study of the issues of justice, peace, aging, poverty, hunger. The action can be either a catalyst for learning or an expression of the learning. Oftentimes, young people are involved in service but do not have the opportunity to reflect on the experience and opportunities for further study. Many youth ministries organize mission projects, work camps, or service projects.

BI-WEEKLY MODEL

In the bi-weekly model, meetings, courses, or events are scheduled every other week usually for a longer time span (for example, three hours) so as to allow sufficient time for community building and program content. The bi-weekly model allows other programming to take place on the alternate weeks. Some parishes have organized early adolescent catechetical program on the first and third weeks of the month, and older adolescent course offerings on the second and fourth weeks of the month. Early adolescents respond well to the bi-weekly model when it is integrated with other youth ministry programming on the alternate weeks, thereby offering them variety.

FULL DAY MODEL

The full day model brings young people together for an extended period of program time for community building, study, reflection, interaction, prayer, and action/service. This model may be used in a five to eight hour session. It often includes a shared meal, a liturgical celebration, and informal socializing. In the full day model there are two or three learning sessions or program times lasting 1 1/2 - 2 hours each. For catechetical programming, several full day programs can be grouped together on one theme (like a mini-course) or scheduled five or six times throughout the year each with a distinct theme. The length of the day should be accommodated to the abilities of the early adolescent, especially regarding the intensity of the schedule and nature of the theme. You can accomplish in one day what can easily take three weekly meetings to accomplish.

Full day programs call for careful planning. It is recommended that a team of leaders (both adults and young people) meet well in advance to plan each of these days. Some items to be considered are: previewing resource materials; selection of a date with as few conflicts as possible; choice of a location which provides a pleasant environment; plans for snacks and meals, assignment of leaders for each part of the day; plans for liturgy or prayer service.

INTERGENERATIONAL/PARENT EDUCATION MODELS

Several types of family programming can be utilized in early adolescent ministry, for example, programs specifically designed for parents, programs for parents and adolescents. See Chapter 7, "Early Adolescent Ministry through a Family Lens," by Leif Kehrwald for specific ideas.

MINI-COURSE MODEL

The mini-course model can become the bread-and-butter of parish catechetical and ministry programming. Whether you are using a weekly, bi-weekly, full day, overnight, weekend, or full-week model, you can use the mini-course model. This model organizes catechetical faith themes and youth programs into four-six-eight session course offerings. Mini-courses can be offered throughout the year, allowing time between mini-courses for the variety of other programming. Many parishes conduct mini-courses on a six-eight week basis in the fall, winter and spring, allowing plenty of time for other programming. Other parishes conduct the first three weeks of a six week mini-course, then take a meeting for community building, special event, and/or worship, and then resume the mini-course for the second three weeks.

MONTHLY MODEL

The monthly model can be used in two ways: monthly meetings or monthly full day programming (described above). In the monthly meeting approach, sessions are scheduled for a longer time span (three-four hours) so as to allow sufficient time for two learning or program sessions, community building, prayer. A typical six-eight session course would take three-four months to complete. The monthly model allows other programming to take place during the month. Many parishes gather young people monthly (often because of distance) for four hours, offering them a variety of faith themes in mini-course format for which they can select. In addition time is provided for socializing and community prayer. Early adolescents respond well to the monthly model when it is integrated with other programming on the alternate weeks, thereby offering them variety. One of the drawbacks of the exclusive use of the monthly meeting model can be the infrequent contact among the young people. This can be overcome by offering a variety of programming during the month.

OVERNIGHT MODEL/WEEKEND MODEL

The weekend or overnight model of youth programming utilizes many of the dynamics of the retreat weekend — extended time for the building of relationships, the forming of community, sharing of religious experiences, prayer, and liturgical experiences. The weekend or overnight model can be used for all of the components of early adolescent ministry: catechesis, evangelization, prayer and worship, justice/service, guidance/healing, enablement or leadership development. The weekend model allows for six 2 - 2 1/2 hour sessions available to planners; the overnight model allows for three-four 2 - 2 1/2 hour sessions. In addition, time for community building, recreation, liturgy, and prayer must also be scheduled.

Like the full day model, the overnight/weekend model calls for careful planning. It is recommended that a team of leaders (both adults and young people) meet well in advance to plan the weekend. Some items to be considered are: previewing resource materials; selection of a date with as few conflicts as possible; choice of a location which provides a pleasant environment; development of a schedule for all the components included, plans for snacks and meals, assignment of facilitators for each part of the day; plans for liturgy or prayer service.

The length and intensity of the weekend model may place demands on the early adolescent that he or she may not be able to sustain. The overnight model, however, is quite applicable to the early adolescent. Camping trips provide another format for weekend or overnight programming. Organized with the same care, camping trips provide an outdoor setting for youth programs.

SEASONAL MODEL

The seasonal model organizes programming using fall-winter-spring-summer seasons. The seasons of the year help to organize the programming in three or four month units. Within these units, the various program offerings are organized. The liturgical seasons offer two other regular times during the year for catechesis or special youth programming. These Advent and Lenten offerings can easily parallel parish-wide programs. They also offer the possibility of integrating liturgy, study, parish involvement, and service into a concentrated time span and thereby tapping the richness of the Advent or Lenten season.

STUDY TOUR/TRIP MODELS

The study tour model offers planners the ability to use learning opportunities outside the parish community. For example, one course on the Judeo-Christian tradition was designed by visiting each of the churches/synagogue in town, listening to a presentation by the minister/rabbi, and touring the church/synagogue. Another course on Church visited a variety of Catholic churches in urban, suburban, and rural areas to explore how they were organized and the variety of their ministries. This course also explored the ministries of the diocesan Church (e.g., social ministry). Such tours provide opportunities for first hand experience and can be combined with classroom presentation, discussion, and reflection.

WEEK-LONG MODEL

The first option for week-long programming is a weeknight program for three-five nights, 1 1/2 - 2 hours per night. This option takes the weekly meeting model and condenses the time frame into one week. Parishes which use this option offer several mini-courses or program topics in this time frame and repeat these week-long mini-courses throughout the year. The big advantage of this option is concentration and continuity. They take careful planning, especially in selecting weeks which do not conflict with community or school events or with exams or special tests at school. You may want to even clear the dates with the school and parish administration so that nothing will be scheduled during these special week-long programs.

The second option is a full day (and possibly overnight) week-long program during school vacations or summer. Many parishes have adapted the vacation bible school concept for their younger adolescent catechetical program, offering several thematic courses in three-four weeks during the summer. In addition to morning and afternoon learning sessions, there is time scheduled for recreation, socializing, prayer, and service-action. This three-four week summer program replaces the year-long early adolescent catechetical program, allowing time during the year for a variety of other programming. A second variation on this full day option is similar to summer camp. Young people spend an entire week at a retreat or camp site studying, recreating, and interacting. One or two themes can be offered during a week-long program. These summer models respond well to the life situation of early adolescents who are not working at a summer job.

WEEKLY MODEL

The weekly model may be the most commonly used approach to programming in parishes, but it is not the only approach. In parishes, courses or meetings are scheduled on weeknights or Sunday evenings. Sessions can be designed to last 1 1/2 - 2 hours. Anything less than 1 1/2 hours is not desirable with adolescents. A weekly meeting model for catechetical themes or extended topics should be short-term (four-six-eight sessions). Courses can be offered throughout the year. The timing of programs following this model makes a difference. Some parishes find it better to have these sessions following the same schedule as the school semesters in their area. Other parishes prefer to organize the program into distinct blocks of four, six, or eight weeks for which the adolescents enroll each time around. The description of the seasonal and mini-course model explains this "block approach" to programming.

WORSHIP/CELEBRATION MODEL

Like the youth community model, the worship/celebration model offers a context for catechesis and youth programming. The *first context* involves young people in liturgy planning and as a consequence the adolescents will be involved in studying and reflecting on the Scriptures; studying the meaning of liturgy: the rites, the symbols; and planning liturgy — the ways the message of the Scriptures affects song selection and prayers. Whether it involves planning for a Sunday or seasonal (Thanksgiving) or special event (senior graduation), liturgy planning offers a marvelous opportunity for catechesis.

A *second context* is within a celebration (Church season or special event). For example, the celebration of Pentecost can be the context for catechesis on church as well as empowerment for justice and service. At homily time the young people can be organized into small groups and explore a particular faith theme, like Church (perhaps the mission and characteristics of the early Church as described in the Book of Acts). The results of that learning can be shared at the presentation of gifts — through creative art, gesture, song, and audio-visual. If the adolescents are also involved in planning the liturgy, this celebration will become a tremendous learning experience.

A *third context* is a weekly program based on the Sunday Scripture readings. This program can be conducted after the Sunday Eucharist or on Sunday evening. Using the Sunday readings, a theme is developed which connects the life experience of the adolescent with the Scriptures. Through activities, discussion, and reflection the meaning of the Scriptures are applied to the life of the adolescent.

EVALUATING YOUR PROGRAM

Just as planning programs with youth, and not just for them, builds a sense of ownership, the same results come from evaluation. Young adolescents must be invited to share freely their reactions to particular events and to the overall program. Those who have some ownership for a program attend more regularly and participate more actively in what is offered.

Young adolescents are not the only ones who should be involved in program evaluation. All adult leaders who have been a part of programs during the year need to be consulted. Parents need to have a chance to offer feedback and give input as a part of the year-end evaluation.

Evaluation can take place in a variety of ways using a variety of tools. The most common form is written questionnaires or surveys. This is probably the preferred approach for young adolescents. Avoid using "mail-home" forms, instead distribute them at a gathering and provide time (and pencils) for them to be filled out.

Verbal evaluation can be very effective when a group or individual is comfortable enough to speak openly. In a group, this approach allows each person involved to add on to another person's comment or offer a different perspective of his or her own. Individual interviews of youth or adults provide the opportunity to gather more detailed information whenever a response is not completely understood. Individual conversations provide the most personal feedback.

Third, do not ignore your own personal observations and reflections. Review your own experiences of the past year and trust your instincts and your insights. Yours may not be the most objective evaluation but take time to listen to yourself and keep a written record of your own thoughts.

SAMPLE METHODS OF WRITTEN EVALUATIONS

A) Rating Forms

Rate each component of the Junior High Program using the following scale: 1—Great, 2—Good, 3—OK, 4—Not so good.

Classes	1 2 3 4
Prayer Services	1 2 3 4
Christmas Celebration	1 2 3 4
Meeting at 7:00 p.m. was...	1 2 3 4
The speaker was...	1 2 3 4

B) Open statements

What I liked best was...
What I liked least was...
In the future I hope we can...

C) Reactions

What is your overall feeling about this program or event? (Circle any words that apply)
Excited Good Discouraged Satisfied Bored Irritated Happy Confused Surprised Worried

D) Specific Questions

The most important thing I learned is...
The activity I will remember the longest is...
The topic I would like to learn more about is...

SAMPLE VERBAL EVALUATIONS

A) Ten minute verbal evaluation

Take the last few minutes of a meeting and ask the group to respond to three simple questions:

1. What were the strengths of the program?
2. What were some weak points?
3. What word would best summarize your feelings about the program? Record the responses on a chalk board or on an easel pad.

B) Two hour evaluation meeting (for example, parent night)

Step 1. Provide a written and a verbal overview of the program to be evaluated.

Step 2. Divide into small groups to gather feedback on general content of program, specific events or sessions, and logistics (time, place, etc.). Provide a worksheet.

Step 3. Re-gather in a large group to hear a summary of small group reports.
Step 4. Brainstorm ideas for future programs in a large group or form new small groups for this task. Participants should be asked to generate possibilities and suggestions, not to make decisions.

CONCLUSION

Young adolescents learn from a variety of experiences. Service projects, mini-courses, field trips, worship experiences, social activities, and retreats can all be integrated into a total ministry effort with early adolescents. The most important ingredient, however, is caring adults: catechists/teachers, youth ministers, program leaders who take the time to get to know young adolescents and affirm them.

END NOTES

[1] These models are adapted from Chapter 5, "Learning Models for Adolescent Catechesis" in *Adolescent Catechesis Resource Manual* by John Roberto (New York: Sadlier, 1988).

WORKS CITED

Dorman, Gayle. *3:00-6:00 P.M.: Planning Programs for Young Adolescents.* Carrboro: Center for Early Adolescence, 1985.

Lefstein, Leah, William Kerewski, Elliot A. Medrich, and Carol Frank. *3:00-6:00 P.M.: Young Adolescents at Home and in the Community.* Carrboro: Center for Early Adolescence, 1982.

A Vision of Youth Ministry. Department of Education, USCC. Washington DC: USCC, 1976.

RESOURCE BIBLIOGRAPHY: PROGRAMMING

Baumgarten, Bruce,et al. *On the Move: Activities for a Year of Early Adolescent Ministry.* New Rochelle: Don Bosco Multimedia, 1991.

Bright, Thomas, and John Roberto, editors. *Access Guides to Youth Ministry: Justice.* New Rochelle: Don Bosco Multimedia, 1990.

Brown, Carolyn C. *Youth Ministries - Thinking Big with Small Groups.* Nashville: Abingdon Press, 1984.

Dorman, Gayle. *3:00-6:00 P.M.: Planning Programs for Young Adolescents.* Carrboro: Center for Early Adolescence, 1985.

The Challenge of Adolescent Catechesis. Washington, DC: NFCYM Publications, 1986.

Ekstrom, Reynolds, editor. *Access Guides to Youth Ministry: Retreats*. New Rochelle: Don Bosco Multimedia, 1991.

———. *Access Guides to Youth Ministry: Pop Culture*. 2nd Edition. New Rochelle: Don Bosco Multimedia, 1992.

———. *Teen Media*. New Rochelle: Don Bosco Multimedia, 1991.

Ekstrom, Reynolds and John Roberto, editors. *Access Guides to Youth Ministry: Evangelization*. New Rochelle: Don Bosco Multimedia, 1989.

Fox, Zeni and Marisa Guerin, Brian Reynolds, and John Roberto. *Leadership for Youth Ministry*. Winona: St. Mary's Press, 1984.

Lefstein, Leah and Joan Lipsitz. *3:00-6:00 P.M.: Programs for Young Adolescents*. Carrboro: Center for Early Adolescence, 1983.

Lefstein, Leah and William Kerewski, Elliot A. Medrich, and Carol Frank. *3:00-6:00 P.M.: Young Adolescents at Home and in the Community*. Carrboro: Center for Early Adolescence, 1982.

Martinson, Roland. *Effective Youth Ministry: A Congregational Approach*. Minneapolis: Augsburg Press, 1988.

Ng, Donald. *Asian Pacific American Youth Ministry*. Valley Forge, PA: Judson Press, 1989.

Robins, Duffy. *Youth Ministry Nuts & Bolts*. Zondervan/Youth Specialties, 1990.

Reed, Sharon, editor.. *Access Guides to Youth Ministry: Spirituality*. New Rochelle: Don Bosco Multimedia, 1991.

Rice, Wayne. *Junior High Ministry*. Revised Edition. Grand Rapids: Zondervan, 1987.

Roberto, John. *Adolescent Catechesis Resource Manual*. New York: Sadlier, 1988.

———, editor. *Access Guides to Youth Ministry: Liturgy and Worship*. New Rochelle: Don Bosco Multimedia, 1990.

———, editor. *Access Guides to Youth Ministry: Leadership*. New Rochelle: Don Bosco Multimedia, 1992.

Roehlkepartain, Eugene C. *Youth Ministry in City Churches*. Loveland CO: Group Books, 1989.

Shaheen, David. *Growing a Junior High Ministry*. Loveland CO: Group Books, 1986.

Strommen, Merton and Irene. *Five Cries of Parents*. San Francisco: Harper and Row, 1985.

A Vision of Youth Ministry. Department of Education. Washington, DC: USCC, 1976.

Chapter 7

Early Adolescent Ministry through a Family Lens

Leif Kehrwald

How can we practically apply a family perspective in ministry with early adolescents and their families? What concrete, practical application does the information on family in the foundational essays of this *Access Guide* have for my ministry with adolescents? How can I put on a family lens to evaluate my current ministry?

The intent of this essay is to analyze these questions by exploring the interconnecting system of youth, youth ministry, and adolescent families. These systems are highly interrelated although they may not always appear to be. They all operate according to the rules of systems theory. An adequate understanding of these systems and their interdependent relationships can reveal interesting and valuable insights for working with adolescents and their families.

THE FAMILY SYSTEM

A system is any collection of parts organized in such a way that whatever affects one part affects all other parts. (Braun) In a system, all parts are connected and interdependent, meaning the relationships between the parts are more important than the parts themselves. The experts simply say that the basic idea of systems theory is that the whole is greater than the sum of its parts. (Power 4)

Some systems are static, mechanical and (given sufficient knowledge of the parts and their interdependence) therefore completely predictable, such as automobiles and computers. Family systems, however, are organic, alive, and fluid, making it impossible to have total knowledge of the parts and their interdependence. They are not completely predictable, but they will follow the "rules" of systems theory in a lively dynamic way. In his book, *Family Matters*, Thomas Power states,

> ...members of a family system...function together for two common goals: the emotional well-being of the adults and the growth and development of children. This inter-dependence means that members of a family need each other to get along. ...Family members are connected by the things they share and the things they do for one another. ...[T]he most important connections are the feelings they have for each other. (Power 5)

These emotional connections are so strong in most family systems that they determine the personalities and pathologies of family members and the family as a whole. These characteristics can last for generations.

There are numerous principles encompassing the whole of systems theory. Stemming from the description above, some basic principles include:

* Parts of the system maintain their own identity, rendering the whole system greater than the sum of its parts.

* Change in one part of the system affects all other parts and the whole.

* All systems strive for equilibrium and thus resist change.

* Systems relate to their environment with some degree of openness or closeness. Healthy systems are normally more open.

* All systems have boundaries for adaptiveness and cohesiveness which help the system determine its own identity and relationships with other systems.

Using a systems approach to view the family, we can see that there is a dynamic interplay of relationships within the family as members confront change, maturity, faith growth, and day to day life. It is the emotional push and pull within a family that serves as a catalyst for change and growth, but also provides focal point(s) for struggle and pain.

A FAMILY PERSPECTIVE IN MINISTRY WITH EARLY ADOLESCENTS

This section provides a transition from the foundational concepts to practical application in a variety of early adolescent ministry settings. We will do this by exposing the unspoken assumptions we may hold about ministry and family life. We will then take a look at our posture of youth ministry with respect to family life. This will lead to a reflective tool with questions that help you examine your youth ministry efforts through a family lens and discover possible adjustments. We will conclude our "bridging" process by surfacing a number of practical tips and suggestions for bringing a family sensitivity to youth ministry.

BLIND ASSUMPTIONS IN YOUTH MINISTRY

What are your assumptions about family life as you do youth ministry? Have you ever tried to name them? Sometimes we do ministry based on attitudes of which we are not fully aware, and which are not healthy or proper. As soon as we expose them, we realize their folly and can work toward eliminating them. Below are descriptions of eight common "blind" assumptions that many in ministry hold at one time or another. Review your attitudes toward adolescence itself, ministry programming, and your vision and praxis for faith formation.

Adolescence is pathological. When you hear the phrase "teenagers and their parents," what words come to mind? Conflict, rebellion, communication gap? If you think of only problem words, then you're probably guilty of this myth: that is, having teenagers in the household always spells trouble.

Yet, if other words like crazy, fun, emotional, busy, friendly, frustrating, and trusting also come to mind, then your assumption is probably more balanced and realistic. Adolescence is a highly developmental stage for teens and parents, rendering many adolescent families somewhat tumultuous and chaotic.

Yet most teens deal with their adolescence (all those self-image questions and relational/emotional ups and downs) with about the same degree of success as adults in day-to-day life. Adolescence is not automatically problematic. But if we expect trouble from them, they will deliver. If we expect growth toward maturity, they will deliver that instead.

Adolescence is transitional. This myth is widely held in our American society. How often do you hear remarks like, "It's just a stage she's going through. Not much we can do for her now." When a teen experiences a first love lost, severe facial blemishes, or a failed driver's test, it does not feel "transitional" to him or her. These are real (albeit common) experiences for teens which sometimes make the present moment seem like eternity.

Teens have both the need and the right to express the wide range of their emotions. Parents, youth workers, and the entire community must validate adolescent experiences and the feelings which accompany them. Too often we short circuit their feelings with, "Don't be sad. It will pass." "You'll be over him, and interested in someone else by next week." These statements may be true but render injustice to a teen's emotional development.

Adolescence is foundational rather than transitional. All the emotions, mood swings, life questions, ambiguities, and rebellions help form the base of maturity essential for adulthood. It's the stuff that shapes individual identity, perhaps the single most important task for adolescents. If these processes are not allowed to take their normal course during the teen years, they will rear their heads in much more challenging ways during mid-life. Adolescence is not just a stage.

More is better. The best youth programs sponsor the most activities, right? That's what I believed as a parish youth ministry coordinator. Some kids in my group were so active they joked about never seeking their parents. That gave me a sense of pride then, but I've since realized more is not always better.

You can have an impact in teens' lives without sponsoring tons of activities that gouge family prime time and burn out volunteer help. When the minister recognizes the family and household limitations of time, energy, and space, he or she will be more selective about the quantity and quality of programs sponsored. If you filtered all your activities through a family lens, would they all be necessary? Careful planning which recognizes family limitations will yield a balanced and dynamic youth program. And you might get a night off!

Effective ministry with individuals obviously benefits their families. This is a common assumption because it seems logical and may actually be true sometimes. Yet, if the ministry is solely focused on the individual without respect for household life, then that ministry is quite likely causing stress for the family.

Effective ministry with individuals implies change and growth in their lives. Recall that families, as systems, resist change even if it is positive. Your good work with teens may meet with resistance at home. Yet if you provide "bridger experiences" between your ministry efforts and the households of teens, your efforts will be more effective and will also enrich family life. (More about "bridger experiences" in a following section, "Principles for Bringing a Family Sensitivity to Youth Ministry.")

Effective community building automatically enriches the families of the community. Like the previous assumption, this one seems logical, and, if done correctly, will be true. But if the focus is solely on building community among teens, family life is undoubtedly fragmented in the process.

This fragmentation happens when teens are continually called out of the home for all sorts of activities and when volunteers are drained of energy and motivation with endless demands. Community building efforts can provide positive faith enrichment for teens, but the minister must always keep in mind (and encourage) the faith value of the home. If the church of the home is ignored, then the faith community building efforts in the parish or school will be far less valuable and legitimate.

Parents cannot really pass on faith to their children (especially teenagers). Few ministers would openly profess this statement, but many who work with children and teens continually encounter parents who appear completely apathetic about their child's faith formation. It can cause the minister to truly wonder about the capabilities of today's parents in transmitting faith. Studies show, however, that the home is often the most powerful faith influence in a person's life. Gather any group of adults and have them reflect and share on the beginnings of their faith journey. The majority will always cite experiences relating to parents, family, or home.

Somehow, faith is transmitted from generation to generation in the home. Some ministers, particularly those who work with teens, fall guilty to this assumption in subtle ways; i.e., believing that we mark the beginning of a young person's faith life, or becoming convinced our programs are crucial to the spiritual health of teens. Granted, many parents do not invest themselves in either their child's faith formation or their own for that matter. Yet rather than relinquish them from that responsibility, we must challenge them to accept it. Youth ministry should be done in a posture that seeks a partnership with parents in the faith nurturance of young people.

Without question, I can certainly transmit faith and values to young people. Perhaps the most dangerous form of youth ministry is the "Lone Ranger," "guru" approach that attracts young people to a single individual who personally leads them on their Christian journey. Personal relationships between teens and significant adults is very important to faith nurturance, yet we must always remember that our Christian faith is communal in nature, not isolationist and individualistic. The significant adult in a teen's life must lead him or her into a relationship with the community as well as a personal relationship with Jesus Christ.

Again, we cannot forget the value of the household as Christian community. God is fully present in our homes, just as God is present in church on Sunday morning and at our youth catechesis programs. The more we can bridge these forms of Christian community together, the more effectively we will transmit our faith to the next generation.

Do any of these assumptions hit home for you in your work with adolescents? Just naming the attitudes out of which we minister can sometimes reveal our shortcomings. Be sure to take the time to work through the questions in the Reflective Tool.

YOUTH MINISTRY POSTURE

In his book, *A New Design for Family Ministry*, Dr. Dennis Guernsey describes four approaches to ministry in relationship to household life. These approaches lie on a continuum from negative and self-serving to positive and relational. The four approaches are described below. Check your posture of ministry in your work with teens and their families.

On the far negative side of the continuum, Guernsey describes the *parasitic* approach to ministry. This posture demands unfailing commitment to all programs and activities. As a result, the virtue of service gets turned around: families serve and sustain the programs, thus allowing the minister to feel needed and successful. This approach may even go so far as to equate one's level of Christian commitment with his/her participation in the programs.

Few, if any ministers are blatantly parasitic in their work. Yet when the minister becomes so enthused about a particular program, movement, or renewal, recruitment efforts may take on this characteristic.

The *competitive* approach is less severe but far more common in all parish programming, particularly youth ministry. Picture the calendar as battlefield over which we skirmish for the best nights for activities and programs. Working around school, sports, and community events, we schedule our programs during remaining family prime time, because "that's when we can get them to show up." Families are caught in the middle and feel frustrated. If they want quality time together, they are forced to "do battle" with all the institutions that are supposed to be serving their needs: school, community, parish.

Before long, family motivation begins to wane, and participation dwindles. Ministers find themselves asking, "Why don't folks come to our programs? We're doing good things." Program quality isn't a problem, but quantity and posture may be. If the minister continually feels cynical toward parents and families while conducting programs, that is a good indication of a "competitive" approach to ministry.

Moving to the positive side of the continuum, we come to the *cooperative* approach which attempts to work within the rhythms and dynamics of family life. It recognizes that the individuals in any given program have strong connections to family and household members, and those connections will influence the program. It attempts to learn about these family influences and adjust the program accordingly. At times, just a slight schedule change or personal encounter can make the difference between success or failure.

Guernsey uses the image of "friendship" to describe the cooperative approach. A friend is someone you know well enough to know how to ask them to be involved or lend some assistance. For example, in recruiting volunteers a cooperative approach may place more emphasis on tapping the gifts and talents of the folks than filling the vacant job slots. Another point here is that a friend can say "no" without feeling guilty. Too many people agree to participate only to avoid feeling bad for saying "no." And too many ministers capitalize on that.

On the far positive side is the *symbionic* approach to ministry. At this level, there is a mutual interdependence between program and the families involved in the program. The health or illness of one is reflected in the other. Granted, this model is idealistic, but it can be experienced in small groups where there is less distinction between minister and those ministered to. Efforts in peer ministry programming can reflect a symbionic approach.

What's your ministry posture? Where do your activities lie on the continuum line? How can you move them farther to the positive side? You may reflect on these questions and pertinent others when you get to the Reflective Tool.

PRINCIPLES FOR BRINGING A FAMILY SENSITIVITY TO YOUTH MINISTRY

A family sensitivity in youth ministry means looking at our ministry and service efforts through a "family lens" and making appropriate adjustments. It means doing all we can for teens and their families without creating new programs. Pope John Paul II in his Exhortation on the Family, *Familiaris Consortio*, captured the essence of family perspective when he wrote, "No plan of organized pastoral work at any level must ever fail to take into consideration the pastoral area of the family."

More specifically, a family perspective in youth ministry seeks to do three things. (Kehrwald)

1. *It seeks to sensitize the minister to the realities of marriage and family life.*

Today's family is not what we were raised to believe it should be. Nearly every household has been impacted by divorce, remarriage, dual careers, high mobility, and/or a serious family dysfunction. There is a myriad of family forms present in our parishes: blended families, single-parent, dual career, etc. Youth ministry leaders are generally aware of these trends, and yet some youth ministry programs fail to fully involve folks from non-traditional family forms. At times we tend to label all but a small minority of families as "broken" when actually, all families are broken and wounded in one way or another. Thus, all households deserve to be embraced and accepted.

How can parishes and youth programs respond to the realities of marriage and family life today? One parish provided *Family Background Sheets* for all their catechists and youth workers. The sheets indicated how many students were from single parent families, or blended families, or dual career, how many were oldest or youngest in the family, etc. The idea was to provide information about students and their families so the catechist could tailor the lessons to their lived experiences at home.

Other parishes have used a simple strategy called *Family Life Awareness Raising*. This involves using the various forms of parish communication to raise parishioner consciousness of everyday household realities. Through means such as the Sunday bulletin, prayers of the faithful, notes home through students, and even pulpit announcements, parishioners are exposed to the many forms and functions of family in our society.

2. *A family sensitivity in youth ministry seeks to sensitize those who serve individuals to broaden their perspective by viewing the individual through the prism of adolescent household life.*

Here we must remember a couple of key principles of family systems theory. All families seek a balance of relationships. This means there are particular patterns for interacting with each other as well as those outside the family. Also, there are particular "roles" that family members play. This balance is called homeostasis. Whether healthy or not, most families resist anything that might upset their particular "balance."

When one family member experiences change, all others must adjust in order for that change to be lasting. In other words, the whole family must seek a new balance to accommodate an individual's change. Most families will try to change the individual back the way he or she was, rather than seek a new balance.

The primary goal of youth ministry is to help individuals respond to God's activity in their lives, that is, *change*! Most of the programs and activities are focused on individuals: retreats, confirmation preparation, informal counseling, catechetical classes. This is not wrong. On the contrary, it is appropriate and necessary. The challenge, however, is to help families adjust to the changes the programs are trying to encourage in the lives of individuals. Families resist change, even if it is a positive one. If ministers cannot help them adjust, then the changes for individuals will not be lasting.

How do we do this? The obvious answer would be to involve the entire household in the program in which the individual is enrolled. Some gallant efforts are being made here, particularly in the areas of family catechesis.

Yet, for many aspects of youth ministry, it is just not realistic for the whole family to participate. Therefore, some parishes are working to create *Bridger Experiences*. They provide exercises designed to "bridge" the experience of the particular youth program with the individual's home life. Family members can adjust to the changes in the individual if they can be kept abreast of, and connected to the progress of the ministry activities.

One parish developed a very effective bridger experience for young adolescents preparing for confirmation. They were given a 50 question review of the Catholic Faith, and told to take it home and ask anyone to help them answer the questions. The catechists were not so interested in correct answers as they were in spurring dialogue about our Catholic Christian faith in the home. The strategy worked beautifully.

As another example, a parish youth ministry program designed a *Retreat Re-entry* session for parents of teens returning from the youth group retreat. Their goal was to sensitize parents and family members to the powerful faith experiences which occurred on the weekend and give practical advice on nurturing on-going growth at home.

These bridger experiences can connect the evangelizing and catechetical work of youth ministry to the delicate balance of home life.

Along these lines, families will also benefit from opportunities to draw support and encouragement from others having like experiences. Families find it easier to adjust to the change and growth of an individual (finding a new balance) when they interact with others dealing with similar tasks. For this reason, parish like-to-like support groups are extremely valuable, particularly at the adolescent stage of family life.

3. *A family perspective in youth ministry helps adolescent families become better partners with the many institutions they deal with regularly...including the parish itself.*

There was a time in generations past when the family maintained both responsibility and control over the most important human functions: education, religious formation, health care, recreation, work, child bearing and rearing, personal nurturing, etc. In the agrarian society of 200 years ago, the family, in conjunction with the small community, fulfilled all these major functions.

With the dawning of the industrial revolution, families moved into the cities, and employment was found outside the home and family farm. Families were fragmented when the work place was separated from the home. This fragmentation has only escalated as society has shifted from industrialism to high technology and vast information exchange. As our lives have become computerized, so our lifestyle has become compartmentalized. In our high mobility, our household numbers have shrunk. Consequently, we have created institutions to fulfill the functions families used to perform, for example, school sports (recreation), physicians groups (health care), and parish religious education programs (religious formation).

Today, the family has held onto only two important functions: child bearing and personal nurturing. Even the personal nurturing function is often shared with child care agencies among single-parent and dual-working families. With all the other functions, the family must *partner* with various institutions of society to receive their services. Coordinating these *partnerships* is a harrying, stressful experience for many households, especially when one or more of these institutions are not particularly family sensitive in their manner of providing service. Complications often arise over issues of scheduling, child care, communication. Does the institution serve the family, or does the family serve to sustain the institution?

Parishes and youth ministry efforts have two challenges here. First, they must look at their own relationship with families. How are the services and ministries of the youth program made available to families? This may sound like an absurd question, but when we focus most of our energy on serving individuals and/or building community among teens in the youth ministry, the question is worth asking because families often become fragmented in the process. When we're more concerned about parish policies than pastoral presence, chances are we're not very family sensitive.

From the other side of the coin, families are challenged to fulfill their end of the partnership. When they view the youth catechesis program as just a "sacramental service station" with no real sense of ownership or membership, they hinder faith growth for all. If they contribute to the life and vitality of the community, then they demonstrate their effective partnership.

The second challenge is to support and advocate for adolescent families in their relationships with other service organizations. The parish can provide a forum for families to gather together and speak as a united voice to the community concerning societal issues facing teens and their families today, for example, drug use, sexual experimentation, unhealthy media exposure.

The youth ministry program can also help create an atmosphere of support for families that helps them prioritize their activities, say "no" to some of society's demands, and rediscover the value of home life. When the minister emphasizes quality home life, it will surely enrich the ministry as well.

YOUTH MINISTRY AND FAMILIES: A REFLECTIVE TOOL

The reflective questions below will help anyone who works with adolescents assess how he or she considers families of adolescents. The questions are based on information presented above regarding blind assumptions about youth ministry and household life, your posture in ministry, and the three principles for bringing a family sensitivity to youth ministry. These family impact assessment questions will help the minister look at all aspects of service and programming through a family lens.

You may wish to work through these questions by yourself or with your ministry team. They can be particularly helpful if addressed in the process of future planning. One caution: do not be tempted into planning a lot of new programs which incorporate parents and families. Remember, more is not always better. Perhaps the most family sensitive decision you can make is to do less. The questions below are designed to help you look critically at your existing programs, and see what possible adjustments can be made.

1. What is your overall attitude toward early adolescence and early adolescent families today?

2. Can you recall an incident when you may have been guilty of assuming that early adolescence is pathological?

3. Can you recall an incident when you may have been guilty of assuming that early adolescence is transitional?

4. How can your ministry, service, and programs better reflect the healthy and foundational nature of early adolescence, and the realities of early adolescent families today?

5. How do your programs improve the capacity for families to master the challenging developmental issues of early adolescence?

6. Concerning early adolescent ministry programming, have you ever been guilty of assuming that more is always better?

7. Are there any activities or programs that could either be eliminated, reduced, or adjusted with a greater family sensitivity in your early adolescent ministry effort?

8. Have you ever been guilty of assuming that whatever good things you do in ministry for early adolescents will automatically benefit their families?

9. Do your ministry programs have a process for helping early adolescents and their families deal with the change and growth your programs encourage?

10. Do any of your youth community building activities fragment household life in the process?

11. Have you ever been guilty of assuming that parents cannot pass on faith to their early adolescents?

12. How are the parents of early adolescents involved in your program's planning, implementation, and evaluation?

13. Have you ever found yourself assuming that a young person's faith life was completely dependent on your spiritual guidance?

14. Does your work with early adolescents show any signs of being the "Lone Ranger" style of ministry?

15. When you consider Guernsey's four postures of ministry toward household life (parasitic, competitive, cooperative, symbionic), what is your posture?

16. Has your ministry posture shifted in the last six months? If so, how?

17. Can you think of any changes in your programs and activities that would help you shift to a more cooperative posture?

18. Does your program address only the early adolescent's needs, the needs of the adolescent in relation to his or her family, or the overall needs of the entire family?

19. Are you aware of the different family forms represented by the early adolescents in your program (for example, single parent, blended, dual career)? Does your program account for these different household situations?

20. What underlying attitudes concerning the family situation are built into your program?

21. Does your program, in any way, advocate for the needs of early adolescents and their families within the parish/school community or the civic community at large?

22. How would you respond to these four statements?
* Our early adolescent ministry program hinders family life when...
* Our early adolescent ministry program strengthens family life by...
* Families hinder the early adolescent ministry program when...
* Families strengthen the early adolescent ministry program by...

23. In light of your responses to the above statements, how can you create a better partnership with early adolescent families?

24. What is one immediate adjustment your program can implement to become more family sensitive?

25. What is one long-term goal your program can incorporate to increase its sensitivity to families?

PRACTICAL TIPS AND SUGGESTIONS

Below are some first-step ideas for bringing a family sensitivity to early adolescent ministry. They do not call for developing new programs, but rather to shift the posture of your youth work toward a better partnership with early adolescent households.

Meet early adolescents on their "home turf." Contact work with kids is important for developing relationships: going to games and concerts, meeting them at school for lunch, hanging out where they hang out. Have you considered spending time in their homes, getting to know their parents and families? You can learn a lot about a person by simply being in his or her home for a short while. It takes some time and energy, but if you are already doing contact work with early adolescents, be sure to include meeting them in their "home turf."

Be involved with parents. Instead of lamenting that age-old question "How can we get more parents involved with our programs?", ask first how you might be more involved with parents. Many parents are struggling through various stages of development just as their early adolescents are. They may not be in a position to lend much emotional or practical support to the program. Also, many early adolescents send messages that parent participation is not welcome. No wonder it is tough to get them involved.

Yet if the minister shows an understanding of the stresses and struggles of parents, attempt to get to know them personally, and provide opportunities for support, a solid partnership can emerge. The better you know parents, the easier it is to know just how to invite their participation. They will also be more motivated to contribute.

Regularly assess your ministry. Be sure to periodically re-visit some or all of the reflection questions in the preceding section. These may periodically reveal the need for a variety of adjustments in your programs and activities. The questions are best used as you plan the next phase of your early adolescent ministry effort. Ask them of parents too. You may get an abundance of advice.

Parent advisory group. Parents should have a voice in the scope and shape of the early adolescent ministry program. Consider inviting them to be part of a parent advisory group. The role of this group is to help the coordinator and volunteers choose the best ways to meet the needs of early adolescents and their families. It may meet only a couple of times a year, but it helps parents stay connected without having to chaperone dances drive for retreats.

Parallel needs assessment. If you survey the needs of early adolescents in planning your program, consider developing a parallel survey for parents, asking them what topics and issues they would like their early adolescents to learn about and discuss. You might want to bring parents and early adolescents together for a couple of topics of common concern.

Early adolescent retreat re-entry. A re-entry session for parents of early adolescents following a retreat may help bridge the powerful spiritual experience of the retreat with normal home life. It may also help parents and family members accept whatever changes their teen may have experienced. The re-entry session can be simple; giving parents ideas and suggestions for how they might interact with their teen upon return from the retreat.

Brainstorm ways to bring parents and early adolescents together without calling them out to the parish. How many ways you can think of getting early adolescents and their parents talking without sponsoring an activity or holding a meeting? For example, sponsor an electricity fast where families are encouraged to spend an evening together without using electricity. You'll be amazed how creative folks can be. If this is too austere, sponsor a "No TV Tuesday," where folks pledge not to watch TV on a given Tuesday night and spend the evening together.

Family life awareness raisers. Use the parish bulletin to provide interesting facts, statistics, tips and quotes about adolescent family life. If done on a regular basis, this simple strategy communicates to all parishioners a genuine concern about early adolescents and their families. And you are not asking anyone to volunteer or come to anything, which will certainly stand out in your parish bulletin. You can also do awareness raising through the Sunday Liturgy's "Prayers of the Faithful." Volunteer periodically to write these prayers for the congregation about adolescent family issues.

Parent education programs. Organize programs which will address the specific learning needs of parents with early adolescents. These programs can include the development of new parenting skills for adolescence; a better understanding of early adolescents, the family life cycle, and the key concepts of family systems, especially family change; and the development of skills for communication and faith sharing with early adolescents. Be sure to make use of community and church resources to assist you in sponsoring and conducting these programs. Often times it is better to utilize pre-designed programs (print and video) or outside resource people to conduct a program. Be sure to conduct a needs assessment of parents to determine the exact topics and best timing for a program.

Parent education programs would do well to assist parents in strengthening the four essential elements of a close family life as outlined in the research of Merton Strommen: 1) parental harmony — demonstrating love and affection in their relationships with each other; 2) effective parent-youth communication; 3) a consistent authoritative (democratic) parental discipline — valuing both independence and disciplined conformity, and affirming an adolescent's own qualities and style while setting standards for future conduct; and 4) parental nurturing — showing affection and respect, building trust, doing things together, and developing family support systems. (Roberto)

Programs for parents and early adolescents. One way to integrate parents and a family perspective into programming is to design certain programs with built-in parent sessions. For example, a course on human sexuality for early adolescents might follow this sequence: a parents-only session, followed by three youth sessions, another parents-only session, then three more youth sessions, and finally a parent-teen closing session.

Other possibilities for programming include: a) family activities and programs which build communication, trust, and closeness; b) parent-teen programs that discuss moral values and promote discussion; c) providing structured times of worship (Sunday worship, celebrations, rituals) in the parish that have a parent-early adolescent focus; d) worship and scripture resources for parents to use in the home with early adolescents; e) justice and service projects that involve the whole family (perhaps at regularly scheduled times during the year); f) parent-early adolescent retreat experiences; and g) home-based advent and lenten programs (as individual families or clusters). (Roberto)

Parallel programs for parents and early adolescents. Parallel programs offer the opportunity for parents and early adolescents to experience the same program content but in formats geared to their needs and life stage. For example, parents could take an adult course (like morality or Scripture) while their son or daughter was participating in an adolescent course on the same topic. For many parishes, this could be the beginning of an adult education program. Another example of parallel programming can be support groups, which provide parent and adolescent groups on the same topics or crisis situation, for example divorce or separation. (Roberto)

Parent resource center. Parents are realizing that they cannot "go it alone" in today's society. Parents are realizing that it makes sense to draw on the skilled resources of outside experts when problems arise. There are many critical situations that demand outside help today, for example, drug use, alcohol use, sexual activity, suicidal tendencies, child abuse, and other out-of-control behaviors. For parents needing help with critical situations, early adolescent ministry can establish a parent resource center which provides information and videos on adolescent problems, referral assistance to expert and trusted counselling resources, a link to support groups (like AA or Al Anon), and information on community educational programs that address critical adolescent situations. (Roberto)

These are just a sampling of ideas that you might consider. Hopefully, they have stimulated your own creativity. Family perspective adjustments are endless if you continually filter all your efforts through a family lens.

CONCLUSION

Take a moment for reflection. Try to recall the days when you were 10...13...15...17. Who were the key persons in your life? How did you feel about your parents, siblings, and extended family members? How did your family relate to faith nurture, religion, and the Church?

For many, family life has been a place where they encounter holiness, experience Christian community, and discover a call to ministry or service.

The church of the home can be the most effective disciple-maker. It stands to reason then that the parish church (and beyond) must partner with the home in this faith-building and disciple-making endeavor. The church of the home can never be the entire expression of Church, but it is an essential link in transmitting faith and values from one generation to the next...even for adolescent families.

Early adolescent ministry in the future will have a stronger multi-generational dimension. It will not isolate early adolescents from their families and parishes. It will bridge the youth program with the homefront, exposing early adolescents to persons and experiences that stretch them beyond the boundaries of their youth culture, and exploring ever more creative ways to bring parents and early adolescents together in the context of Christian community.

In short, a family perspective in early adolescent ministry will not only enrich household life, it will also greatly benefit the field of youth ministry.

WORKS CITED

Braun, Mary. Lecture on Family Systems Theory. Regis College, June 30, 1987.

Guernsey, Dennis B. *A New Design for Family Ministry*. Elgin IL: David C. Cook Publishing, 1982.

Power, Thomas A. *Family Matters: A Layman's Guide to Family Functioning*. Meredith NH: Hathaway Press, 1989.

Roberto, John. *Principles for Ministry with Youth*. Network Paper #26. New Rochelle NY: Don Bosco Multimedia, 1989.

Strommen, Merton and Irene. *Five Cries of Parents*. San Francisco: Harper and Row, 1985.

RESOURCE BIBLIOGRAPHY: MINISTRY WITH PARENTS AND FAMILIES

Ambrose, Dub, and Walt Mueller. *Ministry to Families with Teenagers*. Loveland CO: Group Books, 1988.

Canter, Lee, and Marlene Canter. *Parents on Your Side*. Santa Monica CA: Lee Canter & Associates, 1991.

Condon, Camy, and James McGinnis. *Helping Kids Care — Harmony Building Activities for Home, Church, and School*. St. Louis: Institute for Peace and Justice, 1989.

Curran, Dolores. *Working with Parents*. Circle Pines MN: American Guidance Service, 1989.

——. *Traits of the Healthy Family*. San Francisco: Harper and Row and New York: Ballatine Books, 1983.

Durka, Gloria. "Family Systems: A New Perspective for Youth Ministry." *Readings in Youth Ministry*. Washington DC: NFCYM Publications, 1986.

Guernsey, Dennis B. *A New Design for Family Ministry*. Elgin IL: David C. Cook Publishing Co., 1982.

Farel, Anita. *Early Adolescence: What Parents Need to Know*. Carrboro NC: Center for Early Adolescence, 1982.

McGinnis, Jim. *Helping Families Care*. St. Louis: Institute for Peace and Justice, 1989.

McGinnis, Jim and Kathleen. *Parenting for Peace and Justice — Ten Years Later*. Maryknoll NY: Orbis Books, 1990.

NCCB. *A Family Perspective in Church and Society*. Washington DC: USCC, 1988.

Power, Thomas A. *Family Matters — A Layman's Guide to Family Functioning*. Meredith NH: Hathaway Press, 1989.

Roberto, John, ed. *Growing in Faith: A Catholic Families Sourcebook*. New Rochelle: Don Bosco Multimedia, 1990.

Sawyers, Lindell, ed. *Faith and Families*. Philadelphia: The Geneva Press, 1986.

Small, Stephen. *Preventive Programs that Support Families with Adolescents*. Washington DC: Carnegie Council on Adolescent Development, 1990.

Steinberg, Laurence, and Ann Levine. *You and Your Adolescent — A Parent's Guide for Ages 10-20*. New York: Harper and Row, 1990.

Stinnett, Nick, and John DeFrain. *Secrets of Strong Families*. Boston: Little, Brown, and Co., 1985.

Strommen, Merton and Irene. *Five Cries of Parents*. San Francisco: Harper and Row, 1985.

Chapter 8

Ministry with Racial/Ethnic Minority Youth

David Ng

BEING A TEENAGER IN A MULTIFACETED WORLD

In our mind's eye our image of a house may be simple and sentimental. But we also know that a close inspection of any house will reveal much complexity. How much more complex and multifaceted would be a whole housing compound! In a similar way, the initial simplicity and sentimentality we imagine for youth ministry gives way to a more realistic realization of its complexity, depth, and multifaceted character, especially when the youth ministry is multicultural. A ministry that involves young persons from several cultures is complex, multifaceted, and potentially rich with possibilities. And very difficult to accomplish! Building one little cottage is one thing; building an apartment complex is something else. Building a youth ministry to serve the needs of teenagers who are Hispanic, African American, Native American, Pacific Asian American, or any other type of racial, ethnic, and cultural minority is challenging indeed. This article offers a theological and sociological stance from which to view ministry with minority youth and to provide some perspectives on such ministry.

Suppose we visited a medium sized city that once was an agricultural center but is, like so much of life today, "multi"—a mixture of economies, types of work, people, and cultures—multicultural in many ways. In one small apartment in that city lives a 14 year old girl with her family. It is a large family—an extended family in that some aunts and uncles and cousins live in the same apartment complex. But it is not a complete family in that some members died during the Vietnam war and others could not or chose not to emigrate to the United States.

In the apartment we are visiting, the 14 year old girl, Tran Thi-Mai, lives with her parents and two younger brothers and a sister. Her older brother, born six years before her, was killed by a land mine in Vietnam.

Thi-Mai was born in a refugee camp in Thailand, and her younger siblings, who are now eight, six, and three, were born in the United States.

The residential section where the Trans live is in transition. It always has been, and has experienced wave upon wave of new immigrants who stay only long enough to gain the wherewithal to move to better housing. The Trans have been in the neighborhood for seven years and enjoy the company of extended family, but hope some day to move into a house of their own, in a quieter place. The neighborhood has its good points: it is primarily residential, with small houses built in the 1920s and small apartment buildings of post-World War II vintage. Small grocery stores, a few restaurants, and other shops and services are nearby. However, Thi-Mai has to take the bus to attend the junior high school two miles away.

The school reflects the community. There are Southeast Asians, Hispanics, many Filipinos, some African Americans, and some Caucasians (whom everyone calls "Anglos.") The cliche the school principal loves to use is "Garfield High is a mini-United Nations."

THE JOURNEY OF IDENTITY FORMATION

As with virtually every adolescent growing up in North America, Thi-Mai is in the process of identity formation. Her body has changed in recent years and is noticeable even on her spare 5' 2", 105 pound frame. Certainly Thi-Mai knows that she has experienced change and physical growth. Her "mind" is in a state of change too. She senses some satisfaction that she has had physical and sexual growth but is not sure that change and growth are complete; another inch here and there would be nice. Her "mind" is also changing in that she is now raising more questions about how things are done—they really are questions of <u>why</u> things are done as they are. Given her home situation, many of these questions are internalized; she knows better than to ask too many "how come" and "why not this way" questions of her parents, especially of her father.

Identity formation is the nearly universal task of young persons to deal with the questions of "who am I," and "what do I believe and value," and "how will I relate with others in a way that maintains my own independence." Thi-Mai's journey of identity formation is taking many of the twists and turns familiar to most teenagers. With her basically pleasant, positive personality, the identity formation journey has been fairly smooth.

THE TURNS AND TWISTS OF CULTURAL IDENTITY

However, one stretch of that road is different from that of many North American adolescents. Thi-Mai is a person of minority racial/ethnic and cultural background. She is Vietnamese American. She will not be as tall or heavy as the Anglo girls at school or as women are portrayed in movies, television shows, and glamor magazines. Even if others pay sparse attention to her physical characteristics, Thi-Mai is very conscious of them. She is aware, through personal experience if not through informed, studied knowledge, that she is different in cultural background and worldview. Her family has a religious background that is Buddhist even though they are now Christian; their social ethics are Confucian; their philosophy of life is Taoist.

An example of each religious and cultural dimension can illustrate how different Thi-Mai is from others in her school who are not from Southeast Asia. Her parents grew up with the religious attitude that life includes much suffering which must be overcome through enlightenment. Becoming spirit (not just becoming more spiritual) is a goal in life. Thi-Mai and her brothers and sister have been taught that they are not to do anything that will bring shame to their parents and their family, or to their country, that is, to Vietnam. Whether or not she realizes it, her worldview is that of "yin-yang." All of life is in balance and harmony. Opposites are held in tension: male/female, good/evil, strong/weak, bitter/sweet, growth/decay, day/night, and so on. Every item and every aspect of life is connected and balanced in a harmony of life. This Asian "both/and" view of life contrasts greatly with the Western "either/or" way of viewing life and having to make choices either for or against. In contrast to her Anglo schoolmates who are taught to be independent minded and decisive or even aggressive, Thi-Mai grew up learning to be accepting of life or "fate," to avoid conflict, and so seems not at all assertive to the Anglos.

Many of Thi-Mai's Anglo schoolmates experience times when their families seem almost unimportant. Outside activities and organizations often take precedence over family life and obligations. Thi-Mai, however, lives in a family system that is top priority. In that regard she is like the Filipino and Hispanic youth at the school. Thi-Mai's life is dominated by her family and her attitudes and practices center on the family. The family is her main unit of relationship. Her parents, particularly her father, have authority over her. Now that "big brother" is dead, she has assumed authority and responsibility over her three brothers and sister. The way they are called reflects that hierarchy: they are "little brothers and little sister; she is "big sister." Her mother is subordinate to her father, but she has an unambiguous honored role. The children are to obey the parents and revere ("venerate") their elders and ancestors. They have an obligation to care for the family, especially the parents when they are older. Decisions are made in the light of what is good for the family; no one is an independent agent making a decision solely for the individual.

Thi-Mai is very involved in the family matrix. She has obligations such as caring for her younger brothers and sister. Her decisions about studying, spare time, college, and career are communal decisions. Family activities and celebrations such as attending observances of birth, marriage, and death are obligatory. In these and many other ways Thi-Mai is drawn into a net of relatives and community.

Years from now Thi-Mai may look back on this pervasive family system and be glad for its support. Right now she harbors ambivalent feelings, because in her surge toward identity formation and personal independence, she feels the constraints of family pressures. Something that is supposed to be good often is bad, at least in terms of personal freedom and self-esteem. It seems they always have a family celebration the same night there is a school function or special program at the church!

THE IMMIGRANT EXPERIENCE

Another facet in Thi-Mai's multifaceted life is her immigrant experience. Like many other racial/ethnic minority people in North America, Thi-Mai was not born here; her family immigrated from another country and another culture. They have had to adjust to a country and a culture new to them. There was great discomfort in leaving the homeland. The oldest son (the most valuable child) was left behind in a grave. Major social, economic, and cultural adjustments had to be developed quickly. The English language was very foreign and hard to learn. The Trans found themselves in a society that holds individualistic and materialistic values. The changes and adjustments have been hard for the parents. For the children they are confusing. For Thi-Mai the immigrant experience compounds her task of identity formation.

THE UPHEAVAL OF BEING REFUGEES

Even more traumatic is the experience of having to flee one's country as a refugee. Life in the homeland was so intolerable and the suffering so great that the Tran family left in a desperate search for a better life. For all their love and loyalty for their native country there is little hope of returning to Vietnam. Ambivalence infiltrates their refugee experience. They are grateful for the opportunities, however, meager, in the United States. But this is the same country that tried to save their country by bombing it back to the Stone Age. Life in the United States is somewhat safer and no one is starving. A few of their friends and relatives are regaining economic security. But this is not home nor the life they knew.

THE DEVASTATION OF WAR

Perhaps the most traumatic experience for the Tran parents is that they are refugees who survived a cruel and devastating war. We who were not there can only imagine, with the help of what we saw on television and in recent movies, the horror and pain of the people who experienced the

Vietnam War. But for refugees like the elder Trans, war is not something they viewed from a television screen in the comfort of the living room. They were in the middle of the bombing, under the guns of soldiers, and they know relatives and friends who are maimed or dead. Thi-Mai was only three years old when she came to the United States, but she lives among people whose collective memory is vivid and haunting. Interestingly, Thi-Mai has learned something of the trauma of war from two friends at school, Margarita and Miriam Garcia, who fled El Salvador just a few years ago.

THE PERVASIVENESS OF RACISM

Thi-Mai is self-conscious about being Vietnamese American, one of the multitude of minorities in North America. While she senses she is different, her experience of most "Americans" is that they are kind and friendly to her and her Vietnamese companions. There even are persons who show sympathy for the traumas they have endured as Vietnamese. But unfortunate incidents occur often enough to instill in Thi-Mai a sense that she cannot trust Anglos and Anglo culture. Some incidents are mean: being called derogatory names, being victimized by surly service or being taken advantage of because of a lack of language and knowledge. Other incidents are "unintentioned," such as being questioned about her name, being talked at as an outsider, and being given the impression that her culture is inferior. It is hard to say whether the sharp pain of mean acts or the constant dull pain of unintentional acts is easier to bear. Occasionally Thi-Mai thinks to herself, "Anglo kids don't have to go through any of this s___."

ON THE WAY TO BEING THE MAJORITY

In many sections of Canada and the United States, the Caucasian, European-background majority percentage of the population is falling and there is a noticeable rise in the population of the so-called minority racial/ethnic peoples. In California it is estimated that by the year 2032 "Anglos" will be a minority and other racial/ethnic peoples will be the majority. This change reflects the growth in numbers of people from Mexico, Central America, the Pacific Islands, and Asia. Tran Thi-Mai often is treated as an outsider, a minority person who has to earn her way into the American society. But she and millions of others in her region are no longer satisfied with such treatment in society or in the church. And in both society and church there are many encouraging signs of openness to the idea that our world, our societies, and our churches are multicultural and should be.

A MULTICULTURAL CONGREGATION

Thi-Mai experiences multiple stress: being an adolescent in search of identity, living in a family with some difficulties in communication and cultural values, being an immigrant and refugee in a majority culture that wittingly and unwittingly asserts dominance over her—these are not easy years for Thi-Mai. Poverty and limited economic and social opportunities add to the difficulties. For all this, St. Patrick's Church in her neighborhood is one very positive experience for Thi-Mai and her family. Only four blocks from her apartment, St. Pat's is a place of comfort, acceptance, and hope. This congregation, fortunately, has members and leaders who offer pastoral care and nurturing programs that have enabled people like the Trans to feel that they are persons of worth and esteem.

While not perfect, the approach to youth ministry at St. Pat's is exemplary in three respects. It is based on sound theological and ecclesial foundations. It has a sympathetic understanding of the developmental tasks their adolescent members are working on. And of great significance for the racial/ethnic minority members of the church, St. Pat's has an appreciation for the unique situation of these people.

THEOLOGICAL AND ECCLESIAL FOUNDATIONS FOR YOUTH MINISTRY

No matter who is included in the church's youth ministry, be it so-called majority or minority persons, the basic question must be raised: Why youth ministry? Not surprisingly, the unstated answer to this usually unstated question comes out weakly: "Because we've always done it." No serious reflection on the basic question has been done for years. Some happy surprises are in store for those congregations that will ask the basic question and seek theological and ecclesial resources for responding.

Certain theological themes are rich with potential for informing why we do youth ministry. Among many themes are those of *creation*, *personhood*, *community*, *faith*, and *mission*.

The programs and opportunities for study in youth ministry can help young people to know the world as the good creation of God and to know themselves as a part of that creation. This understanding of themselves and their world provides a basic framework for understanding life and its purpose. Identity formation includes the forming of a sense of self in relation to life and the things of life. A young person needs to think through for one's self the reason for one's existence and the ways one relates to all else in this world, including other persons, nature, and the rhythm of birth, growth, work, and death. To know God as the creator of all of this and as the giver of life, talent, and purpose to one's self is to have a positive, purposeful view of life and of self. This good news about life is to be shared with our young persons.

Thus personhood—personal, individual identity in relation to others—is framed by this positive view of creation. A good God created a good world and gave us a the gift of life and of personhood or identity, so that we can make something worthwhile of all this. Certainly not every person experiences gloom, doubt, and despair while going through the time of adolescence! But many if not all of them benefit from assurances that they will grow up, will form a mature personality, and will find reasons for living and working. The Church, through its tradition and particularly through the messages of the Bible, not only can give such assurances but gives the very model of fully realized humanity, even Jesus Christ himself. In Jesus Christ each person's own identity as a human being is defined and challenged toward fulfillment. Identity formation is a big issue for every adolescent, and the Church's theology at its core has the richest resource for persons searching for identity.

Another large part of the Church's story of creation, again presented rigorously and vividly in the Bible, is that we are made to live in community. To be human is to relate to other humans (and to all of creation) in a loving manner, giving and receiving love and nurture. This major theological theme also informs youth ministry and guides how it will be organized and achieved. To do youth ministry is to involve young persons in meaningful nurturing relationships.

Identity formation is also faith formation and values formation. Adolescents are reviewing what they know and believe about themselves, their families, and about God and the Church. As they go through this exploration it is timely for the Church to walk with them on this journey toward the discovery and affirmation of personal faith. Adolescents, with newly honed skills of abstract thinking, can be critical and analytical, and can recast older, more naive perceptions of God into fresh understandings of a God of grace who gives life, offers forgiveness, and calls for commitment. Young people are notorious for being hard questioners of all things, including the doctrines of the Church. In youth ministry we are glad for these questions and doubts and we thank God that we have the privilege of working with teenagers during this critical time of faith development. We understand that faith is a theological theme of crucial importance in youth ministry.

Mission, vocation, call, discipleship, and similar words provide further rationale for doing youth ministry. Driven by the need for identity formation young persons will ask,"What is life's meaning?" and "What is the meaning of my life?" The Church's story of creation tells of the purposes for which we were created. All of creation and all of us creatures are to love God and enjoy our life and relationship with God. Each young person is to be challenged, through youth ministry, to see creation and life purpose this way and to respond in commitment to fulfilling this purpose. Each young person is to be called to a life and to work that will serve God and God's creation. Youth ministry presents the challenge of vocation and mission.

Certainly other significant theological themes can be considered as bases for building an approach to youth ministry. Sexuality and sex, values, family, justice, and other topics need to be understood theologically, and their theological implications presented to young people. However a congregation lists its theological issues, what is at stake is for it to see that its ministry with youth is grounded in its theology. To answer the question of why youth ministry we start with what we understand God is about and what God desires for our young people.

In our imaginary congregation, St. Patrick's, the youth ministry leaders did not become "theological" overnight. But they did take an "overnight"! At a leaders' retreat over a weekend they were led by a parish staff member in a study of the five theological themes above. Biblical passages that highlighted these themes were discussed. A recurring question was "How does this passage support the young persons we know as they work on their sense of identity?" The leaders were introduced to several books for study and further discussion. These books did not merely give directions for how to do activities in youth ministry; they placed youth ministry upon theological and ecclesial foundations. These were "why" books, not just "what" or "how-to" manuals. (See bibliography at the end of this chapter, pp. 151-152.)

ECCLESIAL CONCERNS FOR YOUTH MINISTRY

Related to theological concerns are the ecclesial—those concerns that have to do with enabling young people to become active and productive members of the Body of Christ. In answering more fully the question of why youth ministry the Church responds by stating its desire for young people to be members of the worshiping community of faith. Acknowledging that the cup of cold water is freely offered to anyone in need, and that helping a young person with personal growth is itself a worthy goal, the Church also acknowledges that it proclaims the Gospel and invites young persons to become Christians and to fulfill their calling to worship and serve God as a part of the community of faith.

In many cases racial/ethnic minority persons have not been baptized and have not grown up as Christians. Youth ministry seeks to present a religion that is attractive and challenging, so that young people feel invited to join. For those who already have Christian associations, youth ministry invites growth and deeper involvement, ultimately challenging young persons to minister in the name of Christ through their work and their lives. In youth classes, programs, and special activities such as retreats and field trips, worship is explained, often through guided instruction and participation. Nurturance and Christian education are required parts of any youth ministry program.

Throughout the churches, Roman Catholic and Protestant, confirmation is being aimed at middle adolescence, to provide persons of that age and developmental level the occasions for faith review, exploration, and personal decisions about faith and mission. Part of the answer to "Why youth ministry?" is given through the purposes of confirmation. That program of the congregation meets young people during their questioning years and helps them in their personal search and personal decision-making about what faith is for them, and how they hope to relate to Jesus Christ and his Church.

Many people think of youth ministry as a time for helping young people with their personal and relational needs. Adult leaders can see their involvement in youth ministry as opportunities for listening, advising, gently leading young people, and as ways of helping young people help each other through peer ministries of care and support. Pastoral care is one more significant rationale for youth ministry.

Our imaginary church, St. Patrick's, learned the hard way that doing youth ministry without attention to theological and ecclesial concerns led to programs that were routine and repetitive, and to leaders who were poorly motivated and on the verge of burnout. Youth ministry is hard work—impossibly difficult if a leader does not have sufficient reasons for doing it. However, youth ministry can be the means of sharing with young people the joy of knowing our place in God's creation and our call to work with God in proclaiming this good news to all. Seen in this light, working with youth is truly a ministry and in many instances a very joyous ministry.

DEVELOPMENTAL ASPECTS OF YOUTH MINISTRY

Youth ministry can be structured on the framework of adolescent development. The major task for young persons, especially in early and middle adolescence (approximately ages 12 to 15), is to form a sense of identity that is satisfying to the self and to significant others such as family and peers. In that undertaking a young person takes stock of the values and practices that were handed down by family, school, church, and other institutions. Using more developed modes of thinking, including the propensity to question and to think hypothetically, the adolescent relies less on the ways and thinking of the past. More and more she or he chooses for one's self what to think and to do. The movement is toward independence.

The most common question for the adolescent is "Who am I?" Other questions closely relate to this: "What are my beliefs and values?" "How shall I express my personality?" "Who are my friends and how do I relate to them?" "What will I do with my life?" "To what will I be committed?"

It is hardly an exaggeration to claim that no matter what the subject of discussion, the early and middle adolescent will view that subject through the personal lenses of identity formation. Is the subject sex and sexuality? The viewpoint of the adolescent is that of wondering how he or she is affected by or will behave regarding sex. Is the subject war and peace? Homelessness? AIDS? Church history? The adolescent will engage each subject in terms of personal needs or a desire to develop a personal perspective, opinion, or understanding of the subject. Such is the stimulus of identity formation. The young person is establishing her or his independent grasp or control of the subject.

The facts of personality development, sexual growth, glandular change, and how this all affects the intellect, emotions, and personal spirit as well as the body, make for fascinating learning. Such learning is absolutely necessary for effective youth ministry. Numerous resources are available for those who wish to learn the details of adolescent development. This article will only highlight two concerns related to identity formation: relationships and decision-making.

DEVELOPING RELATIONSHIPS

We all know of the tremendous influence of peers at this age. As a young person strives for independence, there is the natural desire to avoid the ties and controls of earlier relationships such as with parents and other authority figures. Peers provide support for a teenager's trial efforts without seeming to control. That peers often become new authorities and tyrannies is a risk that too often happens. When an adolescent's peer group is a gang, that form of control can have dangerous or even violent results. The presence of peer relationships calls for the church to be transformative rather than condemnatory. Youth ministry may be a place of hope for a teenager who needs the intimate caring support of a small group but also needs to escape from the tyranny of the gang. Intimate relationships are greatly needed and extremely difficult to achieve in youth groups comprised of youth of diverse cultures, schools, and styles of life. Youth ministry must be relational ministry.

Relationships with peers need to be transformed to become wholesome, supportive, and nurturing. Often such relationships start with the quiet work and guiding examples of adults who serve in youth ministry. Adults may be needed to be models of what it means to care for one another and to "be there" when a young person is in need. So much of life and relationships is new to the adolescent that many do not know how to relate. Worse, the examples offered by secular society may be directed by selfishness, manipulation and exploitation, and immaturity—or by angry resentment toward people in authority.

Adult leaders in the church need not be the stereotypical multitalented, flashy all-stars or attractive pied pipers who can gain a loyal youth following. Of more value to young people are adult leaders who are moving toward mature faith and relationships. Such leaders have enough maturity to not take over the young people's lives but to respect them and try to help them develop wholesome relationships. Leaders may need to offer alternatives to unhealthy ways of being a group, such as a gang would, that exercises power through violence. Leaders also need to help young people cope with the changes in relationship they are making with their parents and families, and with other adults. Without taking sides, leaders can teach about such changes and offer themselves as role models of persons who try to be loving, accepting, and forgiving as they relate with others. The word "guarantor" often is used to describe such persons whose own lives and ways of life assure young people that their lives can be wholesome and loving in similar fashion.

THE SKILL OF DECISION-MAKING

It is imperative for a young person developing a sense of identity to learn the skill of decision-making. Implicit is the power to make decisions for one's self. As that power is gained there needs to be a development of the ability to make good decisions. Some of this is "nitty-gritty" ability to define the question or issue, lay out the facts or factors, and then to choose. The logic of making decisions is available to most teenagers, and a rational procedure can be practiced to perfection. For example, a counterperson at a fast food restaurant can learn decision-making procedures quickly and exercise those methods with rapidity and success. But we all know there is more to decision-making than logic. When the facts or factors are laid out, on what basis do we choose? Deciding whether to eat a hamburger or cheeseburger may be simple enough. Or is it that simple? Is our choice based on taste, cost, peer pressure, appearance, or nutritional value? Or some combination? What combination, in what priority? How much more complex and profound will be the decision when it has to do with how a young person will spend a summer, or whether or not to go to college, or how she will relate with her boyfriend.

The dimension mentioned earlier—the Church's theology—is needed here as a basis for decision-making. An adolescent will have a more mature sense of identity when she or he has secured a faith and values that offer the basis for making choices.

Youth ministry is of great service to young people when it helps them to learn how to make decisions. In our imaginary example, St. Patrick's Church, their method was practice, practice, practice! Throughout the youth ministry program young persons were given opportunities to make decisions. They had to choose which games to play, which topics to discuss. They had to choose whether to meet next Sunday or to take a break. In their formal studies they had exercises where they had to choose from various options. Role playing and case studies required choices, often between plausible possibilities or between two "evils." Reflection and evaluation, and the possibilities of trying again, all were a part of teaching the profound skill of decision-making. Faith itself was presented as a choice to be made.

The youth ministry program at St. Patrick's truly honored the young people by taking them seriously and taking seriously their need for wholesome relationships and the development of decision-making skills.

COLORFUL COMMUNITIES: THE CHALLENGE OF DIVERSITY

Having established the groundwork of theological concerns and the framework of developmental needs, we now consider the inhabitants of the "house" we call youth ministry. Youth ministry today includes people of diverse racial/ethnic and cultural backgrounds. We need to identify that reality, affirm it, and be sensitive and creative as we minister with young people of various minority backgrounds.

AFFIRMING DIVERSITY

There was a time when questions about racial/ethnic and cultural identity were "out of the question" and there still are churches today that do not ask them. It does not occur to such churches that the United States and Canada are, to use the Canadian term, "mosaics"—nations that are artistic creations of people of multiple dimensions, colors, shapes, and textures. Or some churches may have noticed the diversity of people but simply assumed that the "solution" to that "problem" is for everyone to "be like us"—"us" usually meaning Euro-American Caucasian or "Anglo."

Step one is to acknowledge that we are a multicultural society and a multicultural Church, and that every one of our members happens to be of a race, ethnicity, or culture that differs from others. Step two is to acknowledge that such differences do not mean that those who are different are inferior to or need to become like the majority people. Lockstep with this acknowledgement is the affirmation that people of different races and cultures have worthy contributions to make to the whole human race.

Recalling the Church's theology of creation, we understand the world and the Church to be multicultural—because that is how God made it. Youth ministry is multicultural too.

IDENTIFYING OUR YOUNG PEOPLE

Specifically, who are our young people? What are their specific racial/ethnic, and cultural backgrounds? How do the specific characteristics influence the young people, particularly as they establish personal identity, seek relationships, and make decisions and commitments? For the sake of God's multicultural Church and the sake of each young person we need to be aware of cultural identity.

The example of Tran Thi-Mai, sketched earlier in this article, illustrates some things to look for as youth ministry leaders try to respect each person's cultural identity, and especially as young persons of minority racial, ethnic, and cultural background are brought into the church's community. In Thi-Mai's case attention was given to her age characteristics—she, like most other young persons, is engaged in adolescent identity formation. That task is compounded by being a "minority person," a Vietnamese American. Even in brief sketch we looked at certain dimensions of Thi-Mai's life:

* her race
* country of origin
* family
* major cultural values
* worldview as informed by history, religion, and culture
* important social customs, rites, and celebrations
* learned and preferred styles of relationships
* lines of accountability and authority in family and similar institutions
* roles of persons including family roles and gender roles
* experiences of living in this country, including place of birth and degree of assimilation into the culture of this country
* conditions and economic opportunities for the particular minority group
* education, facility in English, and communication skills
* exposure to social problems such as racism, poverty, political and social marginalization
* conditions in the home and community
* relationship with and experiences in the church

Knowledge of these characteristics of the young people in the church would help the leaders to be sympathetic to their needs and aspirations. The style and content of the youth ministry program can be planned in response to these conditions. In response to the worldview and styles expressed by Thi-Mai and her Vietnamese family and friends, the program could try an approach that is low-keyed, in which people are given time for reflection and consultation with each other prior to individual decision-making. The program could offer opportunities for young people to discuss, indirectly and somewhat impersonally, issues of communication with parents and other elders. Rather than pressuring young people from Asian cultures to talk about themselves and their families, they can be encouraged to look at and discuss the situations of other people and then be given time for personal comparisons, reflections, and applications. There could be role playing, discussing television programs and movies, and reacting to written vignettes of young people who have experienced immigration, prejudice, and cultural confusion.

With some other groups, such as Native Americans or Hispanics, similar attention to their cultural values and styles may yield relevant possibilities. It may be appropriate to tell stories, legends, and myths to get at significant truths and values. Expressing personal thoughts through music and art may be helpful. Having young people record oral histories and stories of immigration or moves from one community to another can help the young people to feel more rooted and to gain appreciation for the integrity and wisdom of their elders.

Oral tradition is also strong with African Americans. Reading and similar literary pursuits are not necessarily the preferred modes of communication, so young people may benefit from having a variety of ways to share and to express their thoughts and reflections. African Americans have done much to trace their African roots, the history of involuntary immigration, of great suffering and courageous triumph over oppression. But every generation needs to hear the story, and every African American young person can incorporate these stories into his or her own story and identity.

Including these racial, ethnic, and cultural materials in the content of youth ministry fosters pride and sense of identity for young people. The Church rightly includes this in its curriculum because it is called to proclaim release from captivity and liberation for membership in the realm of God, the new creation.

DIVERSITY WITHIN DIVERSITY

Every young person is unique. Within every convenient category of people, each member of that category has the right to one's own character. The generalities that may characterize a racial/ethnic group, such as the "Hispanics," are useful for the purposes of developing broad approaches to ministry. But we must be sensitive to the fact that the term "Hispanic" itself cannot do justice to the wide variety of nationalities, cultures, and histories of the Spanish-speaking, Spanish-surnamed people we label as Hispanics. In youth ministry we need to be aware that someone from Mexico may have quite different views than one from El Salvador. And a

Puerto Rican born in the United States may have needs and wishes far different than a person born in Puerto Rico. In one family there can be a multicultural mix! Grandparents may be very traditional regarding native culture, and have very little facility in English. Parents may have their feet placed in two cultures, and children may favor North American culture, have no facility in the native language, and no desire to respect the native culture. The church's youth ministry becomes a ministry to all the factions of such polarized families. Sensitivity and creativity are needful in such situations.

It seems that almost every adolescent in North America could be labeled a "youth-at-risk" in that two or more characteristics of being at risk are present: failure in school, feelings of depression, experiences of physical or emotional abuse, problems of substance abuse, problems with the law, immature sexual behavior, and so forth. Racial/ethnic minority young people often are pushed into being at-risk because of social and economic conditions. For example, many Laotian and Cambodian young people in Southern California find it necessary to join a gang and engage in violent gang activity as the only form of self-protection available to them. Unfortunately violence begets violence and some of these young people end up in jail (these places have benevolent names like "juvenile centers") even though they are basically "good kids." Also unfortunate is that often one race is pitted against another in these gang encounters.

Many of these "kids" are desperate for alternatives. The church's youth ministry may be that alternative. The friendship and role modeling of adults, the warmth and security of small groups, and even simple programs such as field trips, camping, and work projects, may provide at-risk youth with the alternatives they need to break with the past and to find hope for the future.

TOWARD A COLORFUL YOUTH MINISTRY

For a final time we will use the device of an imaginary church doing youth ministry for imaginary young people who are racial/ethnic and cultural minority people—St. Patrick's Church where Thi-Mai and her Vietnamese American friends participate. The following handout, summarizing some ideas for youth ministry, was created for the leaders in that youth program to suggest how they could minister appropriately:

MINISTRY WITH MINORITY YOUTH

1. Have a biblical-theological and sociological base for ministry with racial/ethnic and cultural minority young people.

* Be informed by theological understandings of creation, community, personhood, faith, and mission.
* Describe our young people sociologically.

2. Find out about our young people.
   * Ask them to tell their own stories.
   * Listen, listen, listen.
   * Visit, visit, visit.
   * Find out their needs.
3. Be a community of support.
   * Support the young people as they try to be Christian.
   * Have one-on-one and small group ministries.
   * Provide opportunities for small group Bible study and prayer groups.
4. Offer wholesome alternative activities.
   * Provide recreation and sports.
   * Offer study halls, tutoring, counseling about education.
   * Challenge young people to serve others. Involve young people in work and service projects.
   * Offer field trips and other activities away from the neighborhood.
5. Serve as guarantors and role models.
   * Be an extended family.
   * Make the church a place of rest, haven, and comfort.
   * Enact "aunt and uncle roles."
   * Help young people to relate to others.
6. Stress vocation and mission.
   * Develop the leadership of the young people.
   * Work with a core group of youth.
   * Challenge individuals to reach their potential.
   * Insist on mission and service.
   * Challenge and guide regarding vocation and career choices.
7. Relate identity and culture.
   * Deal directly and often with ethnic and racial identity and affirmation.
   * Deal with justice issues such as racism, poverty, etc.
   * Challenge the young people regarding vocation and mission to their own people. For example, ask, "How will your life make a difference in this neighborhood? Among the _________ people?"
8. Help with spiritual formation.
   * Help the young people find appropriate spiritual expressions.
   * Encourage them to worship with the community of faith.
   * Find a spiritual support group for yourself.
   * Share your spiritual quest and discoveries with the young people.
   * Expect weariness and guard against burnout.
9. Expect to learn from the young people and to be enriched by them.

RESOURCE BIBLIOGRAPHY: MULTICULTURAL EDUCATION AND MINISTRY

Banks, James A. *Teaching Strategies for Ethnic Studies*. Fifth Edition. Boston: Allyn and Bacon, 1991.

Banks, James A., and Cherry A. McGee Banks. *Multicultural Education: Issues and Perspectives*. Boston: Allyn and Bacon, 1989.

Bowman FSPA, Thea, ed. *Families: Black and Catholic, Catholic and Black*. Washington DC: USCC, 1985.

Department of Education. *Faith and Culture: A Multicultural Catechetical Resource*. Washington DC: USCC, 1987.

Deck, Allen Figueroa. *The Second Wave: Hispanic Ministry and the Evangelization of Cultures*. New York: Paulist Press, 1989.

Edwards SM, Rev. William. "Ministry in the Black Community: A Base Community Approach." Network Paper #27. New Rochelle: Don Bosco Multimedia, 1989.

Fitzpatrick, Joseph. *One Church, Many Cultures*. Kansas City: Sheed and Ward, 1987.

Foster, Charles R., ed. *Ethnicity and Education in the Church*. Nashville: Scarritt Press, 1987.

Foster, Charles R., and Grant S. Shockley. *Working with Black Youth: Opportunities for Christian Ministry*. Nashville: Abingdon Press, 1989.

Gollnick, Donna M., and Philip C. Chinn. *Multicultural Education in a Pluralistic Society*. Columbus: Merrill Publishing Co., 1990.

Herrera, Marina. "Toward Multi-cultural Youth Ministry." *Readings in Youth Ministry - Volume 1*. Washington DC: NFCYM Publications, 1986.

Jones, Nathan. *Sharing the Old, Old Story - Educational Ministry in the Black Community*. Winona MN: St. Mary's Press, 1982.

McCray, Walter Arthur. *Reaching and Teaching Black Young Adults*. Chicago: Black Light Fellowship, 1986.

Myers, William R. *Black and White Styles of Youth Ministry: Two Congregations in America*. New York: The Pilgrim Press, 1991.

__________________. *Theological Themes of Youth Ministry*. New York: The Pilgrim Press, 1987.

Ng, David. *La Juventud: Discipulado para Hoy*. Adaptado por Victor M. Vazquez. Valley Forge: Judson Press, 1989. (Also in English: *Youth in the Community of Disciples*.)

Ng, Donald. *Asian Pacific American Youth Ministry: Planning Helps and Programs*. Valley Forge: Judson Press, 1988.

Program Agency, Presbyterian Church (U.S.A.). *My Identity: A Gift from God.* (In English, Spanish, and Korean.) Seoul: Publishing House of the Presbyterian Church in Korea, 1987.

Tiedt, Pamela L., and Iris M. Tiedt. *Multicultural Teaching: A Handbook of Activities, Information and Resources.* Third Edition. Boston: Allyn and Bacon, 1990.

Roehlkepartain, Eugene C. *Youth Ministry in City Churches.* Loveland,CO: Group Books, 1989.

Warren, Michael. *Youth, Gospel, Liberation.* San Francisco: Harper and Row, 1987.

Chapter 9

Catechesis with Early Adolescents: Curriculum

Bruce Baumgarten

INTRODUCTION TO ADOLESCENT CATECHESIS

As research into early adolescents and their needs has expanded, early adolescent ministers have tried to translate their new-found knowledge into models and strategies for effective programming. Throughout that effort the area that has received the greatest attention is catechesis. The last 10-15 years of work in the development of our understanding of early adolescence has been paralleled by an ever-increasing growth in our understanding of catechesis in general and adolescent catechesis in particular. Much of that growth in understanding came together in the publication of *The Challenge of Adolescent Catechesis: Maturing in Faith* in 1986 and its ongoing implementation in years since.

In *The Challenge* document we have a consensus statement by the four main national-level youth-serving agencies. The document would be important simply for that collaborative impact. But there is much more. It has become a significant resource because it reflects and is consistent with the best of our catechetical tradition, while integrating the most current understandings of adolescent development especially for our purposes here, early adolescent development.

Restricting our attention to early adolescents then, we can find in *The Challenge* and the books and articles written since its publication, the foundations for developing effective catechetical ministry with early adolescents — a goal sought by religious educators, youth ministers, parents, and early adolescents alike. Brian Reynolds attests to the fact that this goal is so surely needed when he states, "catechetical curricula, class environment, and learning methods have often ignored the developmental needs of young adolescents. A tremendous amount of energy has been spent trying to control young adolescents rather than motivate them." (Reynolds 14)

After five years of working as a diocesan trainer and consultant in early adolescent catechesis, I have come to identify the struggle for effective catechetical programming as a task of clarifying definitions and aims followed by developing with equal attention the complementary issues of curriculum and teaching (or "being a catechist"). Quite simply, there is still a great deal of confusion about what we actually are about in catechetical programming for early adolescents — what *is* adolescent catechesis and what are we trying to *do* with it? *The Challenge* document offers clear and concise direction in the effort to define catechesis and specify its aim. I will present a brief summary of these points below.

After the definition and aim questions are resolved, we are still left with the great "so how do I make it happen?" issues. I truly believe that this is a matter of two complementary parts of the same whole. I explore this using the image of taking a picture with a zoom lens camera. The resolution of the definition and aim questions is like setting up the shot, focusing and clarifying exactly what the picture is. By dealing with the issue of *curriculum* we are attending to the wide-angle of catechetical programming; by taking up the issue of *being a catechist* we are moving in for a close-up on the major element of an effective catechetical experience. By seeing these as complementary issues, I am asserting that the goal of *effective* early adolescent catechesis can only be reached by attending to both. For this reason, each of these issues will receive treatment in the chapters which follow.

DEFINITION AND AIM OF ADOLESCENT CATECHESIS

The Challenge of Adolescent Catechesis defines catechesis as "a systematic, planned, and intentional pastoral activity...directed toward the kind of teaching and learning which emphasizes growth in Christian faith through understanding, reflection, and transformation." (*The Challenge* 5) In articulating such a definition the document draws directly upon Pope John Paul II's apostolic exhortation, *Catechesi Tradendae*, and remains consistent with the vision of the US Bishops' *Sharing the Light of Faith — the National Catechetical Directory* (the NCD).

Such a definition does not deny the catechetical dimension in other ministerial activities (what some call "informal catechesis"). It simply sets its parameters around those activities within the catechetical enterprise that are more deliberate and formal. At the same time it does not equate catechesis with "schooling" — a presupposition many make when they read "systematic, planned, and intentional." The definition merely directs ministerial leaders to the discipline of creating catechetical programs that are doctrinally and developmentally sound, have deliberate objectives, are ordered coherently, and are based in sound planning. Such characteristics can be found in a variety of creative educational programs that bear no resemblance to the image of traditional "schooling." Indeed, one of the central conclusions of *The Challenge* is the need for variety: in programming, content, format, and method.

Having acknowledged "what" catechesis is, the next question we must answer is "why" should we engage in it? This is the question of "aim." According to *The Challenge*,

> The primary aim of adolescent catechesis is to sponsor youth toward maturity in Catholic Christian faith as a living reality... We have two tasks: to foster in youth a communal identity as Catholic Christians and to help them develop their own personal faith identity. To accomplish the first task, we present the faith convictions and values of the Catholic Christian tradition and invite adolescents to adopt and own these values and convictions. To effect the second, we help adolescents respond to God in faith, in prayer, in values, and in behavior. (*The Challenge* 8)

By speaking about the aim of faith maturing, *The Challenge* echoes a message that is consistent with the major Church documents in catechesis (see NCD #33 and *Catechesi Tradendae* #20).

Since the publication of *The Challenge*, many catechetical and youth ministers have related this aim and twofold goal to a very concrete image developed by John Nelson. In speaking about the tension between personal identity and corporate identity, Nelson says that we can be both "midwife" and "adoption agent." We are midwife when we are "helping adolescents give birth to their own personal convictions and values." We are adoption agent when we "present to them convictions already born within the Catholic Christian tradition" which we represent. (Nelson 98)

This is an extremely rich concept and one with direct implications for those seeking to develop effective catechetical curriculum and catechists in early adolescent ministry. The struggle is to keep the tension or balance between both task in sponsoring faith maturity, between being midwife and adoption agent. Though most individuals (and even courses and curricula) tend to gravitate toward one or the other, it is a central tenet of adolescent catechesis that we try to maintain both equally. I believe that the presence of early adolescents as the ministry group simply magnifies the importance of this insight.

With a solid foundation, I turn now to the complementary issues of curriculum and teaching. In this chapter, I will explore the principles and process of curriculum for early adolescents. In Chapter 10, I will explore effective teaching with early adolescents.

EARLY ADOLESCENT CATECHESIS: CURRICULUM

In his foreword to Maria Harris' book on church curriculum, *Fashion Me a People*, Craig Dykstra anticipates the less-than-enthusiastic greeting most people give to the topic of curriculum:

> "Curriculum" is, unfortunately, a debased word. Its mention generates little interest or energy in most people... The very word "curriculum" conjures up images of boxes pile on top of each other in out-of-the-way places, packed with dull workbooks for children to fill out endlessly in Sunday school. (Harris 7-8)

I would take the prediction one step forward: mention curriculum in connection with early adolescents and the reaction is one of either fear or outright disbelief. How can we ever get an interesting and helpful curriculum for early adolescents? It's a downright oxymoron!

By pointing out that such reactions are based in a mistaken understanding of curriculum and by directing us to Harris' use of the term, Dykstra helps us move beyond this fear:

> Curriculum is about the mobilizing of creative, educative powers in such a way as to "fashion a people." Maria Harris uses this wonderful image... in order that we may see afresh how deep and broad, how intricate and complex, and, finally, how interesting and beautiful is the work of forming and re-forming the "course" of the church's life. Curriculum is not, in any of its most important senses, reducible to resource materials, no matter how good and how useful. Rather, curriculum is an activity, a *practice*, of a people. (Harris 8)

In my own experience of working with religious educators and youth ministers in the development of their catechetical programs with early adolescents, I have come to affirm Dykstra's reading of the situation and of the response. Nevertheless, the predominant question on the minds of most busy parish ministers is "what's the best book for them?" And even though it increases their initial frustration, I continue to turn the question around. I do not believe that the "book" question is a bad one to ask. It's simply being asked at the wrong time. The selection of books, or more realistically, varying types of catechetical resources, is one of the final questions that must be asked as part of the process of curriculum development. "How do we *develop* an effective curriculum for early adolescent catechesis?" is by far the better question with which to start.

In this chapter I would like to explore that question. To accomplish this task I will first return to *The Challenge of Adolescent Catechesis* to review its "Principles for Developing Adolescent Catechesis." Though the document was written to guide *all* adolescent catechesis, my survey of the principles will relate them directly to the issues awaiting early adolescent ministers. Next, I will examine the development of curriculum as the result of a deliberate process enacted for that purpose. Third, I will comment on the tasks and roles of ministerial leaders in the process. Finally, I will conclude the chapter with some brief words on catechesis in the Catholic school setting.

GUIDING PRINCIPLES FOR EARLY ADOLESCENT CATECHESIS

As a document, *The Challenge of Adolescent Catechesis* combines and integrates the best of: a) our contemporary understanding and the Church's teaching on the ministry of catechesis; and b) the most recent findings on adolescent development. Because both of these were held in tension and integrally developed by the writers of the document, foundational and operational principles were able to be clearly articulated to guide the development of effective adolescent catechesis. Together with the definition and aim of adolescent catechesis explored earlier, these principles are the starting point for any discussion on developing an effective catechetical ministry with early adolescents.

FOUNDATIONAL PRINCIPLES

Principle 1: *"Adolescent catechesis is situated within the lifelong developmental process of faith growth and ongoing catechesis. The entire catechetical effort is committed to the continuing faith growth of the individual."* Enacting this principle in the development of early adolescent catechesis means a switch in starting point for some. This "lifelong" principle asks us to approach our early adolescent ministry in the context of a lifelong faith journey and lifelong catechesis. In a word, we must do away with our "finish-line" mentalities: a mistaken belief that we must "get it all in" before a young person reaches a certain age or grade (like 8th or 12th grade or whenever confirmation is celebrated).

Though a "banking" model of religious education was the primary model in the Church's practice for many years (we "deposit" a lifetime's worth of instruction in the childhood years so the individual can "withdraw" it in later life), this "lifelong" principle is firmly rooted in contemporary Church teaching on catechesis. It echoes the *National Catechetical Directory's* statement: "While aiming to enrich the faith life of individuals at their particular stages of development, every form of catechesis is oriented in some way to the catechesis of adults, who are capable of a full response to God's word." (NCD #32) Likewise, the "lifelong" principle recalls Pope John Paul II's apostolic exhoration, *Catechesi Tradendae*, when he says of adult catechesis: "This is the principal form of catechesis, because it is addressed to persons who have the greatest responsibilities and the capacity to live the Christian message in its fully developed form." (#43)

How is catechesis planned and developed out of this attention to a lifelong perspective? Quite simply, we are called to catechize within the context of the needs of each stage of development while the person is in that stage of development. We catechize to the needs of children while they are in childhood, to the needs of early adolescents while they are in early adolescence, to the needs of later adolescents while they are in later adolescence. Instead, we catechize to the needs of adults beginning a married life while they are in that state, we catechize to the needs of midlife while people are in midlife, etc.

One way of imaging this can be found in the title of the *National Catechetical Directory — Sharing the Light of Faith.* I think of this "sharing" not only as a description of the action of the community but as a context for the *direction* of that sharing: with what/whom must the light of faith be shared? In childhood faith must enlighten the life and needs of a child. In midlife the light of faith must be shared with the needs of adults in those years, for example, career, family, or sexuality concerns. And for early adolescents, that faith must enlighten early adolescent needs: developing identity, relationships, sexuality, etc. We must avoid the temptation to catechize to a full lifetime's needs in a few short years of youth.

We cannot overestimate the importance of this first principle — it is, in one sense, the root of them all. When we do not recognize this foundation, I believe we engender a self-fulfilling prophesy, often phrased like, "we must teach them all these things before we lose them." The truth seems to be that in overloading the curriculum in such a way, we tend to alienate our early adolescents and, in fact we do lose them (from our programs, not from God).

Principle 2: *"Adolescent catechesis fosters Catholic Christian faith in three dimensions: trusting, believing, and doing."* This "3-D" principle simply calls us to root our catechetical ministry within the best understanding of our faith as something that is not limited to either the affective, cognitive, or behavioral dimension but is truly a synthesis of all three. Thus, our catechesis must be developed in such a way that it promotes growth in all three areas. Good catechesis is not simply a question of correct answers, warm feelings, or good deeds, but a process designed to challenge and encourage growth in "head, heart, and hands" simultaneously.

For early adolescent ministers, this principle can be both comfort and challenge. Because early adolescents are such diverse individuals and come in such diverse groups, the comprehensiveness of this approach to faith encourages creative, dynamic catechetical strategies. At the same time, because of that very diversity, meeting our catechetical objectives can be a complicated venture often with less-than-consistent results.

Principle 3: *"Adolescent catechesis supports and encourages the role of the family, and in particular, the role of the parent in the faith growth of the young person and involves the parent in formulation of an adolescent catechesis curriculum and in programs to strengthen their parenting role."* In this principle on "the family factor," especially the role of the parent, we find some important direction for early adolescent ministry. As we have discovered in the foundational essays, the role of parents and family in early adolescent lives is great. Responding to this, we can take our cue from the text itself. Three directions are suggested, all of which could serve an early adolescent catechetical program well: support/encouragement, involvement, and programs for parents themselves.

We must provide ongoing support/encouragement for parents and families. This can include everything from newsletters and articles of interest for parents of early adolescents to simply thanking and recognizing them for their assistance (even if it is just to drive the young person to the program). Making such statements in front of the young people themselves is even more effective. Involvement of parents, however, means more than asking their help in teaching or transporting. Parents have a right to be involved in the actual setting of the curriculum (see the section on curriculum development p.167) and in its ongoing evaluation. Given our concerns about involvement, I am continually surprised at how many times curriculum decisions are made by a single person (ordering the books) whether or not they understand the needs of early adolescents. Finally, we must consider it within the scope of an early adolescent ministry to provide programs or learning opportunities for parents themselves.

Principle 4: *"Adolescent catechesis respects the unique cultural heritages of young people and builds upon the positive values found in these cultural heritages, while at the same time engaging young people in examining their culture in the light of faith and examining their faith in the light of culture."* This principle asks us to take seriously the context within which our early adolescents are found and out of which we must engage in our ministry. Once again we see the need to understand curriculum development as a task much greater than obtaining books and resources. Despite many gains over the past few years, many such resources do not take adequate account either of the ethnic/racial culture of significant numbers of young people or of the presence and predominance of the "youth culture" to which many early adolescents are subject.

Beyond that attention to context, this principle calls adolescent catechesis to a genuine dialogue of faith with culture. Frequently this can be related to the twofold task of the aim of adolescent catechesis which began this examination: the need to be both midwife and adoption agent for faith maturing. It is often in and through the cultural context that young people will give birth to their personal faith and adopt our communal faith. This cultural context is not a peripheral concern in our ministry, but a foundational principle.

Principle 5: *"Adolescent catechesis is integrated and developed within a comprehensive, multifaceted approach to a ministry with youth."* For many early adolescent catechetical ministers this principle can be "reality check!" As the last of the Foundational Principles, this statement calls us to the realization that even in some of the best of our catechetical programming, we cannot meet all the needs of all our young people. Those needs are diverse and they require a ministry that is diverse, a ministry encompassing all the components of *A Vision of Youth Ministry.*

For several years this was the principle that required much attention by those who were struggling to provide programs that met the needs of early adolescents. Often, a total youth ministry program was what awaited young people of high school age while early adolescents had only a catechetical program. As early adolescent ministry has grown, that situation has begun to change. One result of that change has been the further realization that such integration demands collaboration on the part of all those involved in the ministry to early adolescents (see the section on Leadership p. 171). Now we see more and more early adolescent ministry programs with a variety of components, of which catechesis is but one part.

Nevertheless, we are challenged to make that part as responsive, effective, dynamic, and faithful as possible. The above five Foundational Principles, together with a clear definition and aim for the ministry, provide the ground on which an early adolescent catechetical program must be built. Our task now is to review the Operational Principles and their application in an early adolescent program.

OPERATIONAL PRINCIPLES

The Operational Principles are just that — principles to help us in the "operation" or programming of a catechetical ministry with early adolescents. In reviewing them, we can comment more fully on each and seek direct application for the work of the coordination minister.

Principle 6: *"Adolescent catechesis responds to the developmental, social, and cultural needs of adolescence. Related to that, the curriculum respects the changing developmental and social characteristics of the various stages of adolescence, providing a significantly different content and approach for young and older adolescents."* As the first Foundational Principle called attention to the lifelong horizon against which adolescent catechesis is developed, this first Operational Principle calls attention to the ground from which it springs: adolescent experience itself, its characteristics and, in particular, its needs. This "developmental needs" principle makes it absolutely clear that the catechetical enterprise must not be divorced from the real-life experience of young people:

> The ministry of adolescent catechesis is viewed through the prism of developmental research and the social/cultural analysis of youth today. Understanding Christian faith as a lifelong journey means that catechesis first discerns a young person's developmental journey and social/cultural situation and then designs catechetical experiences that respond to the young person's particular faith needs. (*The Challenge* 10)

In concurring with *The Challenge* document and asserting that early adolescent catechesis is a response to needs, I believe we are uncovering implications that are welcome for many and challenging to some. First and foremost, as we develop early adolescent curriculum, we are required to pay as much attention to the needs and experience of our young people as we do to our doctrinal concerns. This is not to deny the importance of doctrine or to suggest it be diluted in any way. It is, as we explored in the "lifelong" principle above, to maintain that the message of our faith must be clearly and pastorally related to the needs of the catechetical participants. At this point in time it is becoming clearer why much of the new catechetical material for early adolescents looks different from previous resources. As we learn more about the needs of this age group, we are challenged to provide catechetical experiences that respond accordingly.

Beyond a response to general adolescent needs, this principle calls us to remember that even within the category "adolescence" there are significant differences between the characteristics and needs of early adolescents and those of later adolescents (as the existence of this very book symbolizes). However, this is truly easier said than done. On the one hand is the need to develop early adolescent materials that are genuinely different in content and approach from those used for primary grade children. On the other hand is the knowledge that it is no more effective to take the group/topic formats used with some high school youth and "water it down" for young adolescents. "It is important that programs for young adolescents 'look' different..." (Reynolds 14)

One final way of examining this principle might be to look at a situation in which many catechetical and youth ministers found themselves during the past two decades, a situation in which some still find themselves today. Faced with young people who had been exposed to excessive content often unrelated to their real needs of early adolescence, these ministers began providing high school programs that sought to increase the affiliative dimension of the young people's faith and thus, "bring them back" to the

Church from which they seemed so alienated. However, there are two problems that occur in this approach. First, such strategies do little to appeal to the new-found abstract cognitive abilities and searching style of faith prevalent in later adolescents. Second, the strategy does nothing to deal with the situation that gave rise to the problem: the lack of effective catechesis, responsive to needs, in early adolescence.

As we implement this operational principle, we are almost reversing the above pattern. We are developing catechetical experiences for early adolescents that better speak to their affiliative needs (that are, literally, about "me" as much as they are about "the Church"). As we accomplish this for early adolescents, we will be able to provide better programming for later adolescents which meets their needs to search, question, and think through their faith more deeply.

Principle 7: *"Adolescent catechesis respects the variability in maturation rates and learning needs of adolescence."* —If there has been anything gleaned from the research on early adolescents, it is that diversity is the key and "inconsistency is consistent." However, our catechetical programs have tended to group these young people in age-graded approaches that assumed that every young person of the same age was ready for the same content at the same time. Enacting this principle requires us to provide substantially different approaches for early adolescents.

This goal is partially achieved when we respect the requirements of the above principle and provide an early adolescent catechetical program that is different in form and content from both the children's program and the offerings for later adolescents. Nevertheless, offering different minicourses or topics to combined groups of 7th and 8th graders is not the entire solution either. Catechetical experiences for early adolescents, if they are to respect the variety of maturation rates and learning needs in the age group, must provide variety in format, setting, method, material, etc. Effective early adolescent catechesis will include as many opportunities for nonverbal expression as it does questions for discussion.

From the point of view of basic research into early adolescent development, we can see that this is one of the most difficult principles to program. It is one thing to recognize the difference in the developmental needs of early adolescents as opposed to later adolescents, and even to recognize the diversity within a single group of early adolescents. It is something else to deal with the inconsistency that can exist within an *individual* early adolescent. For example, an early adolescent who has achieved a high degree of physical maturity may not have achieved a corresponding cognitive growth. Or, a young person who is cognitively advanced may still be socially/emotionally immature.

Of course, the "perfect curriculum" that meets all these needs does not exist. In addition, the development of a curriculum that attends to this principle must be accompanied by adequate training for the catechist who will teach it. As catechetical leaders attend to both issues, we can expect new, creative approaches that handle and respect the diversity that is early adolescence.

Principle 8: *"Adolescent catechesis respects the expanding freedom and autonomy of adolescents."* As we approach this principle, it is important to remember the aim of adolescent catechesis and its twofold task of being both midwife and adoption agent to adolescent faith. With such a goal before us, it is easier to reflect on the implications of this principle. In accepting the aim of sponsoring youth to maturity in faith, we must also accept the fact that such maturity is not gained with a simple nod of the head. It is the reality of human development that as we grow past childhood our ability to question, choose, and exercise our freedom grows with us. This is as true of adolescent catechesis as it is of any human enterprise. Adolescent catechesis "recognizes and respects the essential freedom of young people to question, doubt, rebut, and perhaps even temporarily reject the Catholic Christian faith. Catechesis must avoid coercion and manipulation." (*The Challenge* 10)

In my experience this principle has been more respected by those catechists who have been well-trained, particularly in the area of adolescent development, than by curriculum planners. But having pastorally sensitive teachers is not enough if the overall catechetical program does not also respond to young people's growing needs for freedom and self-direction. Adolescents, including early adolescents, tend to "vote with their feet," absenting themselves from programs with which they feel no connection. If it happens that an early adolescent is required, by a parent for example, to attend a program that is unresponsive to his/her needs, he/she will find ways to "leave" the program — if not physically, then mentally or spiritually! To develop ownership and commitment, programmers plan with early adolescents, not for them.

It is not my intention, however, to suggest that effective catechetical curriculum is simply a matter of letting young people create and then take whatever they want. There are ways on a programmatic level of enacting this principle. Involving early adolescents and their parents in a needs-assessment and interest finding process gives them ownership into the learning experiences, increasing the likelihood of their participation. Such inquiry can go beyond topic and content questions to a survey of desirable times, places, and formats. Offering a variety of short-term learning experiences (mini-courses, day- or weekend-long programs) from which to choose also increases the opportunity for adolescents to exercise freedom.

One important implication of this is presented in *The Challenge*: "adolescent catechesis must be attractive, interesting, creative, and responsive to adolescents' learning needs and must offer a variety of faith themes, learning formats, environments, schedules, and educational techniques to encourage participation." (10) For many catechetical ministers, this means that we must expect the same (if not greater) level of attention to "marketing" early adolescent programs as we expect in adult programming. I have often wondered how many adults in the average Catholic parish would show up for a catechetical program if they were told that they "must" attend it, that the class would meet every week for a whole year (holidays excluded), that they have no say in what would be taught or how it would be taught, and that only by participating in the program would they be allowed to attend the adult dances and parties held throughout the year. I doubt many would attend; they may even leave the parish! Obviously, early adolescents are not adults (in fact, with early adolescents we potentially have greater opportunities for dialogue with both them and their parents about making good choices), but in the desire for ownership and the God-given need for some degree of autonomy, they are quite similar. This operational principle may present a challenge to some, but in reality I believe it is more an invitation to a golden opportunity — if we but take it.

Principle 9: *"Adolescent catechesis uses a variety of learning formats, environment, schedules, and educational techniques."* This principle is a natural progression upon the former operational principles. If we are attentive to the concerns expressed above, we must develop early adolescent catechetical curriculum built upon variety — in every aspect. Enacting this principle means that we must move beyond the assumption that there is only one way of doing catechesis, especially if that way is simply a 60 to 90 minute-a-week class format for a year-long, one-book, one-course program. In fact, there are more possibilities for learning than most programs could contain. In his book *Adolescent Catechesis Resource Manual*, John Roberto has included a chapter on "learning models" that suggests 16 different possibilities for adolescent catechesis. (68-75) In a later chapter on "learning methods," the book presents dozens of techniques varying from "Field Trips" to "Reaction Statements" to "Discussing a Rock Song." (80-101)

In my work with parish leaders, I have found that the biggest surprise for many is the realization that they *do* have a choice in their planning and programming. This can be welcome news, especially if the program they have is getting mixed reviews. Brian Reynolds has phrased it this way:

> In the past, religious education programs for the middle school years looked very much like the primary grade programs. When given the opportunity to evaluate their programs, most catechists (and parents) believed their efforts were not very effective in meeting the needs of

> seventh and eighth graders in particular. Catechetical curricula, class environment, and learning methods have often ignored the developmental needs of young adolescents. (Reynolds 14)

Likewise, *The Challenge* itself sees variety as the answer to the needs of both program and participant:

> The particular needs of parish adolescent catechesis suggest short-term, rather than long-term, programming. Young people have increased demands placed upon their time. Catechists adapt to their world by offering a diversity of faith themes in a variety of short-term formats. Short-term learning opportunities actually increase the participation of youth and encourage them to engage in multiple learning experiences throughout the year. (10)

In addition, those who offer such experiences report a "qualitative" difference as well. Too often catechists experience the frustration of spending a significant portion of class time settling early adolescents and preparing them for the experience, only to spend an equal amount of time readying them to leave. In contrast, a day- or weekend-long program provides opportunities for significant community building activities, meaningful prayer experiences, and quality catechetical ministry. Whatever the format, model or technique, it is imperative that early adolescent catechetical experiences integrate the seven developmental needs as often as possible.

Finally, the experience of those trying out a variety of short-term learning experiences suggests a beneficial side effect: recruiting catechists often becomes easier as adults are more willing to commit to short-term experiences rather than long-term classes. Undoubtedly, facilitating this may take a little more organization, needs assessment, and planning time on the part of the coordinator, director, or planning team, but the results appear worthy of the effort.

Principle 10: *"Adolescent catechesis best responds to the learning needs of adolescents when it is focused on particular faith themes."* — In this final principle we again find an almost sequential development from the preceding principles. After responding to developmental needs, variability in maturation rates and learning needs, expanding freedom and autonomy, and after providing variety in format, content, and method, the next logical step is to offer a "faith theme" approach:

> It focuses the exploration of a faith theme on selected topics (content) that provide possibilities for exploring the theme in some depth. Instead of surveying the broad scope of a particular faith theme, this approach selects a primary focus and key topics in keeping with the adolescent's developmental and social readiness. (*The Challenge* 10)

Seven faith themes are presented in *The Challenge* as an appropriate basis for an early adolescent catechetical curriculum. They are presented below with a brief summary of their focus. Consult the document itself for more detailed information on their focus and suggested content.

Church — understanding and experiencing the story and mission of the Catholic Christian community and becoming involved in its life and work.

Jesus and the Gospel Message — developing a more personal relationship with Jesus, learning how to follow him, concentrating on the person and teaching of Jesus, and responding in a more personal way.

Morality and Moral Decision Making — learning the skills for decision making; learning and applying Catholic Christian moral values in their decisions.

Personal Growth — developing a stronger, more realistic self-concept and exploring who they are and who they can become.

Relationships — developing more mutual, trusting, and loyal relationships with peers, parents, and other adults; learning the skills that enhance and maintain relationships.

Service — understanding Jesus' call to loving service that is integral to discipleship, developing a foundation for a social justice consciousness, and participating in service involving relationships and concrete action.

Sexuality — learning about sexual development, understanding the dynamics of maturing as a sexual person within a Catholic Christian's value context, and discussing sexuality with their parents using a Catholic Christian value-based approach.

Because the writers of *The Challenge* document integrated contemporary research on the needs of adolescence into their exploration of the catechetical ministry, these faith themes represent a significant foundation in the development of an early adolescent catechetical curriculum. Nevertheless, an individual parish or school's curriculum development process may uncover additional learning needs that result in other faith themes or other ways of presenting the above faith themes. For example, some parishes have included within their curriculum courses on media awareness, communication skills, or an intergenerational faith growth experience for early adolescents and their parents.

In the conclusion to its explanation on the "faith themes" principle, *The Challenge* document states:

In the context of lifelong learning, these faith themes for young and older adolescents have been selected because of their particular importance at this stage of a person's life. This approach to adolescent catechesis builds on the foundations developed in childhood and looks to young adult and adult catechesis for continued opportunities for learning. (10-11)

Ending its description of the last operational principle, the document returns to the theme of the first foundational principle — lifelong context. As both a foundational concept and an operational practice, this lifelong context focuses our attention upon the subjects of the curriculum: the early adolescents themselves and asks us to do nothing more than pay attention to the needs of early adolescents within the very substance of our early adolescent catechesis. As leaders in the ministry of early adolescent catechesis, perhaps we can take our cue from that portion of the Sermon on the Mount which is often titled, "Trust in Providence." In its conclusion Jesus says, "Enough, then, of worrying about tomorrow. Let tomorrow take care of itself. Today has troubles enough of its own." (Mt 6:34) Not a bad philosophy for early adolescent catechesis!

CURRICULUM DEVELOPMENT: A PROCESS

If we take these principles seriously and attempt to program accordingly, one undeniable conclusion presents itself: there is more to providing effective catechesis for early adolescents than selecting a book to use in seventh or eighth grade (or, as some would have, selecting a K-8 textbook series and simply using the grade seven and grade eight texts in that series for the seventh and eighth graders). Something much more is required if we are going to provide effective early adolescent catechesis. That "something" is a process whereby a parish or school can combine the accumulated wisdom of *The Challenge of Adolescent Catechesis*, and those members of the field who have addressed its implementation, with the needs of their young people and the experience of the parents, adults, and planners involved. It is a process of curriculum development. Such a curriculum would then be faithful to the demands of good catechesis and good early adolescent programming. It would enable early adolescents to learn about themselves and their faith. It would be accountable to the developmental needs of early adolescents and the goals of a catechetical ministry that is an integral part of the mission and ministry of the Church.

While the task sounds great, it is, in fact, quite basic. Indeed, the word "curriculum" itself is derived from the Latin word meaning "to run," as in a course that is run. Curriculum development is not new. In fact, the very existence of the textbook series described above is evidence of some type of curriculum development. That is, it is the result of a process that determined the course of religious and faith development to be "run" by a child/young person through the years that he/she is in grades K through 8.

The idea that is new, perhaps for some, is that such development is incomplete for it results in offering early adolescents two or three survey courses when a faith themes approach is desirable. Or, it demands that early adolescence be seen as an extension of childhood and that the catechetical content for early adolescence be nothing more than a continuation of that offered to children. That such curriculum was developed in the past is nothing to denounce. It was developed based upon the prevalent understandings in catechesis and developmental research. But now, in light of *The Challenge* document and its implementation, and especially in light of our most current understanding of the needs of early adolescents, we can do better.

Like most good ministry, the key is planning. Catechetical curriculum development is simply a more concise and "educational" term for basic youth ministry planning of formal learning experiences. Curriculum development will be familiar to many youth ministers, for the process is similar to the planning process offered by many youth ministry resources. (see for example, Fox, et. al.; and McCarty and Tooma). Though the phrasing of specific steps of the process vary from author to author, in general all planning processes proceed as a response to needs. They generally include the following basic planning steps:

* education toward a vision of ministry; proposing a framework for the ministry
* needs assessment
* prioritizing needs and brainstorming responses (programs)
* developing and planning the programs
* organizing the program sequence/structure; creating a calendar of individual programs/events

After these steps, the basic process usually includes an articulation of the steps which must be taken to actually conduct the programs and evaluate the results:

* leadership development (articulate needs for, recruit and train leaders)
* conducting the program
* evaluation

In a curriculum development process we proceed in much the same fashion but the object of our planning is not a mixture of programs/events within a total youth ministry program but a variety of courses and learning experiences within an overall curriculum. In the last several years a number of resources have been published that provide processes for developing catechetical curriculum. They vary from developing general curriculum for the entire community (Harris 167-183) to developing adolescent catechetical curriculum for both early and later adolescents (Roberto 34-63) to developing an early adolescent curriculum using a specific published program (Carotta 49-53). As noted above, the basic process used by each author is similar. (For a process that closely follows *The Challenge* document's definition, aim, and guiding principles while facilitating a diversity of resulting programs and resources, see John Roberto's *Adolescent Catechesis Resource Manual*. And for more detailed information on any of the above examples, consult the resource cited.)

In applying the general planning process described above or in using any of those cited, we see that the first step in an early adolescent curriculum development process is one of education and framework: we must be firmly rooted in the definition and aim of adolescent catechesis found in the chapter introduction and in the principles reviewed above. Next, we must get a firm grasp of the needs of the learners. In my experience, this includes both general information about the learners (e.g., developmental research like that of the foundational essays in this book) and specific information about the participants in the local setting (e.g., needs assessment and interest finding at the parish/school). From there, we proceed in a dialogical fashion, combining our understanding of catechesis, especially the suggested faith themes of *The Challenge*, with the needs of the early adolescents themselves to produce some general ideas for curriculum content (faith themes, courses) and form (a curriculum model). The process continues refining and specifying the objectives of the faith themes, choosing which published programs to use or draw on for newly designed experiences. Finally, the pieces are brought together into an organized way (final development of scope and sequence) and a calendar is prepared.

In his *Adolescent Catechesis Resource Manual*, John Roberto has suggested three principles to guide the process of curriculum development:

> *First*, this process relies on gathering a *team* of curriculum planners who are committed to planning. This team should include the key leaders who are responsible for adolescent catechesis in your setting....
>
> *Second*, the process of planning is as important as the product. This team approach to planning emphasizes collaboration and shared decision-making which builds a strong sense of *ownership* among team members. This ownership extends the responsibility for catechesis beyond the coordinators and catechists/religion teachers to the community-at-large.

> *Third*, planners need to pray for guidance, courage, creativity, and obedience to the Spirit in their decision-making. Curriculum planning needs to be a reflective, prayerful experience. (Roberto 34)

It is important to note that the entire process is collaborative and dialogical. There is neither a slavish adherence to curriculum developed by publisher or expert, nor is there an automatic assent to "the top 10" uncovered in a needs assessment. In working with curriculum development teams in my own diocese, I have adapted an image used in our diocesan youth ministry planning conference which spoke of the "voices" to which planners need to listen. In this process of curriculum development, I suggest the planners listen to four voices: 1) *The Challenge* document, its principles and faith themes; 2) the "field"—those who have written about adolescent catechesis and are implementing and building on *The Challenge*; 3) the needs of the learners—our best understanding of their developmental needs and the specific results of a local needs assessment and interest finder; and 4) the wisdom and experience of the development team and the Holy Spirit working in and through their midst. In this way, the curriculum is built upon the best insights of each contribution together with an interaction between them: literally, a whole greater than the sum of its parts.

Another curriculum concept, particularly relevant to early adolescent catechesis, is found in a principle of curriculum design articulated by Maria Harris: "The curriculum must take into account three forms: the explicit curriculum, the implicit curriculum, and the null curriculum." She elaborates on the terms, citing Elliot Eisner, from whom they are derived:

> The explicit curriculum refers to what is actually presented, consciously and with intention…The implicit curriculum, in contrast, refers to the patterns or organization or procedures that frame the explicit curriculum: things like attitudes or time spent or even the design of a room…The null curriculum is a paradox. This is the curriculum that exists because it does not exist; it is what is left out. But the point of including it is that ignorance or the absence of something is not neutral.…The null curriculum includes areas left out (content, themes, points of view) and procedures left out (the arts, play, critical analysis). (Harris 68-69)

If we use this concept to reflect on the curriculum offered to early adolescents in the past, we uncover some interesting things. Confining our thoughts to 12-13 year olds, we find an explicit curriculum that concentrated on Jesus in 7th grade and Church, usually Church history, in 8th grade. The implicit curriculum seems to include ideas like: catechesis is a lot like schooling; it is only important during the school year; and catechesis is not related to our feasts and seasons, since the programs close down during Christmas and Easter time. Also, because catechists were frequently ignorant of the developmental needs of early adolescents, the implicit curriculum included punishments for having the need to move around or to express oneself in non-verbal ways. Finally, the null curriculum in such catechetical programs included many of the themes and processes called for in our review of *The Challenge* principles: exploration of relationships and self-concepts, sexuality education, and programming that involves parents, to name a few. As a curriculum development team goes through their planning process they should ask themselves if the explicit, implicit, and null curriculum are in agreement with each other. The curriculum planners must see if this three-fold analysis of their curriculum is in line with the program's catechetical goals and if, when taken together, these three curricula represent and help develop a consistent, responsive early adolescent catechesis.

In applying these curriculum concepts and principles, we can begin building the effective early adolescent catechesis we so strongly desire. It means looking beyond a simple purchase to enacting a dedicated process. It requires putting off a phoned-in order — "just get me the books" — in favor of establishing teamwork and collaboration to develop ownership. And it means forgoing haste and a "we've always done it this way" attitude in favor of reflection, prayer, planning, and a real attention to the needs of early adolescents.

LEADERSHIP FOR EARLY ADOLESCENT CATECHESIS

Parishes and Catholic schools throughout this country benefit from the gifts and talents of many well trained and educated leaders. In providing catechetical programs for early adolescents, the Church has drawn and continues to draw upon these dedicated professionals and volunteers alike. In my experience with parishes seeking to provide more effective early adolescent catechetical curriculum, I have found that such leaders can be one of the most significant elements in the process.

However, a problem frequently occurs — not with the leaders themselves, but with the structures in which they often work. For example, in many parishes it is the job of the director or coordinator of religious education to oversee the parish's catechetical program (which, for a long time, was the only programming offered to the early adolescent age group). A youth minister or youth ministry team may oversee the other components of youth ministry (now reaching out to early adolescents). And, a principal of a Catholic school (where present) may have responsibility for the religion curriculum for the seventh and eighth graders in that school. In this structure, it is possible for each of these leaders to perform their tasks without encountering or sharing in the responsibilities of another.

Into this mix comes the new initiatives in early adolescent ministry and catechesis. In fact, the vision of *The Challenge* document itself suggests that adolescent catechesis is collaborative by nature, boasting a shared ownership by youth ministry, catechetical, clerical, and Catholic school personnel alike. The image that best expresses this reality is that of an intersection point or a crossroads. Providing more effective early adolescent catechetical curriculum does not require any ministerial leader to give up or change their responsibilities. Rather, the implication of the definition, aim, and principles of early adolescent catechesis which we have explored is that collaboration is the necessary key. Providing a ministry that is, to use the image above, right in the middle of a busy intersection requires that we work together to select the best path.

I have witnessed situations that run the gamut of this collaboration. In a parish where a youth ministry team received training in early adolescent ministry but where neither the school principal nor the DRE had similar experience, the early adolescent ministry was quite separate from the other formation programs. Sensing the need for a more effective catechesis, the team in this small parish began offering one of the newly published minicourses for early adolescents on the theme of relationships and personal growth. The result was an increase in participation, especially among the youth from the Catholic school who already had religion classes during school hours. It is ironic and just a bit sad that these young people are coming for two catechetical sessions — they do not even know it, and neither, it seems, does the DRE or principal. With a little collaboration among all the ministers involved, the parish could offer a creative, holistic early adolescent ministry and an integrated, responsive catechesis in both school and parish settings.

And this is happening in many places. There are many success stories coming out of parishes that have made a commitment to having their leaders trained in the most recent methods of early adolescent ministry. In these parishes it is not uncommon to find DREs and youth ministers working with dedicated teams of planners to develop an attractive, exciting curriculum. In some schools principals and religion teachers are drawing on the expertise of their youth ministers and DREs to improve the quality of their religion classes. Slowly, but surely, more effective early adolescent catechesis is creeping and crawling, stretching and squirming, leaping and bounding through our parish communities. Much like the early adolescents themselves!

A NOTE ON CATHOLIC SCHOOLS

While the above signs of hope and prosperity are quite real in many parishes, we must acknowledge that there is still work to be done in implementing *The Challenge of Adolescent Catechesis* and the many developments in early adolescent catechesis cited above. Much of that work lies in developing those early adolescent catechetical programs that take place in the context of a Catholic school. *The Challenge* document was written to assist schools, where they exist and where they include adolescents among the student body, in their ministry as well. While everything I have stated above can apply equally to a Catholic school setting, there are some things that can be added.

Judging by the research being done in both the areas of early adolescent development and education, the time is ripe to attend to our school-based catechesis for early adolescents. New initiatives in the other educational disciplines are being tested with early adolescents with much success. The interesting thing to note is that many of the formats, models, and methods being considered are quite similar to the type of programming for which *The Challenge* called.

Based on my experience with teachers/catechists in Catholic elementary schools in my own diocese, we are not far from the mark — at least on the level of practice, if not planning. Often, these teachers are given a full-year course and textbook to teach, but then find that year being broken up with other curriculum units (in substance abuse education or sexuality catechesis, for example) to be covered during the time that religion is normally taught. What is happening in reality is that an overall curriculum is being developed based on mini-courses and short-term learning experiences. The missing piece in this situation is some planning work on the "front end." When introduced to the concepts and principles found in this chapter, most teachers with which I have worked responded enthusiastically. In fact, many note that these principles and processes put words to their experiences in or dreams for their religion classes.

There is work required in the development of effective early adolescent catechesis. That is true of both parish and school alike. Through honest collaboration and dedicated effort genuine curriculum development can be accomplished. And the doubt or fear which may have first greeted the suggestion can be turned into faith and hope.

WORKS CITED

Carotta, Michael. *Director's Manual for the Discovering Program.* Winona MN: Saint Mary's Press, 1989.

Catechesi Tradendae (*On Catechesis In Our Time*). Apostolic Exhortation. Washington DC: USCC, 1979.

The Challenge of Adolescent Catechesis: Maturing in Faith. Washington DC: National Federation for Catholic Youth Ministry, 1986.

Fox, Zeni, et. al. *Leadership for Youth Ministry.* Winona MN: Saint Mary's Press, 1984.

Harris, Maria. *Fashion Me A People: Curriculum in the Church.* Louisville KY: Westminster/John Knox Press, 1989.

McCarty, Robert J. and Lynn Tooma. *Training Adults for Youth Ministry.* Winona MN: Saint Mary's Press, 1990,

Nelson, John. "Faith and Adolescents: Insights from Psychology and Sociology" in John Roberto, ed. *Faith Maturing: A Personal and Communal Task.* Washington DC: National Federation for Catholic Youth Ministry, 1985.

Roberto, John. *Adolescent Catechesis Resource Manual.* New York: William H. Sadlier, 1988.

Reynolds, Brian B. "Ministry with Early Adolescents". Network Paper #36. New Rochelle: Don Bosco Multimedia, 1990.

Sharing the Light of Faith: National Catechetical Directory for Catholics of the United States. (NCD) Washington DC: USCC, 1979.

RESOURCE BIBLIOGRAPHY: CURRICULUM

Brown, Carolyn. *Developing Christian Education in the Smaller Church.* Nashville TN: Abingdon, 1982.

The Challenge of Adolescent Catechesis. Washington DC: NFCYM, 1986.

Groome, Thomas. *Christian Religious Education.* San Francisco: Harper and Row, 1980.

Harris, Maria. *Fashion Me A People — Curriculum in the Church.* Louisville KY: Westminster/John Knox Press, 1989.

Harris, Maria. *Teaching and Religious Imagination.* San Francisco: Harper and Row, 1987.

Little, Sara. *To Set One's Heart.* Atlanta: John Knox Press, 1983.

Roberto, John. *Adolescent Catechesis Resource Manual.* New York: Sadlier, 1988.

Rogers, Donald, ed. *Urban Church Education.* Birmingham AL: Religious Education Press, 1989.

Seymour, Jack and Donald Miller, editors. *Contemporary Approaches to Christian Education.* Nashville TN: Abingdon Press, 1982.

Warren, Michael. *Faith, Culture, and the Worshipping Community.* New York: Paulist Press, 1989.

Addendum

Effective Religious Education Programs

A Research Project by the Search Institute

Peter Benson and Carolyn Eklin

The Search Institute study, Effective Christian Education (1990), *found that nothing in congregational life has more potential for increasing faith in young people than quality religious education. The following summary describes the findings regarding the effectiveness of religious education. This research project provides a strong empirical base for the importance of effective religious education programs and reinforces the two essays by Bruce Baumgarten on catechesis with early adolescents.—Editor*

THE NATURE OF CHRISTIAN EDUCATION EFFECTIVENESS

We have learned that involving adults and youth in effective Christian education is essential if congregations are to increase faith maturity and loyalty. The key question now is: What makes Christian education effective? Does content matter? process? leadership?

Both the survey results and the site visits to effective congregations give strong clues as to the elements of Christian education that, when present, are linked to growth in faith maturity. Twelve findings about effectiveness are important:

* The effectiveness factors are additive. That is, the more a congregation has them in place in its adult or youth program, the greater the growth in faith maturity.

*The effectiveness factors are associated with growth in faith maturity even though the average time youth spend in formal Christian education programs and events is fairly minimal. Even when youth spend as little as 15 to 20 hours per year in Christian education, exposure to a few effective programs produces greater faith growth than exposure to several less effective programs.

*Involvement in effective Christian education has as positive a benefit for adults as it does for adolescents, in part because faith development is best understood as a lifelong process.

*Effectiveness factors can be grouped into categories: teacher characteristics, pastor characteristics, educational process, educational content, peer interest in learning, and goals/objectives.

* Effective Christian education programs are associated not only with greater faith maturity but also with greater loyalty to congregation and denomination.

* The effectiveness of educational process, in tandem with educational content, suggests that the effective program not only teaches in the classical sense of transmitting insight and knowledge, but also allows insight to emerge from the crucible of experience. (Experience can be fostered by reflection and interpretation of personal religious experience or by involvement in the faith stories of others.) Both ways of learning are powerful, and the two combined produce stronger growth in faith than either one alone.

* Effective programs include both strong pastoral leadership and pastoral involvement.

* Effective programs require strong educational expertise on the part of teachers.

* Effective content blends biblical knowledge and insight with significant engagement in the major life issues each group faces. To a certain extent, these life issues have a value component in which one is called upon to make decisions.

* It is significant that in the list of effectiveness factors, program quantity is not mentioned. Although we looked hard at the issue of program quantity, it does not appear to matter in any systematic way. This suggests that effective Christian education can be transmitted through a small number of programs and events, as long as, in combination , they have effective leadership, process, and content. Accordingly, what matters is how things are done rather than number or range of programs. This finding should be especially encouraging to the small congregation.

* Clear mission and clear learning objectives matter. They have power, in part, because the process of determining and evaluating them builds shared purpose and a sense of team.

* And, finally, for both adolescents and adults, the faith maturity of teachers matters. The greater the faith maturity of teachers, the greater the growth in faith maturity of participants.

Effectiveness in Christian Education for Youth: The Ideal

Teachers ...
are high in mature faith.
care about students.
know educational theory and methods for adolescents.

The pastor ...
is highly committed to the educational program for youth.
devotes significant hours to youth program.
knows educational theory and practice of Christian education for youth.

The educational process ...
emphasizes intergenerational contact.
emphasizes life experiences as occasions for spiritual insight.
creates a sense of community in which people help each other develop their faith and values.
emphasizes the natural unfolding of faith and recognizes each person's faith journey as unique.
strongly encourages independent thinking and questioning.
effectively helps youth to apply faith to daily decisions.

The educational content ...
emphasizes education about human sexuality.
emphasizes education about chemicals (alcohol and other drugs).
emphasizes involving youth in service projects.
emphasizes moral values and moral decision making.
emphasizes responsibility for poverty and hunger.
effectively teaches the Bible.
effectively teaches core theological concepts.
effectively teaches youth about how to make friends or be a good friend.
effectively helps youth develop concern for other people.

Peer involvement ...
has a high percentage of 10th to 12th graders active in Christian education.

Parent involvement ...
involves parents in program decisions and planning.

Goals ...
have a clear mission statement.
have clear learning objectives.

(From *Effective Christian Education*. Peter L. Benson and Carolyn H. Elkin. Minneapolis, MN: Search Institute, 1990.)

Chapter 10

Catechesis with Early Adolescents: Effective Teaching

Bruce Baumgarten

In the introduction to Chapter 9, I examined the definition and aim of adolescent catechesis. I proposed that the goal of providing effective early adolescent catechesis could be accomplished by attending to the complementary issues of curriculum and teaching. Having attended to curriculum, I will now articulate some foundational and practical guidelines for effective learning and for being an effective catechist/teacher. To use the image of a photograph once more, we have set our sights and focused our picture: effective early adolescent catechesis as discerned through the definition and aim found in *The Challenge of Adolescent Catechesis*. We have attended to the wide-angle of curriculum. Now, we will try to capture a shot of effective catechesis and teaching by zooming in on the ministry of the catechist/teacher and on the practice of teaching early adolescents.

I have developed a set of foundational and practical guidelines from a "praxis" point of view. By that I mean an articulation of statements and principles that can combine both theory and practice and is drawn as much from experience (my own and those with whom I have trained and consulted) as it is from theoretical reflection. As such, it is my hope that in presenting the ten foundational guidelines for the ministry of the catechist/teacher, I can nuance the practical side to each principle. And in offering ten guidelines for effective teaching, I hope to convey a sense of theoretical groundwork. In using this approach, it is my sincere desire that what follows can truly be assistance to those called to one of the greatest ministries in the Church: being a catechist/teacher with early adolescents.

There is one unavoidable limitation to all that follows. Though my goal is to help develop *effective* catechists/teachers, that is, catechists who *do* catechesis effectively, my task is to *write* the following for you to read and use. Yet, it has been my experience that many who aspire to be effective in what they do, achieve that objective "through the doing." Therefore, the measure of helpfulness for these pages is not in how well they read, but in how well you can use what you read. To that end, I offer one suggestion: find someone who many people regard as an effective catechist/teacher. Watch what he or she does. If possible, see if such a person can be a mentor to you as you exercise your catechetical ministry. Such learning can be invaluable and can make the pages which follow a "complement" to your learning rather than its sole content.

GUIDELINES FOR THE MINISTRY OF THE CATECHIST/TEACHER

The following ten statements are offered as foundational guidelines for the ministry of the catechist/teacher. As befitting the praxis approach and the goal of developing catechesis for early adolescents, I will make specific application to early adolescent situations as appropriate.

1. *A catechist/teacher is a person who has acquired knowledge, skills and abilities for this particular ministry.*

Being a catechist is a ministry, and like all ministries, it is the result of both empowerment and enablement. A catechist is empowered through the universal call to service which comes through water and the Spirit at baptism and through the specific recognition of a call to serve in the ministry of catechesis (discerned by the individual and the community). However, catechists must also be enabled to take up their ministries. Like all ministers, they must develop the competencies needed to fulfill the responsibilities entrusted to them. For some ministers, this process of enablement may be very simple; for others, like priests and lay professionals, years of training and education are required.

Though catechists do not require the level of preparation that is expected of full-time professional ministers, they do require some training — the attainment of knowledge and the development of skills and abilities appropriate to their ministry. I firmly believe that this enablement process requires a two-way commitment. Catechists must commit themselves to training as a part of their ministry, and parish/school/diocesan leaders must commit themselves to provide that training. Though each local Church may set different standards, it is the responsibility of the leadership to be sure that catechists are well trained. Likewise, catechists themselves should be counseled to demand the training they need for their ministry. We must see an end to the days when members of the community volunteer their time and effort to the ministry of catechesis, are given textbooks and teachers' manuals, and are set in front of their charges with no further guidance.

The Challenge prescribes education in the following areas: a) spirituality; b) knowledge of the adolescent; c) skills for adolescent catechesis; and d) content of catechesis. (*The Challenge* 17).

2. *A catechist/teacher is a pastoral minister, sponsoring others toward maturity in faith, leading individuals and the community to live out their faith in action. A catechist/teacher is not a theologian.*

From the first principle above, we can see the need for clarity about who catechists are and what they do. Thus, we can provide the training they require. One of the most important distinctions to be made is the role of the catechist in sponsoring faith maturity, particularly in calling individuals and the community at large to live out their faith in action. One way of expressing this is to see a goal of catechesis as the Christian life lived, not the Christian life known.

This distinction is not meant to be a purely semantic exercise. Through catechetical processes and skills (like those that will be described below), the catechist invites participants of all ages to bring their life into dialogue with the faith of the community. From that dialogue, an effective catechist calls for a response: that the faith shared and reflected upon leads to a different way of living.

By ministering in this way, a catechist follows in a long line of Church tradition. Indeed, one of the most basic truths of our faith is that "the Word was made flesh." A catechist not only teaches, shares, and lives that Word, but he or she leads others to do the same. Literally, the catechist calls for the Word to be made flesh again, in the lives of believers today. A catechist teaches in this way knows why the Acts of the Apostles referred to the new faith of Christianity as "the way," or why that book is called the *Acts* of the Apostles and not the "Concepts!"

By making this distinction, I do not wish to infer that being a catechist is something less than a learning-oriented discipline or that a catechist is unconcerned with doctrine and clear reflection. I am simply asserting that a catechist calls for learning to be lived out and for reflections that lead to responses. Though a catechist employs doctrine and theology, he or she is not a theologian. The NCD expresses it this way:

> Theology seeks fuller understanding of the gospel message through reflection on the life of Christians and the formal teachings of the Church. It employs systematic and critical methods. It uses philosophy, history, linguistics, and other disciplines in attempting to understand and express Christian truth more clearly. Catechesis also makes use of the sacred and human sciences. It does this not as theology does — for systematic study and analyses of the faith — but in order to better proclaim the faith and, in cooperation with the Holy Spirit,

> lead individual Christians and the community to maturity of faith, a richer living of the fullness of the gospel message. (NCD #37)

For early adolescent catechists this is a helpful distinction. A catechist need not produce 12 or 13 year old Thomas Aquinases! He or she must "share the light of faith" with 12 or 13 year old experiences, and invite those young people to live out that faith in the concrete realities of their lives.

3. *A catechist/teacher is more a facilitator of learning than a dispenser of knowledge.*

In my experience as both catechist and trainer of catechists, this foundation represents a summary of the Church's catechetical renewal over the last three decades. Catechesis is a learning *process*, not a delivery of knowledge. Thus, a catechist is a person who leads others through a process — a facilitator of a dialogue between faith and experience that leads to response. *The Challenge* document states:

> In this process, Scripture, tradition, and the contemporary life experience of youth are honored and held in dialogue. Adolescent catechesis encourages young people "to reflect on their significant experiences and respond to God's presence there." (NCD 176d) It enables young people to understand the meaning of their life experience in relation to the Christian faith. (*The Challenge* 9)

The person who has shed the most light upon this is Thomas Groome. In his book *Christian Religious Education*, he described a process of five movements which he called "shared Christian praxis." That process has become the foundation for many catechetical programs published today for children, youth, or adults. In his *Adolescent Catechesis Resource Manual*, John Roberto has described how the shared praxis process can be applied to adolescents:

> This learning process begins with the life experience of the young person, engaging him or her in critical reflection on that experience, and then relating that experience to the Scriptures and Tradition. The process concludes by engaging the young person in reflecting on the meaning of the Scriptures/Tradition for his or her life and what the implications are for his or her belief and lifestyle. The entire learning process can span one session, several sessions, or an entire course. (Roberto 76)

The names given by Roberto to the movements of the shared praxis process are themselves descriptive of the process. After an initial Focusing Activity, the five movements of Shared Christian Praxis include: 1) Experiencing Life; 2) Reflecting Together; 3) Discovering the Faith Story; 4) Owning the Faith; and 5) Responding in Faith. (Groome; Roberto)

This way of viewing the catechetical ministry is reassuring to many catechists. Once again, catechists do not need to be theologians. Rather, they need skills for facilitating a process, for encouraging reflection and dialogue, for presenting the Christian Story and Vision in clear, exciting, and creative ways, and for assembling and managing that process in a meaningful, coherent manner. At the same time, there is also the potential for frustration: by facilitating a process like shared praxis, a catechist is less likely to be a "star" or an "expert." Frequently, he or she spends more time assisting groups in cooperative tasks or individuals in clarifying their reflections than in presenting input. With early adolescents, however, this is certainly the more desirable course. As an age-group that learns best by being actively involved in the learning, early adolescents can profit greatly from a process like shared praxis and from a catechist who knows how to facilitate that learning.

4. *A catechist/teacher teaches subjects, not objects.*

A direct implication of the above foundation and of the shared Christian praxis process is that we honor the participants themselves. They are the "subjects" we teach. As Groome has observed:

> Our students are subjects, not objects. They have an "inalienable" right to be treated with dignity and respect because they possess their own individuality and have the capacity to respond to their own calling... Our students are to be treated as subjects, not from any particular magnanimity of ours or merit of theirs, but because all people are created in the image and likeness of God. (Groome 263).

Though we speak colloquially about having a teacher for this or that "subject," in truth those are the objects of the curriculum. In catechesis, a curriculum might offer a course on Jesus or Church or sexuality. All those courses are the objects of the learning in which we wish to engage. The subjects are always the participants, each with their own story, each capable of their own response.

5. *A catechist/teacher not only educates about Christianity, he or she employs a Christian way of educating.*

Once again, we draw implications from the foundations above. If we accept the role of the catechist as one who calls for the Gospel to be lived out, if we accept the process of catechesis as a dialogical one, and if we accept the inherent subjectivity of the learners, then we must call ourselves to the highest standards of organizing that learning. While we educate about Christianity, we must also educate in a Christian way. In addition to the usual meanings we would take from this language — charity, honesty, concern, respect, etc. — I would draw two additional implications: freedom and incarnation.

By employing a "Christian way of educating" a catechist respects the inherent freedom of the participants. That could mean honoring an individual's choice not to participate in an entire course or acknowledging a person's right to refrain from sharing stories or experiences from their life. It could involve patiently answering questions that challenge the very Christian Story and Vision the catechist is explaining. Respecting a learner's freedom means respecting their right to challenge or even doubt. Above all else, it means respecting each person's response in faith, and never coercing or manipulating individuals into actions or behaviors they do not freely choose. Throughout all of Jesus' teaching ministry, he never compelled or coerced a single person. Rather he invited people to listen and respond, he certainly taught with authority, but never at the expense of another's freedom. This must be said of catechists, too.

Another way a catechist employs a "Christian way of educating" is by revealing the truth of incarnation and leading participants back to it. When a catechist reveals the truth of incarnation, he or she recalls that our God took flesh, was and is Emmanuel — "God with us," and continues to take flesh again in each member of the Body of Christ. When a catechist reveals that truth through discussion and reflection, it is good. When a catechist lives that truth and is, for others, an incarnation of God, it is better. When a catechist helps other to see the God enfleshed in them and calls them to be God enfleshed in the world, it is the best. In that way, a catechist leads his or her learners back to the Incarnation, challenging them to be Jesus once more and to continue his mission: proclaiming and building the Kingdom of God.

6. *A catechist/teacher has respect for him/herself. Though called to selfless love, a catechist must take time to care for his/her own personal needs.*

Part of the excitement in being a catechist is the chance to share in the lives of others and in the life of Jesus. In doing so, a catechist lives and loves as Jesus did, frequently to the emptying of self. In recognition of this fact, I believe it is a foundational reality that catechists must take time for their own needs. If catechists are to empty themselves for others, they must allow the Lord to empty himself for them. Fulfillment must ultimately come not from hours spent or classes taught, but from the God who gives them strength.

I would like to suggest two areas for consideration in this matter. The first is the area of personal spirituality: prayer, reflection, reading, sharing with other believers. A catechist who wishes to nurture all those things in others must start with him/herself. The second area is less personal, and more organizational: catechists must dialogue with the program coordinator, director, or principal about their own needs in the ministry. Though it is the job of the coordinator to provide for such things, catechists should also feel free to raise their concerns. For example, I encourage catechists to seek clear job descriptions and adequate training for the ministry they are undertaking. By attending to such matters, they are ministering to themselves and modeling the Christianity they wish to share.

7. *A catechist/teacher is a collaborator.*

Catechesis is an important ministry, one that requires special preparation and special people. But it is not the only ministry. Of the four main ministries of the Church — Word, worship, community, and service — catechesis is but one form of the ministry of the Word. Or, to use the language of youth ministry, catechesis is one of several components in a balanced, total ministry. As such, a catechist is an important minister in the life of the Church, but he or she is also a member of a community of ministers.

Acknowledging that fact does not lessen the importance of the catechist or any other minister. However, it does call the community of ministers, catechists included, to work together in service of the one Lord, sharing the one faith. It is a call to collaboration. This can be a freeing realization. By recognizing the need for collaboration, a catechist can surrender to God and community the temptation to do it all. Because of the exciting, challenging, and sometimes intimate nature of catechetical ministry, a catechist can frequently feel pulled in many directions. He or she may be drawn to "be all things to all people," or at least, to the learners with whom he or she ministers.

By collaborating with other ministers, catechists can remain focused on their own ministry. They can use the grace and strength God gives them to be the best catechists they can. They can meet the needs that can be met catechetically and they can acknowledge that there are other needs that must be met in other ministries. Finally, they can trust that other ministers will attend to those needs: if not in the present, then in the future; if not by other ministers in the community, then by the One Minister, who works in ways we can never know.

8. *A catechist/teacher recognizes that he or she (or even the Church itself) is not the initiator in the relationship between a person and God; God is always and already active.*

A catechist is frequently the witness, if not the catalyst, to developing relationships between people and their God. By facilitating the learning process described earlier, a catechist leads others to a faith response. Often that response is a renewal or re-affirmation of faith and a deepening of an individual's commitment to live and work for the Kingdom.

The above notwithstanding, it is important for catechists to recognize that they are not the initiator in the relationship between a person and God. They have no "monopoly" over God; they do not "bring" God to the people they catechize. Rather they are called to be witnesses of, and sharers in, the God who has been, is now, and will forever be active in the lives of God's people. Their ministry is as much one of fostering recognition of the God who has been present in the life experience of the participants as it is one of teaching and sharing new faith concepts and responses. One of the greatest gifts a catechist can offer is the gift of seeing the God who is already there.

Given this foundation, it is easy to understand why catechists must facilitate a process like shared praxis or attend to the subjectivity of the learners with whom they minister. Indeed, it makes the call to self-care even more imperative — the more I recognize God's presence in my life, the more I can free myself from the prideful need to be a "messiah" for others. The more I discover the many ways God continually invites me and the many faces God wears, the more I can avoid the mistaken belief that without me and the knowledge I bring, God will not enter the lives of the people I catechize.

9. *A catechist/teacher strives to maintain the balance between fostering personal faith identity and fostering communal faith identity. In the language of adolescent catechesis, a catechist is both midwife and adoption agent.*

Under the aim of sponsoring faith maturity, catechesis seeks to perform a twofold task: fostering both personal and communal faith identities. In the image-laden words of John Nelson, we help people give birth to their own faith identity and we present the faith of the community, inviting them to adopt it and make it their own. Thus, we are both midwife and adoption agent. (*The Challenge* 8; Nelson 98)

The unique and special challenge for the catechist is the ownership of both these tasks and the maintenance of the balance or tension between them. Though individual catechists may feel drawn more to one task or the other, effective catechesis demands that we attend to *both*. Moreover, the balance cannot be achieved by swinging, pendulum-like, from one to the other. Instead, the catechist must be midwife and adoption agent *simultaneously*.

Neither is it true that the midwife task is accomplished through relational, non-learning oriented experiences and the adoption agent role is played out in highly cognitive examinations of doctrine. (Or that courses organized around "personal development" themes are, by nature, midwife experiences, while courses that originate in a "doctrinal" theme are adoption agent experiences). The goal of sponsoring faith maturing and leading people to active faith responses is pursued by balancing the twin roles.

Once again, there is a harmony that can be recognized between the ministry of the catechist and the process of catechesis represented by shared Christian praxis and similar learning methods. Through the dialogical movements of shared praxis, a catechist can balance the midwife and adoption agent roles. As the life experience of learners is reflected upon and the Story and Vision of the Christian Community is presented and placed into dialogue with that life experience, and as that dialogue leads to a decision for future action, participants in the process are simultaneously being led through articulations of both personal and communal faith. The catechist leading that process is, by extension, fulfilling his or her midwife and adoption agent roles. (This balance/tension is not easy, but it is essential).

10. *A catechist/teacher is familiar with the guiding resources of their ministry. In particular, he/she is aware of the essential principles found in the National Catechetical Directory and the documents that have been developed for age/setting specific catechesis.*

As part of their training, catechists must be made aware of the resources that have been developed to guide their ministry, particularly when they are documentary in nature and/or they offer direction that is both practical and foundational. *The Challenge* document is one such resource. As such, an early adolescent catechist should certainly be familiar with its major points. (See my essay in Chapter 9 for a description of the 10 principles of adolescent catechesis.)

GUIDELINES FOR TEACHING EARLY ADOLESCENTS

This section attempts to articulate a set of practical guidelines for teaching early adolescents. By taking the learnings gained from the foundational essays of this book and the foundational guidelines for being a catechist proposed above, I have formulated guidelines for effective catechetical practice. They are, by no means, exhaustive. They are derived from research and from experience — my own and that of others with whom I have had the pleasure of sharing ministry.

1. *Be attentive to the development issues and needs of early adolescents in planning your sessions.*

Use what you know about early adolescents and their needs when you plan. Recognize the diversity that will be present in any group of early adolescents, and plan a variety of learning experiences: use small group discussions at one time, draw creative representations at another. Attend to issues of inclusion and group identity by allowing the young people to occasionally group themselves. Re-channel risk-taking energies into safe opportunities where competence and achievement can be demonstrated: invite a small group to provide a role play or drama.

One of the most practical means for accomplishing this task is a dedicated application of the seven developmental needs articulated by the Center for Early Adolescence. Those needs are: 1) physical activity; 2) competence and achievement; 3) self-definition; 4) creative expression; 5) positive social interaction with peers and adults; 6) structure and clear limits; and 7) meaningful participation. (Lefstein and Lipsitz; Reynolds)

In planning a session, use the seven developmental needs in a checklist fashion. Review the plan to see that as many possible have been met. Other examples that derive from this practice will be presented below.

2. *Clarify the roots of early adolescent behavior before responding.*

Some of the most successful early adolescent catechists I have met attribute their success to "reading" the young people and their situations the right way. Responses to early adolescents behavior must be consistent with the reasons behind that behavior. For example, I once met a catechist who was concerned about the faith development of her junior high students. By her report, they had completely "tuned out" the material they were covering. They were becoming loud and jumpy. Convinced that they were somehow losing their faith, she redoubled her efforts, providing new stories and practices from a variety of religious sources. She thought the behaviors represented a deficiency in faith development and she responded accordingly. However, upon examination of the other major areas of development, we identified many possible reasons for the behavior, most of which had nothing to do with faith development. For each reason, we named some possible responses.

Some of the young people in the above example were undoubtedly experiencing physical needs. Faced with a lack of physical activity in the session, they got jumpy on their own. Some in the group had trouble with the book; while most of their classmates understood the material, they had not achieved the cognitive development needed for the abstract concepts being covered. The catechist began searching the material for opportunities to insert more concrete examples, and she developed reaction sheets on which the young people could write their responses before beginning a discussion. By reviewing the key developmental areas of early adolescence, the catechist revealed to herself the roots of the behavior and the responses she could make.

Following this guideline, you must continually differentiate between behavior that is *disturbed* (which is rare, but when present, should be referred for help) and behavior that is *disturbing* (which may be perfectly normal behavior for the adolescent, but irritating to the adult). Try a variety of ways to channel disturbing behavior, or even ignore it sometimes (remember, it's disturbing to you, but normal to them). Avoid punishing behavior that is normal for the young person. For example, putting a young adolescent out of the room for tapping his feet on the floor or pen on the desk is an extreme response to a normal early adolescent behavior.

3. *While being attentive to your role as a catechist/teacher and not trying to be all things to all people, be open to opportunities to assist growth in non-faith related areas when they arise.*

And they will arise! The natural diversity of the age group assures us that a particular group of early adolescents will include some members with needs in areas of development for which you did not plan. For example, when I was a seventh grade catechist, I had one young man who took advantage of every opportunity to discuss (I might even say, argue) the material we were covering. He did not disrupt the class; rather, he would use break times or steal a few minutes after class to dispute a point. I was beginning to enjoy it; in fact, I thought I had a 7th grade Thomas Aquinas.

I soon realized however that these discussions could be forgotten by the time he reached the door to the parish center. And for all his adept arguing, I discerned no noticeable change in his faith life. I finally understood that I was assisting a period of cognitive growth in the life of this young man. In one sense, he was learning "how to argue," a significant skill for a developing adolescent. I was open to the opportunity to assist this growth.

I offer this guidelines with a reminder — you can not be all things to all people. I would simply like to suggest that you keep an extra eye out for small opportunities. Sometimes, for instance, asking the right three young people to sit together during a prayer service, can help some friendships get started among the very ones who needed that boost in their social skills.

4. *Help motivate early adolescents by developing ownership, fostering collaboration, and building relationships.*

Most catechists/teachers would like to see more motivation in the young people they catechize. Remembering that motivation is strongest when it comes from within, we can still take steps as catechists to meet needs in early adolescents, and thus, motivate them. For example, early adolescents who feel a sense of ownership in a program are going to be more motivated to take part in that program. Build ownership by inviting them to share in your planning. Even if you have a long-term course format, you can scan ahead for topics and draw up an interest finder to discover what areas of the course the young people would like emphasized. When prayer times are coming up, invite suggestions for the prayer — should it be quiet and reflective or should it be a prayer service, should we use guided imagery or readings?

Likewise, motivation is increased when early adolescents experience opportunities for collaboration. This stands in contrast to the fact that most young people of this age are not motivated by competition, which tends to provide unfair advantages for early developers and even punishment to late developers. Catechists can foster collaboration through cooperative learning experiences and group projects. Setting a goal for all to reach and providing an incentive shared equally by all will produce more motivation than a competition with a reward that goes only to the winner.

Finally, as you help early adolescents build relationships, you are laying the groundwork for motivation. Begin new units with community building opportunities designed to help early adolescents get to know each other better. Establish relationships with adult members of the community by inviting parish leaders to share their stories with the young people.

5. *Be organized.*

One of the key developmental needs of early adolescents is structure and clear limits. Beyond helping young people set rules and limits, a catechist can meet this need by simply being organized. When you are organized, you convey a message of safety and security. If you know what you are doing, when you are doing it, and how you are going to do it, the young people feel its safe to enter it. I would venture a guess that their thoughts, if they could be articulated, might be something like this: "You seem to have your act together. If you have your act together, I guess I can give this a shot. At least, I know where you're going with this and when/how I can bail out if it gets too rough! But judging from your organization, I think you'll prevent us from getting that far."

To convey your organization to your group, begin the session by providing an overview of your plan. Tell them if the session will include some creative activities, discussions, or physical movement. You do not need to provide great detail, just enough for them to know that you thought this out very well. As much as possible, avoid last minute planning. Assemble your own materials and order them for use. Early adolescents can be extremely sensitive to a person who is unorganized and extremely responsive to a person who knows what he or she intends to do and how to do it.

6. *Be well prepared. As much as possible, assemble your own "bag of tricks" from which you can select a variety of methods and options.*

Because early adolescents are so diverse, they need a variety of methods, techniques, and activities. But they are also unpredictable, usually responding to events or situations in their lives that change daily. And since a catechist usually does not know all the things that happened during the day or week, he or she may find that the session or method just does not work.

For times like this, you should be as well prepared as you possibly can. While not denying the above guidelines on organization, you should also be flexible. If there is one way to do an activity in a catechetical session, there probably are several. Begin assembling your "bag of tricks" for the times you need to provide options. For example, discussion exercises that focus on choosing images (e.g., different images of the Church, different names for God) can be turned into an opportunity for physical activity by posting the images in different corners of the room and asking people to share their answer by moving to the appropriate space.

A catechist's bag of tricks should also include a variety of ways to respond to disturbing behavior. Try to provide different outlets for such behavior on the part of the early adolescents and different responses to such behavior on your part. (Lefstein and Lipsitz)

7. *Employ cooperative learning strategies; don't be too quick to break up early adolescent groups.*

More and more materials are being published that includes opportunities for cooperative group learning. Be sure to employ some of these strategies in catechetical experiences. For example, in a class of 16 young people, establish four groups of four. Divide the material to be covered into four sections, assigning each group a section. Have them read and discuss their section. Then, reconfigure the students into four new groups, now made up of one person from each of the four former groups. Each group now has the resources within itself to cover all the material. Give each group an assignment drawn from the overall lesson and let them work on their own. Travel from group to group to answer specific questions and help those who might get stuck.

At other times, consider allowing young people to remain in friendship groups. Seldom is something more devastating to a group of early adolescents than the phrase "don't sit with anybody you know." Early adolescents need the security that can be found in the groups they have formed.

8. *Be attentive to time and environment.*

Early adolescents are very sensitive to changes in environment, movement, etc. Be attentive to the subtleties of chair and table arrangement. Allow time for adjustment between activities or change of space. For example, when bringing a group of early adolescents from the parish hall to the church, pause for a minute in the vestibule to allow them time to acquaint themselves with the new space and with any new limits it requires.

Also, keep an eye on time spent in different activities. Even in activities that are going really well, consider how and when you wish to begin a transition to the next activity. For example, in a day-long retreat experience that includes a reflective, imaginative prayer in the middle of the afternoon, pay attention to the depth of the experience. Even in an experience producing an intense reaction, consider moving on if it appears there will be too much incongruity between spirit of the prayer and the activity which follows. I believe it is better to leave them wanting more, than to provide a very deep experience followed by another they will have difficulty entering.

9. *Ask good questions. Specifically, be attentive to the needs of concrete thinkers. Lead with concrete experiences, move to more abstract reflections.*

One of the most difficult areas of diversity among early adolescents is cognitive growth. Frequently, a group of early adolescents will include thinkers who are more concrete and others who have attained some abstract abilities. Provide concrete beginnings to conceptual reflections by connecting to real life experiences, role-playing, or providing simulation experiences. When asking conceptual questions, allow early adolescents time to think of their answers. A more effective method is to provide written instruments on which the young people can first write their answers and then from which they can proceed to a discussion.

10. *Minister to the faith development needs of early adolescents. Don't put them in stances of opposition.*

Early adolescents tend to exhibit an "affiliative" or conventional style of faith, they value membership in the community and seek an understanding of the community's faith and the expectations others have of them. Catechists must remind themselves that the faith needs of early adolescence are different from those of adulthood or even later adolescence. My first experience as a catechist was teaching a seventh grade religious education class while I was in college. Though the parish thought my theology major would be an advantage, they did not tell me enough about the faith needs of seventh graders. I think I was the world's worst seventh grade catechist — at least, that year! I tried to encourage them to question their faith, just as my teachers were doing for me. Little did I know that you can not always question what you do not yet feel a part of, or what you have no ability to understand.

As much as possible, respond to the affiliative/conventional needs of early adolescent faith. Speak about "the community's" beliefs and demonstrate your clear agreement with them. Avoid putting early adolescents into stances of opposition. Rather than asking if they agree or disagree with a Church teaching, present the teaching with clarity and ownership and then ask how hard or easy it is to live out the teaching. The discussion could be just as lively, but the starting point was communal, not confrontational.

CONCLUSION

If I were to sum up these guidelines into one recommendation it would be this: use what you know. The key to being an effective early adolescent catechist is no different than the key to providing effective ministry in any other component. It starts with a solid understanding of who early adolescents are and what they need. And it ends with meeting those needs as best we can in the ministry we have chosen. Let the learning you have gained lead you to action. *And all the while: remember how much you love them.*

WORKS CITED

The Challenge of Adolescent Catechesis: Maturing in Faith. Washington DC: National Federation for Catholic Youth Ministry, 1986.

Groome, Thomas H. *Christian Religious Education.* San Francisco: Harper and Row Publishers, 1980.

Lefstein, Leah and Joan Lipsitz. *3:00 - 6:00 P.M.: Programs for Young Adolescents.* Carrboro, NC: Center for Early Adolescence, 1983.

Nelson, John. "Faith and Adolescents: Insights from Psychology and Sociology" in John Roberto, ed. *Faith Maturing: A Personal and Communal Task.* Washington, D.C.: National Federation for Catholic Youth Ministry, 1985.

Reynolds, Brian. "Ministry with Early Adolescents." Network Paper No. 36. New Rochelle: Don Bosco Multimedia, 1990.

Roberto, John. *Adolescent Catechesis Resource Manual.* New York: William H. Sadlier, 1988.

Sharing the Light of Faith: National Catechetical Directory for Catholics of the United States. (NCD) Washington DC: USCC, 1979.

RESOURCE BIBLIOGRAPHY: TEACHING

Bowman, Locke E. *Teaching for Christian Hearts, Souls, and Minds.* San Francisco: Harper and Row, 1990.

The Challenge of Adolescent Catechesis. Washington DC: NFCYM, 1986.

Foster, Charles. *The Ministry of the Volunteer Teacher.* Nashville TN: Abingdon, 1986.

Griggs, Donald L. *Planning for Teaching Church School.* Valley Forge PA: Judson Press, 1985.

——. *Teaching Teachers to Teach.* Nashville TN: Abingdon, 1974.

Groome, Thomas. *Christian Religious Education.* San Francisco: Harper and Row, 1980.

Harris, Maria. *Fashion Me A People — Curriculum in the Church.* Louisville KY: Westminster/John Knox Press, 1989.

Harris, Maria. *Teaching and Religious Imagination.* San Francisco: Harper and Row, 1987.

LeFever, Marlene D. *Creative Teaching Methods*. Elgin IL: David C. Cook, 1985.

Little, Sara. *To Set One's Heart*. Atlanta: John Knox Press, 1983.

Roberto, John. *Adolescent Catechesis Resource Manual*. New York: Sadlier, 1988.

Schultz, Thom and Joani. *Do It! Active Learning in Youth Ministry*. Loveland CO: Group Books, 1989.

Warren, Michael. *Faith, Culture, and the Worshipping Community*. New York: Paulist Press, 1989.

Chapter 11

Prayer with Early Adolescents

Joanne Cahoon

I was 10 or 11 years old, and we went to my grandparents' apartment for a Sunday meal. It wasn't too long after we arrived that I got into a raging argument with almost everybody there and stomped out of the apartment. I didn't want to be there. Nobody understood me or my perspective on things or appreciated my opinion. I was trapped with adults for an entire afternoon and evening. So I sat out on the step in front of the entrance to the building nurturing my anger. It was good to be angry at someone — anyone. It focused all these energies that were ricocheting inside. And, after awhile of thinking about how mad I was, I started to think about how I could get back inside the apartment without losing face — and still stay mad. I didn't want to give up stomping, but I was hungry and began to plot how to go in for the meal.

As I planned, I began to notice how quiet it was outside. I noticed too the warmth of the concrete step on which I sat and looked up and saw the fountain and flowers at the center of the courtyard I faced. It was really pretty, and I was surprised. The hunger that was in tension with my anger was distracted by the colors and sensory beauty I had just now noticed — helping me to forget the first two for a minute. I breathed the late afternoon spring air and felt spacious inside — and somehow not alone. I enjoyed the feeling and the fountain and the flowers for a moment and then the word "God" came to me and seemed to be what named what I was experiencing. And I became happy. I got up and ran around the apartment building courtyard and walked and looked and the feeling started to subside. But I was convinced that it was God.

Soon I went back inside. I was still hungry. I felt recognized, accepted, and on the inside of a private secret. I did not even have to give up being angry, but I found I was less frantic and fighting. And everything was okay.

That particular Sunday afternoon of my early adolescence was an important one for me. In the midst of my life I found myself introduced to a God who was hanging out waiting for me to notice all the ways around me that God loved me. And God wasn't pushy, but welcoming. God did not require guilt or shame at my behavior, but accepted me. And because of who God seemed to be, I could feel secure and not have to prove or fight so much. I could even exhaust the energy I had with God by running around the courtyard and laughing. I met a God who had a real love for early adolescents. This meeting was one of many to follow which provided the experience for my belief that God "has a thing" for me and for each person — a love relationship specific to each individual. This relationship marks each of us as wholly unique and beautiful and of great worth and implies that we should treat one another as such.

Prayer of a new kind found its way into my living. It was different from Mass on Sunday at the parish and separate from the prayers I had learned to say. This new kind of prayer affected my experience of church and of my familiar prayers. I discovered a God who was present in the middle of my family, in the middle of my emotions, even in the middle of my tantrums and self-centeredness, in my loneliness and confusion, and a God who offered company. Through this new prayer, I began to find the Lord present on my own journey to Emmaus (Lk 24). God did not seem to want or even like being relegated to a thought or a nice idea. God wanted to be in relationship and was offering shared dialogue just as the Emmaus story relates. When my words and emotions were spent, this God offered to speak and to bring silence. This God took part in my frantic energy-spending, celebrating with me.

To nurture growth in prayer is to prompt the individual toward encounter with God who is present in our lives and world. This encounter with God's love invites each individual to love others as God loves us. Fostering growth in prayer is fostering an experience of life and God, not simply teaching a technical skill or specific knowledge about prayer. The goal is to enable the development of a concrete relationship between the human person and God.

How can we develop prayer with early adolescents that will lead them toward an encounter with a loving God? I am proposing six principles that I believe are central to effectively fostering growth in prayer with early adolescents and which can guide the preparation of prayer experiences with early adolescents. Each of these principles has two aspects. The first is a foundational understanding, which grounds our ministry and guides our work with early adolescents. The second explores how to express or celebrate the foundational understanding in all the various contexts in which we find early adolescents: in faith communities; in families; in schools; in specific gatherings of youth for catechesis, for programs, and for activities; in parish liturgies, prayer, and sacramental celebrations; and in parish community gatherings like picnics or socials. Wherever the faith community comes together and finds early adolescents in its midst, there is the opportunity to celebrate intentionally some of these principles.

PRINCIPLE #1:

We must know the early adolescent and provide opportunities for the expression and celebration of who they are.

It is true that to be involved in any relationship you have to first be present. If we want to engage the early adolescent in the relationships that constitute prayer we must be aware of the "I" that they bring to any relationship, i.e., who the early adolescent is developmentally. This is a basic premise of effective youth ministry and the first operational principle of effective adolescent catechesis (*Challenge of Adolescent Catechesis* 9).

Part One of this *Access Guide* described the developmental reality of the early adolescent. In the story which opens this chapter my "I" contained ricocheting energies, confusing desires and interrelationships, and a perceived and frustrating lack of freedom and real belonging. To understand the "I" of the early adolescent "I-Thou" experience, let us summarize some key developmental information.

The early adolescent is in definite flux. Explosions of growth in every possible area of life are normal. There is little stability, little that the early adolescent can call consistent.

Early adolescents will experience a rate of physical growth, second only to infancy, during this stage of life. This time, however, they will live through it self-conscious and self-aware! In addition, their growth may be "crooked," with different aspects happening at different speeds. Early adolescents may be beginning to stretch cognitively as well, varying between black and white concrete thinking and the very beginnings of abstract thought. They are often engaged in cognitive aerobics as they explore and exercise new paths of thoughts asking questions by making statements ("I don't want to go to Mass" rather than "Why do we go to Mass?"), exploring double entendre and puns and plays on words or images. They alternate between a concrete world view and the suspicion that there is another way to see, which they only glimpse now and then and can not hold onto.

The early adolescent's need for connection, affiliation, and identity is strongly expressed in the "who do I belong to?" search. Peers become more than the collection of best friends that an elementary child may have. They are a group in which I find security in conformity, even when everything about me seems to be frustratingly distinct. It has often seemed ironic to me that the developmental journey of older adolescents leads them to the exploration and expression of distinct and unique identities just when their developmental reality can begin to be described somewhat accurately with generalizations (e.g., they have reached physical maturity; the majority begin to become versed in abstract thought). In contrast, the early adolescent finds it extremely painful to be different when developmentally they cannot be otherwise. They need to be "normal" and like everyone else, even when there is no such thing as "normal."

This poignant description Annie Dillard gives of her own early adolescence may cause you, as it does me, to recall the flutter of emotions that went with the piecemeal awakening process, which is early adolescence.

> I woke in bits, like all children, piecemeal over the years. I discovered myself and the world, and forgot them, and discovered them again. I woke at intervals until...the intervals of waking tipped the scales, and I was more often awake than not. I noticed this process of waking, and predicted with terrifying logic that one of these years not far away I would be awake continuously and never slip back, and never be free of myself again. (Dillard 11)

The high energy, the exhaustion, the finding yourself present and in your own way, the sense of being looked at by everyone and the need to get attention — your own and others — on anything and anyone but you, the deep loyalties, the utter embarrassment, these are part of the emotional interplay the early adolescent wakes to. No wonder early adolescents are confusing and somewhat scary to many adults. They are at least doubly so to themselves! I remember particularly frustrating moments when I was in 7th, 8th, and into 9th grade. I would get my 10-speed bike out of the cellar or garage and ride fast and far only to stop somewhere or return home tired and little relieved. As I grew older I realized that part of the purpose of my ride was to get away from me, even though I took me with me!

Knowledge of the early adolescent should lead to more effective planning. Evaluating early adolescent prayer experiences based on their receptivity to the seven developmental needs of early adolescents is basic. (The seven developmental needs are physical activity, competence and achievement, self-definition, creative expression, positive social interactions with peers and adults, structure and clear limits, and meaningful participation.) *These seven developmental needs immediately advocate for experiences of prayer that are active, involving, relational and varied.* They must provide for a diversity of cognitive abilities, enabling early adolescents at all levels of concrete and abstract thought to participate.

The use of symbol and story is an excellent vehicle for enabling individuals to participate, express, connect, and celebrate at whatever level and even mood they find themselves. There is nothing quite as simple or as effective as asking youth (or adults) to discuss a particular symbol as part of an introduction to a prayer experience to discover what it means to them, or on what cognitive level they identify with or give meaning to the symbol. Responses may vary from "my mom has something like that" to "it reminds me of a time when" to "I think it could stand for." Each response provides information on how the symbol functions for them, how they view the theme for prayer, and also provides insight into the cognitive operations level of participants and their personal and family histories.

There is a story I like a great deal that Wayne Rice tells about a father who gave his early adolescent son an archery set for his birthday. They lived on a farm and the following morning the father came out of the house and saw his son shooting arrows at the side of the barn. As the father came around the corner, he saw painted on the side of the barn a number of targets. At the center of a few of the targets were some arrows. The father was extremely impressed and approached his son saying, "Son, how did you manage to get so good at this so quickly? How is it that you shot the center of the targets so easily?" The son explained, "Dad, it was easy. First I shot the arrows and then I drew the targets around where they landed." [3] Alas! Too often I believe we do all levels of early adolescent programming the same way. We shoot an arrow at where we think they should be, instead of where they are, and blame them if they do not respond positively. If we wish to nurture the intimacy and vulnerability that is a relationship of prayer, and encourage worthwhile connections with the faith community in these areas, we must shoot where they are...and celebrate who they are!

PRINCIPLE #2:

We must know and celebrate early adolescents as members of families.

The early adolescent's experiences of faith and prayer are profoundly influenced by the family. Some early adolescents are exposed to patterns of prayer within the family which demonstrate how prayer is valued by the family/parents. Other early adolescents have little experience of prayer within the family and have experienced it as unimportant. Whatever the case, the experiences early adolescents have had and are having in their family setting are a key to their perception of and growth in prayer.

Some of the saddest news is that parents often are unaware of how much influence they still have in their early adolescent's life. Because young adolescents communicate in a manner so distinct from their previous style as children, family members may begin to believe that only their peers have impact and influence on them. In addition, society groups children almost exclusively with their peers in school and in recreational programs. We in the church have frequently copied this pattern in religious education and youth program settings. Few programs gather early adolescents, consistently, in intergenerational and family-based groupings, or give attention to including parents and families with youth.

As I arrived at my grandparents' apartment at age 10 or 11, I had no understanding of family systems as such. There were boundaries and regular systems of communication set up, and I knew how I fit among them. I had little language, but lots of experience in the system. I believe that this reality is a common one among early adolescents.

Robert McCarty, the Coordinator of Youth Ministry Training for the Archdiocese of Baltimore, likes to speak of adults as "experience rich, but language poor" when treating adult learning principles. This descriptor is also true for early adolescents' experience of themselves as family members. While they are in the family system and of the system and learn from the family system how to relate or how not to relate, they do not yet have the cognitive ability to critique the system effectively or to distance themselves from unhealthy patterns.

> In the past quarter century in the United States the family has experienced progressive fragmentation and isolation, along with changes in its structure and child-bearing role. Catholic families have been affected along with the rest...These trends (increase in divorce, one parent families, unwed mothers, families where both parents work, decrease in family size, delay of marriage) appear to be nationwide and are having profound effects on society and religion. They underline the fact that the members of many families need extensive support if they are to grow in faith and live according to the example of Christ and the teaching of His Church. (*Sharing the Light of Faith* 14-15)

The implications are clear. If prayer is primarily relational realities for any human person, and if early adolescents learn the patterns and contexts of relationships largely from family, we as a church community must actively support families in their role as the primary religious educators of their children. Whether or not families accept this role, it is certain that they have the responsibility.

There is a need for creative programming to support and celebrate the early adolescent family and to assist it in understanding itself. Making materials accessible to families can be of great assistance, e.g., parent newsletters that have educational components, parent education sessions, and support gatherings on specific topics, a resource library for parents of books or videos. [2]

The emphasis on celebrating early adolescents as members of families concretely means that those of us engaged in early adolescent ministry need to provide times for early adolescents to gather with their families in parish settings for fun and for prayer. These times need to be well planned and intentional about promoting relationship and fostering family prayer. We need to provide concrete suggestions, resources, and models that encourage families to pray at home simply, yet creatively. We need to model a variety of methods and styles of prayer experiences which involve and engage early adolescents when we gather with them alone, with their families, or with the whole community.

There is something to be said for the "faith is caught, not taught" philosophy as a standard in fostering prayer. Attractive experiences that are simple, meaningful, and involving give the impetus for youth or adult family members to want to try something like what they saw or experienced. That is the rationale behind parish retreats or missions. Special experiences and intentional focuses can provide support for the everyday awareness of God's presence in the family, and the need for gratitude, forgiveness, and celebration.

The desire that parents may have for assistance in fostering their early adolescent's sense of God and prayer life is a real opportunity for adult education and fostering the adult's spiritual journey. It is clear that whatever is done to enable and encourage parents in their own understanding of and commitment to prayer has a direct impact on the early adolescent. Parents will have had varying degrees of experience and understanding of the variety of styles of prayer. To assume that they come from consistent starting points or understandings is as unwise as to assume that their children do. As in every other area of early adolescent ministry, outreach to parents is not optional if our goal is effective ministry with youth.

PRINCIPLE #3:

We must know and celebrate the immediacy of the early adolescents' experience.

Early adolescents live in the "now." They see what is in front of them. They focus on the immediate experience. They are not students of long term outcomes, willing participants in long range planning if there are not immediate consequences, nor are they particularly focused on the experience of yesterday. They are apt to say what they see, to question what they see, to enjoy what they see.

Early adolescents are students of detail in their manner of dress and general appearance. Exhibit A is the early adolescent girl or boy who spends an hour on hair and dress before special events or before school each day! They notice others, particularly their peers, but also the adults around them. Early adolescents notice themselves, and they also notice you noticing them.

The fact that they notice everything brings all kinds of opportunities for concrete expressions of real care for them. They take note of birthday cards sent to them in the mail, they remember a word said specially to them, they notice when adults notice them and comment. The opportunities for ministry are many for those of us who wish to convey care to these young people among us.

They also notice physical environment. In my opening story, it was the warmth of the concrete step that first got my attention. It was nice to sit on but was not hot enough to be uncomfortable. It was that practical detail that led me to look up and around and notice other things — the fountain and then the flowers. It was the enjoyment in these things that led me to a sense of spaciousness that eventually found the name "God." The last step of being able to name the experience as a kind of prayer or something to do with God was not a condition for the enjoyment of the experience. First I noticed it, then I enjoyed, only then did I come to name it. The name did not make the experience. I suspect there were many experiences I will never retrieve because they were just so ordinary for me that they did not seem remarkable. Besides, I was on to the next moment already, not thinking about the last one.

There are concrete implications in all of this. Early adolescents will pray the way they do everything else — as themselves. They will first experience and then maybe have a language for the experience, but the experience is primary. There are moments in the everyday life of early adolescents that they are already experiencing as moments of spaciousness, touches of the love of their God for them. These moments are woven throughout their day and elicit natural responses that are prayer in their own way. We simply do not usually name it that way.

Such an understanding of how prayer is already active in the lives of each of us gives a different focus to how we foster prayer. We need not "create" prayer for them, as much as show them how prayer is already operative in who they are and in their everyday experience. An Anthony de Mello story says this best for me:

> There was a man named Simon who lived in Krakow in Poland. He didn't own a great deal and he lived in a small cottage. One night, while sleeping, Simon had a dream. He dreamed of the faraway city of Prague. He had never been there, but in his dream he saw a bridge which somehow he knew was outside Prague. He could sense too that there was under this bridge some treasure that was meant specifically for him. He didn't know what it was supposed to be, and he couldn't see it, but he found himself looking under the bridge for it. Simon woke and it was still dark. But he remembered parts of the dream, and his sense that there was something he was supposed to find was so strong that he sat up in bed and felt compelled to get up and travel

to Prague. He shook it off though. It was just a dream. And he'd never been there. And it was a long journey by foot. And he went back to sleep.

A week later, Simon had the same dream. This time he could see the road outside of Prague which led to the bridge and found himself traveling it. When he reached the bridge again, he felt strongly that there was a treasure beneath it specifically for him. Still he didn't know what it was, and he woke still in his mind trying to find it. This time it was early morning, and he got out of bed and began to pull some things together to go to Prague. After a few minutes he came totally awake and stopped himself. He said to himself...I still don't know where I'm going, or even really why. You just don't do this. And so he settled for a morning walk and an early breakfast, and went on with his day dismissing the dream.

Another week went by and once again Simon dreamed of Prague, of his treasure, of the bridge. This time when he woke, it was so real to him and the journey so vivid that he decided to go—crazy or not. And so he did. He traveled long, but eventually approached Prague. Sure enough, outside the city was the road of his dream. And it DID lead to the bridge. When he saw it, he could hardly believe it. It was exact. The dream was reality. He approached the bridge and began to walk under it, as he had in his dream. Now he was at a loss. He had never seen what the treasure was or how to find it. He only knew it was there. So he wandered about poking at the beams, restless. "You there...what are you doing?" came a loud and gruff voice. And a man in uniform appeared looking suspiciously at Simon.

"I'm looking for something. I've traveled a long way." "There's nothing here—begone." But Simon only said, "Who are you?" "I am the guard assigned to this bridge. It is my job to expedite travel and to maintain the bridge and report any problems. What are you looking for? There's nothing here. I've been here for years."

And Simon tried to explain. He told the guard about his dreams...and about the treasure he was sure was here. And when he was finished, the guard was laughing loudly. "Do you mean that you made a long journey just to find some treasure of your dream? You ARE foolish. Let me give you an example—you must be sensible about life. Why, for years I've had a dream too about some man named Simon who lives in Krakow—that's far from here—and he has some stove in his small cottage and there's a treasure under it. Now do you think I'd be foolish enough to travel to a city I've never seen and dig up this man's house? No. Begone, man!"

And so Simon did turn and leave. He was confused. He had been so sure that there was something beneath the bridge for him. But the guard's words haunted him. A Simon? In Krakow? And he traveled home. When he reached Krakow and eventually sat in his little cottage, he looked at the old stove that sat in the corner of the room. And he thought. And he decided. So he got up and began to move the stove. And then he painstakingly pried up the wooden floorboards. And sure enough, hidden there beneath the floor, beneath the stove was a treasure.

And it was enough to last Simon for the rest of his life—and to provide for others in Krakow—and many he had never met.

When the Rabbis tell this story, they like to say that all the time the treasure was with Simon in Krakow, but the knowledge of the treasure was in Prague.

I would propose that an essential element of fostering prayer is enabling and encouraging all our "Simons" to uncover that which is already present and looks so ordinary that it hardly gets named — let alone named something religious or prayerful. Carole Goodwin agrees in her profile of Jennifer, an early adolescent who experiences moments of prayer during a "mountain time" (quiet time) in a retreat setting:

> The probability that she will name these encounters "prayer" is minimal. It is only if and when these moments are recaptured during reflection and discussions after the mountain time that she may come to recognize the active presence of God in her life. It is this recognition that will heighten her awareness of herself in dialogue with the other...It is important for us to realize that it is only in retrospect that many of us come to recognize God's presence in our lives. (Goodwin 243-244)

Enabling early adolescents to reflect on their everyday experiences as well as to set aside special prayer times is a skill needed by those working with them. We need to be creative in helping them unearth, uncover and see what they saw. It parallels Ignatian practices of reflection on prayer time. It is important to place "as a goal of our ministry with young people of this age...exposing them to a variety of prayer forms and experiences that lead to prayer, and then to assist them in interpreting the significance and meaning of these experiences for their lives." (Goodwin 244)

How do we help them reflect? We can accomplish this through journaling, the discussion and use of symbols and pictures, role play, general discussion, open-ended statements for completion around a circle, statements where we can ask youth to physically take a stand somewhere on a continuum of "always/sort of/not really/never" with regard to their experience. These kinds of methodologies enable us to help youth reflect on the experiences we have created with them or uncover more consciously the presence of God in their everyday moments. I must add that I see this reflection on experience as primary for it shows a God not just present when we gather for intentional prayer times.

There is another aspect of the immediacy of the early adolescent that requires a word. Their immediacy reminds us that now is indeed the most valued moment. Jean-Pierre de Caussade called it the "sacrament of the present moment" in the spiritual classic *Abandonment to Divine Providence*. More recently Henri Nouwen wrote of prayer as a matter of taking our everyday thoughts and making them no longer monologues, but dialogues. (Nouwen 70-75) The developmental reality of the early adolescent focuses them on change, relationships, and growth. Perhaps the gift of having their attention pivoted to the present needs to be fostered. In fact, it has much to teach the rest of the faith community. Celebrations of the "now" and not only the past and future remind us that now is the only moment we really own in which to celebrate, to give, and to find God.

If we can build on early adolescents' habit of inhabiting the present, we can foster an awareness that is basic to prayer. God is indeed present and our "times" of prayer are our human ways of accessing that presence and relating to God as individuals and as community. Discovering a God in the middle of the early adolescent's life is to foster the beginnings of a basic sense of contemplation. And adults witnessing this may experience the reality hinted at in an old book title "What do you say to a child, when they meet a flower." Wonder may be the early adolescents' gift to the adult community.

PRINCIPLE #4:

We must know early adolescents as individuals who need acceptance, and convey and celebrate their acceptance by God through an expression of the community's acceptance and pleasure in their presence.

Self esteem is the basis of any mature relationship. We can not give what we do not have. To sponsor early adolescents in growth in relationship to God and the faith community is to foster such self esteem.

This is perhaps the time of life when one developmentally stands most in need of acceptance as one is. Experiences of authentic recognition of early adolescents as they are and concrete expressions of our wholehearted acceptance of them enables growth in their sense of and esteem for self. The adults who liked to hang around me in my family, school, or church settings told me it was okay to be me. What an opportunity then for us as faith community to embrace and accept the early adolescent and help him or her to discover the presence of God and of those who share the same journey of faith.

We tell early adolescents we are glad to see them in simple ways. We provide space for them. We invite them to community events. We bring the soda to the parish gathering and not just the coffee.

We also show in our programming an understanding of who they are and the opportunities to belong, celebrate, learn, and grow in age-appropriate ways. All of these things speak to them them of acceptance and belonging at a time when they need affiliation. The kind of belonging church can offer with no strings attached — no designer products to buy, no need to prove themselves as worthy of the group as they may feel they need to do with peers — can be very powerful. We say "you are important just as you are;" "we're glad you're here, teach us too."

How can we communicate the quality of God's acceptance of them as they are? I think we do this best through telling stories that make God's love for individuals concrete. The story of Jacob in Genesis is a central one for me. Here is a young man not at all sure he wants the God of his fathers for his God. He is deceptive, conniving, even a cheat. But:

> The glorious message of Scripture is that we do not have to be perfect for our Maker to love us. All through the great stories, heavenly loved is lavished on visibly imperfect people. Scripture asks us to look at Jacob as he really is, to look at ourselves as we really are, and then realize that this is who God loves. God did not love Jacob because he was a cheat, but because he was Jacob. God loves us in our complexity… (L'Engle 46)

And:

> Jacob does outrageous things, and instead of being punished, he is rewarded. He bargains with God shamelessly: "If God will be with me, and will keep me in this way that I go, and will give me bread to eat, and raiment to put on, so that I come again to my father's house in peace; then shall the Lord be my God."
>
> Jacob also agrees to tithe, but only if God does for him all that he asks. He cheats, but he knows that he cheats; he never tries to fool himself into thinking he is more honest than he is…And yet with all his shortcomings, he is a lovable character…Whenever El Shaddai came to Jacob, he was ready for the Presence...Jacob knew delight in the Lord in a spontaneous manner which too many of us lose as we move out of childhood.
>
> As I live with Jacob's story I see that there is far more to him than the smart cheat, the shallow manipulator. There there are many times when he so enjoyed the delights of God, that he himself became delightful. (L'Engle 25-26)

There are many examples in Scripture where God dares to love people before they feel particularly together and while they are not at all finished. Early adolescents do not feel particularly together and certainly do not feel finished. To tell the stories that speak of God's love for specific individuals in concrete circumstances where God's acceptance of them as they are is clear is to pass on the message.

As a faith community, we do not only own these stories in Scripture. We own them in the stories that each of us can tell. Perhaps those who are oldest among us have more experience from which to draw, but all of us have some stories to tell. We need to make the stories of our own lives accessible to young adolescents so that they can see the love and acceptance of God expressed in the unfolding of the lives or real people. We need them to be engaged in intergenerational faith story telling. Maybe this happens in the context of our early adolescent youth programming and catechetical curriculum. If early adolescents can see and feel the impact of God's acceptance in the life of someone they know, it becomes real.

We can also challenge these same youth with the methods described in Principle #3 about sharing their own stories of God. They have words, perspectives, and experiences that can impact the rest of the church. What a great way to foster their self-esteem by letting them know that we need their voice. A friend of mine likes to say that we have a right to the Christ of one another's heart. He speaks of the uniqueness of each of our relationships with Christ. We need to hear one another. And we need our early adolescents' voices now, not only when they grow up. Do we really believe we are poorer without the participation of early adolescents? Giving youth the skills to speak their own experience is not just good early adolescent ministry — it is essential to who we are and to our life as a faith community. We need to foster these skills in every member of the community.

PRINCIPLE #5:

We must know that early adolescents image God as they understand themselves. In this light, we must help them develop positive images and celebrate the reality of God, themselves, and the Church that gathers us.

Early adolescents do not image God with abstract cognitive word plays. Their image of God is very much connected with their image of themselves. This is actually true for most of us.

> Your reason for selecting one image over all the others as your primary image of God is that it matches your self-image. It works well in relationship to the way you see yourself. (Kimball 37)

Don Kimball makes a case for the concept that all of our images — of God, of church, of ministry, of our direction in life — and our worldview are based in our self-view.

> The key, then, seems to be self-image. Your self-image will dictate all of your compatible images as you construct your view of the world around you. This self-image will affect your selection of friends, spouse, job, peer group, clothes, music, way of life, and even values. Each of your selections will be made from many options, but must coordinate with your self-image. Aren't you unhappy when reality doesn't fit with your view of the world? Would you rather change the world than change your images? Would you rather change God than allow God to change you?...We would rather cling to our images than allow them to change. (Kimball 40)

Gary Chamberlain writes, "Faith is the very mode through which the person shapes new self understandings and new orientations to the world. In this way, faith becomes a constitutive dimension of the human person, and the person's beliefs, values, and actions reveal an understanding of the self and the world which serves as the basic metaphor for life." (Chamberlain 9) That there is a connection between self understanding/image and faith is clear.

It is an interesting activity to ask children and adults of all different ages to image or draw or represent God. The results will vary enormously from clouds to thrones to flowers to abstracts to emptiness to poetry to music to a blank page. It is true that the image you see may in fact tell you more about the individual doing the imaging than about the God they image. You may learn about their histories, their experiences, their family, their particular gifts, their life view. In fact, at times a certain level of resistance can appear in individuals or groups when you ask them to answer an open-ended statement or to image something. What is that? It may be that the methodology they experience is repetitive. But I believe that its origin maybe a resistance to being that visible to others. We know that in imaging God we image ourselves.

Early adolescents' sense of self may be in flux due to the inconsistency that they experience in the process of growth. Their need for group identification and to belong is a search for validation. Their need for acceptance as they are, when they cannot extend this acceptance to themselves, speaks of how important their development of positive self-image is. Focusing on the self-image of early adolescents through esteem programs is important because it is the self that one brings to relationships with friends, with family, with peers, and with God.

Early adolescents have the freedom to try on different images and senses of self in the process of growth. Although this role-playing has made many a parent and youth worker anxious, I would rather see the opportunities for testing exist at this point in development. What a great time to propose positive self-understandings and God-understandings as part of the images to be explored!

This is the time to introduce early adolescents to themselves as individuals who are loved and known as valuable by the God of us. In addition, when we foster growth in one's self-image, we foster a religious process, growth in all of one's life images.

When we gather with early adolescents, we need to celebrate the various images of human persons as loved by God in Scripture, loved by people throughout history, and loved in our own faith community and families. Psalm 139 is a great start. We can also showcase the images God's people have had throughout time, in their own local households and faith communities. If we do not explore these images and show how attractive these images actually are, how can we hope they will try them on?

Helping youth understand the power of images is basic as well. They are surrounded by groups of people attempting to create images for them in a "look," the "right" style of clothing or music. They need to be assisted to see that somewhere beneath the image is the real person, and it is that person that God loves. They need to be given the tools to critique images others would set up for them, and to own or disown them as healthy or unhealthy, knowing that they exist apart from an image. They need to know that just as they cannot be "trapped" or "summed up" in any one image, neither can God. God is beyond our images and representations, but is best revealed in the life, love, and self-giving of Jesus where God expresses the deepest desire to be one with us. Pointing early adolescents to Jesus as one's primary way of "imaging" (seeing) God is not only theologically accurate, it appeals to their need for the concrete. If they want to know about God, tell them about Jesus.

PRINCIPLE #6:

We must know and celebrate the prayer of early adolescents within a context of their lifelong faith journeys.

This principle is reflective of, if not entirely stolen from, the first foundational principle of adolescent catechesis. "Adolescent catechesis is situated within the lifelong developmental process of faith growth and ongoing catechesis." (*Challenge of Adolescent Catechesis* 9). It is a principle reflected in the National Catechetical Directory and, I believe, in any realistic treatment of ministry with youth.

It is not our job in ministry with early adolescents to bring them to an adult prayer life involvement. To try to force their arrival at some level of faith not congruent with what is possible for them given their developmental reality is to operate in a way that cannot help but create frustration for both the early adolescents and the adults.

I often hear "How do we show them how important all this is?" "I want them to know what I didn't at their age." "God is the center of their lives and they don't even know it." I want to ask, and often do, "When did you see it as important? And why? What person, experience, helped you see the connection with your real life? Can you re-create that?" Or "Can they know what you didn't at their age? In fact, should they? What is it that you want them to have? How can you give them a taste that will bring them looking for more as they continue along the way?" Or "They are at the center of their own lives and often painfully so. If we can show them a God who does not just know their story but is *in* their story with them, maybe they will begin to find God in the center with them and not feel quite so alone. Incarnation says God is *with* us. And if they can see adults and members of their faith communities willing to be with them too, then we have the beginnings of church with them in real ways."

Joan Wolski Conn makes the point that only an independent self can offer an authentic self surrender. Early adolescents cannot be expected to have an intact, entirely owned self to commit to anyone. We would not expect a 12 year old to marry successfully in terms of what that commitment means. We must allow time for growth so that an adult understanding of, commitment to, and living of prayer can come about. But we must be cognizant that the adult grows from the youth. We can foster the skills that are basic to relationship, the esteem of the self that is to be offered through concrete acceptance and recognition, the images that are real and engaging while they are young. We must use what we know of early adolescents to connect with them. And invite them to continue their journey.

Early adolescents will not characteristically give us the language that measures where they are in respect to prayer in objective terms. They will tell us if something was "alright" or "pretty okay" or "I liked that" or "stupid." They will tell us if they want to be somewhere, which may tell us if they feel included. They will tell us about themselves in their every physical movement and in what they do not say as much as in what they say. We must continue to learn who they are so that we can effectively engage them in experiences and foster perspectives that will nurture their growth in prayer as faith journeyers.

It would be my hope that these six principles increase the discussion and spark other perspectives on this essential process. In the interim I would challenge each of us who work with early adolescents to pay attention to our own journeys for "unless we ourselves are willing to be transformed, how dare we facilitate, by our engagement in ministry, the transforming movement of the Spirit in others." (Finn 14-15) And as we all are in process in responding to the movement of the Spirit and being faithful to our journeys as best we can, we can know that our youth, like ourselves, are in the care of one who cares for them more than we can even imagine.

END NOTES

[1] An understanding of the unique identity and mission of Catholic families today as well as research and principles that may inform and guide its increasing effectiveness as the primary context for faith growth and sharing may be found in *Growing in Faith: A Catholic Family Sourcebook.*

[2] Two pamphlets from the Center for Early Adolescence I have found particularly helpful for parents: *Early Adolescence: What Parents Need to Know* by Anita M. Farel and *Understanding Families With Young Adolescents* by Laurence D. Steinberg.

[3] Taken from *Junior High Ministry*, the revised edition. This resource provides developmental information on early adolescents and some of Rice's practical advice and ideas for programming implications.

WORKS CITED

The Challenge of Adolescent Catechesis. Washington DC: National Federation For Catholic Youth Ministry, 1986.

Chamberlain, Gary L. *Fostering Faith: A Minister's Guide to Faith Development.* New York: Paulist Press, 1988.

Conn, Joan Wolski, ed. *Women's Spirituality.* New York: Paulist Press, 1986.

Dillard, Annie. *An American Childhood.* New York: Harper and Row, 1987.

Farel, Anita M. *Early Adolescence: What Parents Need to Know.* Carrboro, NC: Center for Early Adolescence, 1982.

Finn, Virginia S. *Pilgrim in the Parish: A Spirituality for Lay Ministers.* New York: Paulist Press, 1986.

Goodwin, Carole D. "Quicksilvers and Prayer." PACE 19 (May 1990): 243-245.

Kimball, Don. *Power and Presence.* San Francisco: Harper and Row, 1987.

L'Engle, Madeleine. *A Stone for a Pillow.* Wheaton, IL: Harold Shaw Publishers, 1986.

Nouwen, Henri. *Clowning in Rome.* Garden City NY: Image Books, Doubleday and Company, Inc., 1979.

Rice, Wayne. *Junior High Ministry.* Grand Rapids, MI: Zondervan Publishing House, 1987.

Roberto, John, ed. *Growing in Faith: A Family Sourcebook.* New Rochelle: Don Bosco Multimedia, 1990.

Sharing the Light of Faith. Washington DC: United States Catholic Conference, 1979.

Steinberg, Laurence D. *Understanding Families with Young Adolescents.* Carrboro, NC: Center for Early Adolescence, 1980.

RESOURCE BIBLIOGRAPHY:PRAYER AND WORSHIP WITH EARLY ADOLESCENTS

LITURGY & WORSHIP

Benson, Dennis. *Creative Worship in Youth Ministry.* Loveland CO: Group Books, 1985.

Bailey, Betty Jane and J. Martin. *Youth Plan Worship*. New York: Pilgrim Press, 1987.

Center for Learning. *Seasonal Liturgies.* Villa Maria: Center for Learning, 1989.

Duck, Ruth C., and Maren C. Tirabassi. *Touch Holiness—Resources for Worship.* New York: Pilgrim Press, 1990.

Hock, Mary Isabelle. *Worship through the Seasons.* San Jose: Resource Publications, 1987.

Huck, Gabe, et al. *Hymnal for Catholic Students: Leader's Manual.* Chicago: GIA Publications and Liturgy Training Publications, 1989. (Includes the Directory of Masses with Children, background essays, and 20 celebrations.)

Krier, Catherine H. *Symbols for All Seasons—Environmental Planning for Cycles A, B, & C.* San Jose CA: Resource Publications, 1988.

Marchal, Michael. *Adapting the Liturgy—Creative Ideas for the Church Year.* San Jose CA: Resource Publications, 1989.

McBride, William and Jeffrey Smay. *Liturgy Models.* Villa Maria PA: Center for Learning, 1984.

Nelson, Gertrud Mueller. *To Dance with God—Family Ritual and Community Celebration.* New York: Paulist Press, 1986.

Reeves SC, Sister John Maria, and Sister Maureen Roe RSM. *Junior High Liturgy, Prayer, Reconciliation.* Villa Maria PA: Center for Learning, 1988.

Roberto, John, editor. *Access Guide to Youth Ministry: Liturgy and Worship.* New Rochelle: Don Bosco Multimedia, 1990.

Warren, Michael. *Faith, Culture, and the Worshipping Community.* New York: Paulist Press, 1989.

PRAYER & SPIRITUAL DEVELOPMENT

Bannon, J.F., et al. *Prayer Forms.* Mystic CT: Twenty-Third Publications, 1987.

Collingsworth, J.B. *10-Minute Devotions for Youth Groups.* Loveland CO: Group Books, 1989.

Costello, Gwen. *Prayer Services for Religious Educators.* Mystic CT: Twenty-Third Publications, 1989.

Fischer, Kathleen. The Inner Rainbow - *The Imagination in Christian Life.* New York: Paulist Press, 1983.

Griggs, Donald. *Praying and Teaching the Psalms*. Nashville TN: Abingdon Press, 1984.

Halverson, Delia. *Teaching Prayer in the Classroom*. Nashville TN: Abingdon Press, 1989.

Hesch, John B. *Prayer & Meditation for Middle School Kids*. New York: Paulist Press, 1985.

Kovats, Alexandra. *Prayer - A Discovery of Life*. San Francisco: Winston Press, 1983.

McDonnell, Rea. *Prayer Pilgrimage through Scripture*. New York: Paulist Press. 1984.

Pennock, Michael. *The Way of Prayer*. Notre Dame IN: Ave Maria Press. 1987.

Reed, Sharon, ed. *Access Guide to Youth Ministry: Spirituality*. New Rochelle: Don Bosco Multimedia, 1991.

Reeves SC, Sister John Maria, and Sister Maureen Roe RSM. *Junior High Liturgy, Prayer, Reconciliation*. Villa Maria PA: Center for Learning, 1988.

Schmidt, Joseph. *Praying our Experiences*. Winona MN: St. Mary's Press, 1989.

Shelton, Charles. *Adolescent Spirituality*. New York: Crossroads Books, 1983.

Smith, Judy Gattis. *Birth, Death, and Resurrection — Teaching for Spiritual Growth through the Church Year*. Nashville, TN: Abingdon Press, 1989.

Stupak, IHM, Rose Thomas. *Youth Ministry Activity Book — For Ages 11-14*. San Jose CA: Resource Publications, 1988.

Warren, Michael. *Faith, Culture and the Worshipping Community*. New York: Paulist Press, 1989.

RETREAT RESOURCES

Carotta, Mike. Junior High: *Growing Selves, Emerging Faith* Minneapolis MN: Winston Press, 1985.

Cooney, Randy. *How to Run Successful Days of Retreat*. Dubuque IA: Wm. C. Brown Company, 1986.

Dockery, Karen. *Jr. High Retreats & Lock-Ins*. Loveland CO: Group Books, 1990.

Doyle, Aileen A. *Youth Retreats: Creating Sacred Space for Young People*. Winona MN: St. Mary's Press, 1986.

Doyle, Aileen A. *More Youth Retreats: Creating Sacred Space for Young People*. Winona MN: St. Mary's Press, 1988.

Ekstrom, Reynolds R., ed. *Access Guide to Youth Ministry: Retreats*. New Rochelle: Don Bosco Multimedia, 1991

Harman, Shirley R. *Retreat Planning Made Easy*. Minneapolis MN: Augsburg Publishing House, 1985.

Junior High Retreats. Villa Maria PA: Center for Learning, 1987.

Kamstra, Doug. *The Get-Away Book: A Handbook for Youth Group Retreats*. Grand Rapids MI: Baker Book House, 1983.

Pastva, SND, Sr. Mary Loretta. *The Catholic Youth Retreat Book*. Cincinnati OH: St. Anthony Messenger Press, 1984.

Reichter, Arlo, et al. *Group Retreat Book*. Loveland CO: Group Books, 1983.

_________ *More Group Retreats*. Loveland CO: Group Books, 1987.

Reimer, Sandy and Larry. *The Retreat Handbook*. Wilton CT: Morehouse-Barlow, 1986.

Chapter 12

Justice and Service with Early Adolescents

Mary Lee Becker

One of the goals of youth ministry is to empower young people to transform the world as disciples of Jesus Christ by living and working for justice and peace. Accomplishing this goal involves educational programs, service action opportunities, and integrating justice and peace perspectives into all aspects of youth ministry. This necessitates an understanding of the foundations and principles of justice and approaches to education for justice. This section will focus on education for justice and service action opportunities as they apply to early adolescents.

Christian service, as modelled by Jesus, involves an attitude and lifestyle grounded in justice, not merely tasks to accomplish. And yet, what is the notion of service experienced by most young people today? In secular settings "community service" is often used as a punitive consequence of undesirable behavior. Many church youth programs present service as a "requirement" of hours, or a one time "do-good" event. The messages we convey to young people by the modelling of our programs is as important as the activities themselves. To offer or require a service activity which lacks the context of faith is to reinforce the notion of service as "task." Such experiences offer little opportunity for youth to believe in and advocate for justice. However, when service opportunities are integrated with faith formation and justice ministry, they develop an understanding of Christian discipleship, encourage an attitude of serving, and identify the need for social change.

Early adolescence is a time of dynamic change and growth. Primary development needs at this age include self-definition and a sense of competence and achievement through positive interaction with peers and adults. Involvement in community service can meet many of the special needs of the early adolescent, including:

* To develop a sense of competence, testing, and discovering.
* To discover a place for themselves in the world, to create a vision of a personal future.
* To participate in projects with tangible or visible outcomes.
* To know a variety of adults, representative of different backgrounds and occupations, including potential role models.
* To have the freedom to take part in the world of adults, but also to be free to retreat to a world of their peers.
* To test a developing value system in authentic situations.
* To speak and be heard, to know that they can make a difference.
* To achieve recognition for their accomplishments.
* To have opportunities to make real decisions, within appropriate limits.
* To receive support and guidance from adults who appreciate their problems and the promise. (Schine 3)

Service/action opportunities meet multiple needs in early adolescents, and are therefore an essential and dynamic aspect of an early adolescent ministry program. Properly planned service opportunities provide an avenue for meaningful participation, which builds competence and self-image while responding to the Gospel message to serve one another. Serving others and discovering the reality of injustice can be a powerful experience for young people for which they need support, guidance, and recognition.

The keys to effective service programming include appropriate justice education, a clear understanding of early adolescent needs, adequate planning, and diversity in activities offered.

EDUCATION FOR JUSTICE AND SERVICE

The overall goal in education for peace and justice is the movement from awareness to concern to action. In a Christian context, it is a recognition of and response to God's call to love one another by promoting peace and justice in our world. Justice education is not just the "what," but the "how." In order for young people to experience the values and skills involved in justice ministry, they must see them modelled in the classrooms, programs and lives around them. [1]

A variety of methodologies are available for teaching youth. [2] In justice education, these methodologies are employed with young people to further an *awareness*.

1. *Awareness of their own giftedness* — both in establishing a positive self-concept and recognizing their gifts and talents as given by God to be shared with others.

2. *Awareness of peace and justice issues* — especially as they relate to their lived experience.

3. *Awareness of the human consequences involved* — making connections between personal and institutional decisions and the lives which are impacted.

4. *Awareness of manipulation/propaganda* — to differentiate between wants and needs and their manipulation by advertising; to develop critical thinking skills which analyze manipulation and propaganda.

5. *Awareness of why evil or injustice exists* — the power and responsibility of free will choosing.

6. *Awareness of Church teaching* — on social justice issues.

7. *Awareness of how social changes take place* — and what creative actions can be taken on behalf of peace and justice.

Awareness in and of itself is not enough. Education for peace and justice involves not just content, but a change in attitude. This process of conversion involves the heart as well as the mind. Nurturing this inner sense of solidarity or *concern* is the link between awareness and action. Four elements are involved in this process:

1. *Experiencing working for peace and justice as a call from Jesus.* We are called as disciples to be compassionate and committed followers of Jesus. It is from this perspective that we can respond to injustices as "prophets" and agents of change. Our educational programs need to enable early adolescents to explore Scripture and discover the values Jesus taught and modelled. And perhaps more importantly, our programs need to help youth foster a personal relationship with Jesus. Since early adolescents are highly relational by nature, this is a primary time to engage them in a relationship with Jesus. Questions relating Jesus and justice might include: With whom did Jesus choose to spend time? What did Jesus teach about justice? How did people respond to him? How did Jesus respond to injustice? What did Jesus work to change? How does Jesus call us to peace? What does Jesus say about being his disciples? How can we be disciples in today's world?

2. *Being touched by the advocates for justice.* People who work actively for justice provide both inspiration and imagination for early adolescents. People who give generously of themselves regardless of risk and with no need for financial gain, offer a powerful counter-model to the materialistic message which bombards youth today. Early adolescents are looking for "heroes" in their lives. What an opportune time to provide them with models who live out the Gospel challenge of peace and justice! Arranging for direct personal encounters with such people is an effective tool in educating youth for peace and justice. Alternative indirect

encounters include reading materials available from such magazines as Maryknoll, or viewing films which profile those who work for justice.

3. *Being touched by the victims of injustice.* Statistics about hungry and oppressed people often do not touch our hearts and move us to action. Images on television may move us momentarily, but can too often be forgotten with the switch of a remote control. But, when statistics and images are concretized by a personal encounter with victims of injustice, the experience can be life changing. Such encounters may be direct interaction with people who are suffering, such as at soup kitchens, food banks, homeless shelters, jails, hospitals, or nursing homes. Or they may be indirect encounters such as letter writing, or buying and/or distributing handicrafts of victims of injustice. Each time a handicraft item is seen or used it can provide a concrete moment of awareness and solidarity. Early adolescents are very "concrete" in their experience of life. This makes experiential learning a most effective model for early adolescent education. Direct encounters with victims of injustice can provide profound "change of heart" moments for young people.

4. *Being supported in community.* Learning and living for justice and peace involve risk. Engaging early adolescents in such experiences requires appropriate adult guidance and support. Although working for justice is an individual choice, it is experienced most fully when shared with a group. Community support helps early adolescents understand that they are part of a larger church community and provides opportunities for intergenerational contact. Other people provide us the support to overcome fears and challenges, and inspire us to take the next step. A group discussion can generate insights beyond that of any one individual's reflections. Such groups also provide early adolescents a place to surface and process their questions, fears, concerns, and achievements. Early adolescents are "social beings" and respond enthusiastically to small group interactions when properly facilitated. Such groups can also provide a place to celebrate new found self-worth and accomplishments.

Awareness and concern for justice are expressed most significantly in *action.* Since no two persons are alike, no one type of action should be expected of everyone. Instead, a balanced range of opportunities for action could include:

1. *Actions of direct service as well as social or structural change.* Direct service actions have immediate results and provide a sense of "doing something." This is especially important for the early adolescent's need for accomplishment. However, exploring the question of "why" such unjust situations exist is essential for structural change and long term improvement of conditions. Although such systemic changes may be difficult for early adolescents to comprehend fully, they are a necessary aspect of justice

ministry. Role-play situations can be a valuable tool in helping early adolescents understand the nature and function of social systems. And writing letters to local and national leaders can be a concrete action directed at structural change.

2. *Actions that focus on local as well as global issues and connect local and global dimensions of the same issues.* Both local and global dimensions are essential to the Christian vision of the whole "Body of Christ" or "family of God." There can be a programming temptation to focus exclusively on global hunger issues, or the local homeless situation, when both are equal realities of injustice. Making a local-global connection for young people is a balanced and necessary aspect of justice education.

3. *Actions that can be done within the home or school as well as the community and larger world.* Justice and service are as much a lifestyle as a specific task. Social action needs to be experienced as a regular part of life, not a special event. To develop an understanding of service as attitude and lifestyle, youth must be involved and invested throughout the experience. The more it is integrated into the daily lives of young people, the more it can become a framework for their choices. This means engaging youth in actions that can be done with family at home, with classmates at school, with friends in the neighborhood and beyond.

EARLY ADOLESCENT NEEDS

In planning service programming as part of an early adolescent ministry it is essential to incorporate the developmental needs and characteristics of this age group. Using the needs as a guide in planning will assure service opportunities that youth will find achievable and meaningful. Key factors to remember when planning service programming include the following development needs of early adolescents:

* *Need for creative expression and meaningful participation.* Include youth in the process of determining what programs will be developed. Early adolescents will be far more invested when they help to create the projects. Creative ideas often come from youth brainstorming sessions. Provide a variety of options, allowing youth to choose those which are of interest to them.

* *Need for physical activity.* Provide for time and space for physical energy to be directed and/or dispersed. We experienced great tension when youth were taken directly from school to a project with the elderly without time to "let off steam" in between. Once we adjusted the schedule to include some "transition time," the attention and attitude toward the project improved significantly. The youth were sincerely invested in the project, but needed to release their physical energy in order to be present to the needs of those they were serving.

* *Need for structure and clear limits.* Be specific with instructions and clear about limits, especially those involving safety. Provide advance training so that early adolescents can better understand the situation in which they will be working and to share helpful skills. Provide adequate supervision and direction during the project to assure feedback, guidance and support. Don't expect early adolescents to make decisions requiring cognitive abilities and experience beyond their development. If adult judgement is needed in a given situation, be sure there is an adult present to make it.

* *Need for competence and achievement.* Projects should be concrete in nature, with specific achievable tasks which provide a sense of accomplishment, and avoid feelings of embarrassment or failure. Provide affirmation during the project, and recognition upon completion. Posters in the church lobby and announcements in the bulletin or newsletters identifying the project and participants can assure support and recognition from the community. Announcements to local newspapers can provide greater recognition and a means of advocating for the value of early adolescents as well.

* *Need for positive interaction with peers and adults.* Service opportunities can be "equalizers" to provide positive interaction, even for youth who don't get along otherwise. When energies are directed together toward those in need, peer "differences" become secondary. Youth who seldom get along can often enjoy each other when sharing a task to help those in need. Adults and youth working together in service can provide an experience of shared responsibility and cooperation often missing in adult-teen relationships. In fact, witnessing the young people give so freely and fully of themselves in serving others in need has transformed many an adult negative stereotype about early adolescence. [3]

The energy and enthusiasm early adolescents bring to a project can transform the attitude of everyone involved, especially the adults. When the youth enter the local soup kitchen the attitude of everyone shifts from somber to lighthearted. Kitchen staff members consistently comment on the life and energy the youth bring, which is uplifting to all, especially those whom they are serving.

* *Need for self-definition.* Identity formation is a primary dynamic of adolescence. "Who am I?" and "What do I have to offer?" are common questions explored during early adolescence. Service/action programs provide a dual benefit of assisting those in need while simultaneously building a sense of self-worth for the young person engaged in service. A strong program of community service provides early adolescents an opportunity to experience the empowerment that comes with making a difference (Schine). When such opportunities are experienced in the context of faith in

action, they can instill a Christian identity grounded in values of justice and peace.

During the drive home from a recent service project, two seventh grade girls were excited and perplexed as they shared with me how a homeless single mother told her two young children that she hoped they would grow up to "be just like these two nice girls." The youth looked at me and said "Can you believe that, she wants them to be like us?!" I affirmed for them the mother's perception that who they were as people was a good model for her children. Their willingness to share themselves had obviously made a difference for that mother and her toddlers. Such an experience did more for the self-image of those two junior high girls than any exercise I could have provided in the classroom.

PROGRAM PLANNING

When developing a service component for early adolescents, *diversity* is a key factor. Individual development and interests vary greatly among a group of early adolescents. Providing a variety of service opportunities will allow for differing needs to be met. Some youth may want to participate in ongoing projects such as "adopt-a-grandparent," while others may choose one time events such as holiday food baskets. The intent is that youth are engaged in serving others with a positive attitude and openness to learn.

Organizing service action programs begins with researching and evaluating available options, as well as surveying the interests of the youth. Church and community agencies provide a multitude of services to those in need, and usually welcome the volunteer help of youth, although some agencies or programs may have minimum age requirements. There is no need to re-create opportunities that currently exist. However, the choice may be to initiate a new project if youth have a concern not being addressed through existing organizations. Once options have been determined, youth are "matched" to projects through a process of orientation, screening and placement. The extent to which screening and placement are necessary will depend on the specific project. A key factor is "choice." If youth are forced into service, their capacity to give of themselves, learn, and grow will be constricted by an attitude of resentment.

Regardless of the activity, preparation and follow-up are essential to the experience.

PREPARATION

Preparing adults and youth for service action is essential for a positive and growthful experience. Time needed for preparation will depend on the specific project, and the experience of those involved. Remember that adult leaders should be appropriately trained in ministering to early adolescents, and justice and peace education.

The purpose of preparation time is to:

* Focus the activity in the context of faith and discipleship.

* Sensitize the young people to the needs and realities of those they will be serving.

* Raise an awareness of the messages conveyed through our actions and attitudes while serving. Comments and actions common to a youth at home or school may be misunderstood and/or offensive in a service setting.

* Train and develop necessary skills for the specific project.

* Develop a spirit of community and cooperation.

* Establish an understanding of expectations and guidelines for behavior/participation, and outline processes for resolving conflicts if they arise.

* Identify roles and responsibilities of leaders and participants.

* Inform and educate parents regarding the purpose, nature and anticipated experience of their youth. The experience the youth have will impact their families, sometimes in very significant ways.

IMPLEMENTATION

As you implement your service project, keep in the mind the following guidelines:

* During the activity, assure adequate adult supervision and availability. Youth may feel uncomfortable in unfamiliar surroundings and need to know adults are nearby for support and guidance.

* Assure that the needs and dignity of those being served are respected at all times.

* Provide structure without stifling the characteristic energy and enthusiasm which early adolescents bring to their interactions.

* Keep the energies of the youth focused on those they are serving, and the purpose of the activity.

* For longer projects (mission trips, service weekends) provide time and means for youth to identify and process the experience. Journals are an effective tool for meeting this need.

FOLLOW-UP

Follow-up to the actual service project is essential. The purpose to follow-up is to:

* "Unpack" the experience and process what people are thinking and feeling about their involvement, and what have they learned as a result.

* Allow questions and concerns to be identified and discussed.

* Reflect on scripture and faith issues of social justice as they apply to the specific experience.

* Share insights and learnings, through the process of social analysis and theological reflection in an age appropriate manner. Social analysis models and processes provide a means to explore questions of "why" situations of injustice exist and what systems and structures perpetuate them. Theological reflection explores questions of what Jesus would say and do about the situation. It also looks at the Church teachings on the issue.[4]

* Identify future needs and responses. Where will this lead to? What's the next step? How will I see and respond to things differently because of this experience? Are there opportunities for continuing or deepening my involvement in this service experience?

* Celebrate the work done, service provided, and community built through the efforts of the project.

* Evaluate the project and make recommendations for future involvement, expansions and changes.

SERVICE / ACTION OPPORTUNITIES

When planning service / action opportunities, consideration should be given to the following elements:

Format....does the project engage youth in *direct* service to those in need, or *indirect* service through collection drives, pen pals, community awareness, etc.?

Involvement...is the project designed for individual or group participation?

Commitment....does the project require a one-time or ongoing commitment of time?

A variety of service-action projects are effective with early adolescents. Here are some ideas to spark your own creativity.

DIRECT SERVICE IDEAS

Direct Service puts youth in direct contact with those they are serving. Such projects may include:

* serving at a soup kitchen
* distributing items at a food bank
* working at a shelter for the homeless
* visiting retirement/nursing home
* working at a hospital or day care center
* sandbagging with flood victims
* helping Red Cross during local emergencies
* working with parishioners (chores for home bound, child care for single parents, visits to the sick, etc.)

* Working with Special Olympics or L'Arche communities for the developmentally challenged

* participating in or initiating environmental programs

INDIRECT SERVICE IDEAS

Indirect Service puts youth in touch with the issues in a different way. It is not always possible to be in direct contact with those in need, and yet needs can still be met through indirect projects such as:

Collection campaigns. Donation drives for food, clothing, money, and supplies are common and needed projects. Direct collection involves youth actively soliciting donations from family, friends, neighbors and bringing them to church. Indirect collection involves providing publicity and collection points at church or neighborhood stores. Youth take responsibility for emptying the collection containers when necessary, and arranging for distribution of items to agencies serving the needy. Collection drives can be done in conjunction with direct service projects, in which youth distribute items directly to those in need. A sense of community support can be created with collection drives, and youth experience a sense of accomplishment when specific goals are set and attained.

Utilize the creativity of the youth when planning collection campaigns. Consider non-traditional or overlooked needs such as socks and underwear, razors, toothbrushes and such. Giving a specific focus to the drive can be a benefit. One local church collected 1000 T-shirts to give to migrant workers when they arrived for seasonal picking. Another church collected small toys (crayons, bubble liquid, small stuffed animals) for the children of the migrant families. At Christmas 300 teddy bears were collected for children in detention centers. One campaign was for diapers and baby clothes for a home for pregnant teens. Often times the more focused the activity, the more energy created by the youth.

Collection campaigns can also be an avenue for raising awareness of justice issues when information flyers are distributed during the collection drive.

Correspondence. Pen pal programs can provide connections to people in need through written correspondence. Establishing pen pals with youth in other countries can be a valuable tool for making global connections. Correspondence can be created with people in prison, care centers, military personnel, missionary workers, political leaders, and others not accessible by direct contact. Relationships developed through pen pals can be as life changing as those experienced face to face.

FAMILY SERVICE IDEAS

Here are several ideas developed by Thomas Bright of the Center for Youth Ministry Development that you can encourage and assist families to sponsor:

Youth, Families and Identity. Develop together a family tree that goes back four or five generations. List people's names and birthdays, occupations and interests, places of birth and residence. (Theme: culture and ethnicity)

Youth, Families and Money. Do a monthly or quarterly family budget review, explaining where and how money gets spent, how family needs are balanced with the needs of others - extended family, church and charitable groups, others in need. (Theme: stewardship, lifestyle issues)

Youth, Families and Roles. As a family, keep track of how family responsibilities are shared at home (who does what, how often, how long). After a month, evaluate what the list tells you about family roles and responsibilities. What criteria is used for deciding who does what? (gender, talent, availability, desire, sharing the tough stuff evenly) Are family tasks shared justly? Why or why not? Discuss any changes needed to make the home a more just and peaceful environment. Try out a new configuration of sharing tasks around home for a month or two, then sit down again to evaluate how well the new system is working. (Theme: gender roles and responsibilities)

Youth, Families and Community Involvement. As a family keep track of how you share your time and energy with others through volunteer service commitments. After a month or two, evaluate what your service involvement says about you as a family. Discuss with one another what you're involved in and why. Do family members think they/you should be doing more or less? Why or why not? Are there ways to reshape present service commitments to allow greater family involvement? What about the balance of home and away-from-home activities? What can you do together to guarantee a better balance of the two? (Theme: service as individuals and family)

Family Service Projects. Talk about your concerns for the local and world communities. After identifying a common concern, find a service project that you can do together as a family, on a one-time or regular basis. Share your learnings, incorporate the service project into family prayer. (Theme: family as domestic church)

Youth, Families and Holiday Celebrations. When celebrating birthdays or other family holidays, incorporate family storytelling and sharing. Tell stories about the individual(s) involved that are humorous (and supportive) and recognize his or her unique contributions to the family. Add a new birthday celebration or holiday to those you presently celebrate, honoring a justice hero or heroine (local or global, unsung or universally recognized). Share and treasure their stories as part of your family's celebration of who it is. (Theme: integrating justice into family life)

Youth, Families and Recreation. Find ways of spending recreational time together that open your family up to different cultural and ethnic experiences. Take part in ethnic festivals and celebrations in your local community. Visit a restaurant that features ethnic cuisine, or have a regular *ethnic cuisine night* at home. Check out art shows, musical performances, etc. that expose your family to the perspectives and talents of different cultural groups. Subscribe to periodicals or magazines that feature stories about people and places from different countries. (Theme: multicultural understanding, local/global connections)

Youth, Families and Justice Spirituality. Incorporate justice in how you pray together as a family. Take turns offering grace before meals. Ask individuals to include three elements in their prayer: a general note of thanksgiving (Thank you God for food, and friends, and family), a specific personal insight or need prompted by the day's experience (thanks, too for the weather) and an element that incorporates a community or global perspective (may this meal strengthen us to continue your work of feeding the hungry or assisting those in ____________ who are suffering from ____________________). (Theme: justice spirituality)

Youth, Families and Peaceful Conflict Resolution. Sharing expectations and developing realistic guidelines for action and discipline before problems arise helps keep family tension under control when times get tough. Institute regular (biweekly, monthly, seasonal) family meetings to assess family needs, discuss family guidelines, ease tensions and plan future family events. Develop an agenda together, keep track of what's been decided, and regularly rotate leadership. (Theme: conflict resolution, participation)

Youth, Families and Ecology. Do an Ecology Home Inspection as a family. Pinpoint things that could be changed to make your home more ecologically sound. Determine ecology priorities, a schedule for improvements, and a responsibility list. (Theme: environment)

ADDITIONAL IDEAS

Other strategies for service-action opportunities include:

"Piggy Back" projects. Many local agencies provide holiday meals for the homeless and hungry. Youth can expand these projects by providing entertainment, atmosphere and activities for those attending. Wall and table decorations can be made reflecting the holiday spirit. Art and craft projects can be provided for children. Polaroid pictures are a treasured gift for

families that have no means for picture taking. Youth can make homemade cookies to distribute at the soup kitchen. It is a powerful experience for an early adolescent to see someone in need share great delight over something the adolescent takes for granted daily.

Awareness Raising. Posters displayed in the church lobby or at coffee hour can illustrate justice issues and needs. Youth can be a powerful witness to the community when sharing their experience of serving by giving talks at liturgy, coffee hour, or religious education programs. Bulletins can be used to publish weekly "Did you know" facts about local and global justice issues. It is also a tool through which to advocate for action toward justice, and invite community support of youth projects.

Non-Traditional needs. It is common for people to focus on holiday campaigns for serving those in obvious need. Youth can undertake projects to meet non-traditional needs such as stationery and stamps for prisoners. Or they can collect Christmas gifts for the families of inmates who are "victims" by circumstance and often forgotten. Contact local agencies to find out what *real* needs there are, beyond what most people assume. When visiting retirement centers, take along shoeshine supplies — it provides a much appreciated service, and gives the youth something practical to do while they visit in what could be an uncomfortable setting.

Youth can also provide service to the blind by recording stories or becoming cassette tape "voice-pals." They can be in direct service by reading to the blind or providing a letter writing service as the blind person dictates.

Early adolescents can be wonderful tutors for younger children or become involved in a literacy campaign.

Extended projects such as *mission weeks* require much organization and planning but should not be overlooked as a powerful means of justice education and service.

Youth can develop, individually and cooperatively, "*sponsorship*" programs providing ongoing service to an individual, family or group. Some churches have "sister parishes" in other regions or countries, or sponsor homeless families as they make the transition into new lives. Such programs can encourage the entire community to become involved in social justice issues.

ENDNOTES

[1] The material presented here is adapted from a chapter in *Access Guides to Youth Ministry: Justice* written by James McGinnis.

[2]The *Access Guides to Youth Ministry: Justice* has resources for understanding effective teaching methods, and outlines a process for education using shared Christian praxis.

[3]Sometimes the adolescent need for positive adult interaction is reciprocated in the adult need for positive interaction with youth. After a summer week-long mission project with migrant workers, in which 20 junior high youth and eight adults lived in community together — including sleeping on the floor and sharing two bathrooms — I asked the adults what they thought of the youth. It was the unanimous opinion of the adults that the early adolescents were wonderfully gifted, fun loving, generous people whom they had come to know and love as unique individuals. A far cry from the rather anxious adults who volunteered wondering how they would survive a week with these seemingly wild kids! It was an experience of enlightenment for the adults, and sincere affirmation for the youth.

[4]The *Access Guide to Youth Ministry: Justice* is a good resource to develop an understanding of social analysis and theological reflection through use of the Pastoral Circle. It also provides guidelines and tools for assessing and planning justice programming.

WORKS CITED

Bright, Thomas and John Roberto, eds. *Access Guides to Youth Ministry: Justice.* New Rochelle: Don Bosco Multimedia, 1990.

Reynolds, Brian. "Ministry with Early Adolescents" Network Paper #36. New Rochelle: Don Bosco Multimedia, 1990.

Schine, Joan. *Community Service for Young Adolescents.* Washington DC: Carnegie Council on Adolescent Development, 1989.

RESOURCE BILBIOGRAPHY: JUSTICE EDUCATION AND ACTION WITH EARLY ADOLESCENTS

The Barrio Video Series: Charo of the Barrio (22 minutes), *Bread for the Barrio* (16 minutes), and *Messages from the Barrio* (21 minutes). St. Columbans NE: Columban Mission Education/Awareness Resources, 1990. (Video program with a leader's manual and two lesson plans; free rental 402-291-1920.)

Bright, Thomas and John Roberto, eds. *Access Guides to Youth Ministry: Justice.* New Rochelle: Don Bosco Multimedia, 1990.

Campolo, Anthony. *Ideas for Social Action.* LaJolla: Youth Specialties, 1983.

Collins, H. Thomas and Fred R. Czarra. *Global Primer — Skills for a Changing World.* Denver CO: CTIR Press (Center for Teaching International Relations, University of Denver), 1986. (Teaching Resource Manual for K-8)

Columban Mission Education Program for Elementary Schools. St. Columbans, NE: Columban Mission Education/Awareness Resources. (Video program with a leader's manual and 5 lesson plans for grades 1-8; free rental 402-291-1920.)

Condon, Camy, and James McGinnis. *Helping Kids Care — Harmony Building Activities for Home, Church, and School.* St. Louis MO: Institute for Peace and Justice, 1989.

Earth Works Group. *50 Simple Things You Can Do to Save the Earth.* Berkeley: Earthworks Press, 1989.

——. *50 Simple Things Kids Can Do to Save the Earth.* Berkeley: Earthworks Press, 1989.

Focus on China. (*Maryknoll World Awareness Curriculum Series*) Maryknoll NY: Maryknoll Mission Education.

Foodfast. Catholic Relief Services, Global Education. Baltimore MD: CRS.

Hollender, Jeffrey. *How to Make the World a Better Place — A Guide to Doing Good.* New York: Quill/William Morrow, 1990.

How to Lobby for Just Legislation. Washington, D.C.: NETWORK, 1987. (806 Rhode Island Ave, NE, Washington DC 20018; 202-526-4070)

Justice and Peace Education Council. *Dimensions of Justice and Peace in Religious Education.* Washington DC: NCEA, 1989.

Keegan, Sr. Jane. *Focus on the Philippines.* (*Maryknoll World Awareness Curriculum Series*) Maryknoll NY: Maryknoll Mission Education. (A supplementary curriculum with lesson plans and activity sheets for grades 7-12)

——. *Focus on Central America.* (*Maryknoll World Awareness Curriculum Series*) Maryknoll NY: Maryknoll Mission Education. (A supplementary curriculum with lesson plans and activity sheets for grades 7-12)

McGinnis, James. *Helping Families Care.* St. Louis MO: Institute for Peace and Justice, 1989.

McGinnis, James and Kathleen. *Parenting for Peace and Justice — Ten Years Later.* Maryknoll: Orbis Books, 1990.

McGinnis, Kathleen and Barbara Oehlberg. *Starting Out Right — Nurturing Young Children as Peacemakers.* St. Louis MO: Institute for Peace and Justice, 1989.

Lewis, Barbara. *The Kid's Guide to Social Action.* Minneapolis MN: Free Spirit Publishing, 1991.

Kohler, Mary Conway. *Young People Learning to Care — Making a Difference through Youth Participation.* San Francisco: Winston-Seabury Press, 1983.

MacEachern, Diane. *Save our Planet — 750 Everyday Ways You Can Help Clean Up the Earth.* New York: Dell Publishing, 1990.

McGinnis, James, Kathleen McGinnis, et al.. *Educating for Peace and Justice*. St. Louis MO: Institute for Peace and Justice, 1985. (3-volume curriculum: National, Global and Religious Dimensions)

Making a World of Difference. Church World Service, Office of Global Education. Cincinnati OH: Friendship Press, 1989.

Neu, Lynn. *Seeking Justice* (The Discovering Program). Winona MN: St. Mary's Press, 1990. (Student booklet and teacher guide)

Operation Rice Bowl Education and Worship Materials. Catholic Relief Services, Global Education. Baltimore MD: CRS. Annually

Rich World, Poor World. Canadian Christian Movement for Peace. Dubuque IA: W.C. Brown, 1987. (A junior high youth justice program.)

Schine, Joan. *Community Service for Young Adolescents*. Washington DC: Carnegie Council on Adolescent Development, 1989.

Shaw, John C. *The Workcamp Experience: Involving Youth in Outreach to the Needy*. Loveland CO: Group Books, 1987.

Withers, Leslie and Tom Peterson, eds. *Hunger Action Handbook: What You Can Do and How to Do It*. *Seeds* Magazine, 1988. (Seeds, 222 East Lake Drive, Decatur, GA 30030)

World Food Day Materials. Catholic Relief Services, Global Education. Baltimore MD: CRS. Annually

Chapter 13

Community Building with Early Adolescents

Mary Lee Becker

When inviting early adolescents to church activities, a typical first response is "Who else is going?" This consistent awareness of others is characteristic of the age group. It could be attributed to their need for identity — I'll go if the "in" kids are going, but not the "rejects." Or to their need for security — I want to be sure I'll know someone so I won't have to stand alone. I believe it also can be attributed to basic human nature — I hear the same response from adults when inviting them to a parenting program. There is an inherent need in us as humans to be in relationship. These relationships are woven throughout our lives at home, school, work, neighborhood, athletic teams, activity clubs, and church. This affinity for relating to others at times weaves a tapestry we experience as "community."

Community is an often used word applied to a variety of situations. It refers to small base communities connected and grounded in faith sharing experiences. Local recreation facilities are often called "community centers." Parishes are identified as faith communities. And youth are frequently called to perform community services. For the purpose of this section, community will refer to those means by which young people are connected to each other and adults in caring Christian relationships through the conduit of youth ministry.

The "community" experience of youth today is a far cry from the comfort and security of neighborhoods and extended families characteristic of past generations. For many youth today, growing up is a world of "don't trust strangers," "just say no," latch-key households, single parent and dual residence, and a shrinking network of support systems. (Elkind) Surroundings once considered inviting have become alienating. With the loss of familial and neighborhood experiences of community for young people, there is the need to conscientiously create such opportunities through youth programming.

As expressed in *A Vision of Youth Ministry*, youth ministry by nature and principle is rooted in relationships. Youth ministry is simultaneously grounded in Christian faith. As Christians we are called to "love one another" — one can not be Christian alone. Youth ministry provides a framework for weaving relationships of young people into an experience of Christian community.

Community building as a ministry is more than fun and games. It is not limited to icebreakers and social interactions. It is not determined by the diversity of names learned or the number of youth participating in a program. These are valid dynamics of creating community, but they do not define it. "Community" is not only *what* we do (activity), but *who* we are (identity) and *how* we interact (relationships).

Creating and maintaining a sense of community is a pivotal aspect of youth ministry, and especially so for early adolescents. Developmentally, early adolescents are immersed in relationships which form a framework for security and identity. Relationships become central in a young person's formation of values and the filters through which they experience the world around them. Although the primary relationships for this age are parents and family, significant emphasis shifts toward peers and other adults. (Carnegie) As early adolescents continue to expand the nature and scope of relationships in their lives, youth ministry can provide them an avenue for developing positive relational skills grounded in Christian values.

When caring Christian community is the cornerstone for youth ministry, a young person is encouraged to develop:

* A healthy perspective of the joys and pains of relationships.

* Skills which promote positive/healthy interaction.

* An attitude of welcoming and acceptance.

* An understanding of Jesus' call to "love your neighbor as yourself."

* An appreciation for both the uniqueness of individuals, and the support of the community united through faith.

I recently asked involved youth the basis for what they identified as positive experiences of church. The two consistent responses were, "I felt like I belonged and was cared about," and "I had fun with my friends." In reflecting on the structure and nature of the program, it became apparent that the primary contributing factors for these experiences were atmosphere, attitude, and actions. These factors experienced through relationships are the basis for creating community.

ATMOSPHERE

When youth identify a place or experience as "okay," it usually means they felt comfortable being there. Their level of comfort is proportionate to their feeling of safety. Young people need to know that they are physically safe, and feel they are emotionally protected and accepted. When this "comfort" factor is perceived, their anxiety lessens, and their ability to be open and relaxed is greatly enhanced. To illustrate, consider why an early adolescent would feel more comfortable in a video arcade than an antique store. Obviously the arcade is a place "for them," where who they are and how they act will be acceptable. An antique store presents an atmosphere with expectations for behavior that are experienced as restrictive at best.

When early adolescents attend church, how often do they experience it as a place "for them"? How many times have you heard adults say "youth are the church of the future — the leaders of tomorrow"? This statement implies that youth have no place in church as young people of today. "We need to recognize that junior highers are a part of the church (today); they too belong to the family of God. Kids don't want to wait until they are "adults" to be a part of the faith community. If God places no age restrictions on us, why should we? When adolescents know that their contributions are welcomed, their energy appreciated, their presence affirmed, they will eagerly participate in activities." (Shaheen 70)

When an atmosphere is created which is inviting, welcoming, safe, and predictable, early adolescents will respond enthusiastically. It is my experience that early adolescents will live up to expectations quite readily when those expectations are realistic, and incorporate the developmental needs of the age.

Early adolescents need articulated guidelines which clearly identify what is expected of them (Shaheen). With too much structure, they are smothered; with too little they become confused. (Reynolds) Early adolescents also need a sense of involvement in what shapes their choices. Inviting their input in setting rules will allow a sense of investment, and encourage self-discipline. "This process may take a little longer, but the young people will grow closer as they struggle with issues such as what's important in the way they treat each other, how they feel about their group's reputation, their care and concern about safety matters, etc. Groups that care about each other are groups that others want to be part of." (Shaheen 75) In summarizing the discussion and creating a list of rules, remember that they need not be extensive to be effective. I have found the simplified guidelines of no put-downs, safety first, and respect people and property, provide adequate guidance for behavior. Creating a "We agree to..." poster and having youth sign it can convey your confidence in them to assume responsibility. Displaying the poster at gatherings is a subtle and significant reminder of the groups commitment to each other.

Physical environment can either enhance or distract from a sense of community. Most church facilities offer little space which looks and feels comfortable for adolescents. If your facility allows for a designated youth room, invite donations of game tables, comfortable chairs and floor pillows. Ask youth to be involved in arranging the room so they feel comfortable.

Room size will contribute to a sense of community also. There is a sense of "closeness" that is created when the space and number of persons present are proportional. Too large a space can leave youth feeling lost in the emptiness and wondering what's wrong since their peers are not there. Too small of a space may feel intimidating and suffocating, although I find youth prefer activities to seem over-crowded rather than under-attended. There are ways to create a welcoming atmosphere regardless of facility limitations. Adjusting furniture and lighting can change the experience. Also, a radio tuned to the top youth station will help to identify the space "for youth." A few nerf balls and time for safe play can also make a significant difference. Perhaps there is a place to install a basketball hoop in the parking lot. The cost is minimal and it provides an ideal space for informal play. It also serves as a reminder to the larger community that adolescents are members too.

ATTITUDE

Early adolescents can be extremely intuitive and perceptive. The emotional and hormonal changes associated with puberty can result in an unconscious yet powerful level of sensitivity. They are keenly aware of the unspoken messages conveyed by those around them. Therefore it is imperative that adults working with early adolescents are aware of the attitudes and perceptions that they may project in their interactions with the youth. Leading adults through a reflection about their own adolescence may help identify unconscious attitudes. It will also increase the sensitivity level of the leaders by getting them in touch with the feelings of being an adolescent. Authenticity needs to be primary in our interactions with early adolescents. Our care and concern must be sincere to be received. Our attitude must be welcoming and accepting to assure that each young person believes that she or he is valued and cared about as a gifted individual.

I often hear concerns about discipline with early adolescents. Actions of youth need to be assessed through appropriate developmental filters. At times behavior may seem inappropriate and even unacceptable by adult standards but not necessarily unexpected of an early adolescent. When behavior is unacceptable, our response needs to convey a message of forgiveness. Often these can be powerful learning moments for a young person. Making a clear distinction between *who* a young person is and *what* they have done in their actions is a powerful tool in identity formation. Adolescents need to clearly understand that what they do may be unacceptable, but who they are as gifted lovable persons is never unacceptable in God's eyes or ours. Although early adolescents may not fully comprehend this concept, it is important that we make the distinction for them. If we do not, talking about a God who loves us unconditionally holds little meaning.

ACTIONS

Our actions should flow from our faith and belief in the value of young people. Our actions need to be grounded in a value system congruent with the Gospel message we preach.

Who we are as persons of faith and how we share ourselves through relationships with youth will have far greater influence than what we teach. Seldom can adults identify the content of their seventh grade class. But when asked to describe their seventh grade teacher, they usually can do so in great detail — positive and negative! We learn about ourselves and life most fully through the relationships we experience. The content of our message will be heard only when it is modelled in our relationships. To teach of peace, forgiveness, acceptance, and love as Gospel values and to identify ourselves as Christians, requires us to live out these values in our interactions with the young people whom we serve. This is the essence of authentic ministry, and the foundation of Christian community. God's kingdom was proclaimed through the relationship of Jesus and continues to be heralded every time we witness our belief in him through the relationships in our lives.

STRATEGIES FOR CREATING COMMUNITY

For youth to feel like they belong, they need to feel they are noticed and known. Therefore, learn names and avoid name tags! One of the least favorite things for an early adolescent is to wear a name tag. If you can not remember a name, acknowledge the youth and ask their name — it lets them know you care.

I have found that the primary criteria used by early adolescents for assessing an activity are: *fun — friends — food.* If activities offered include two of these three factors, most young people will identify them as positive experiences. In addition, *Faith* is a fourth criteria in planning if we are to be a *Christian* community. In ministry, community building includes both the intentional structured programming efforts, as well as the informal (and sometimes seemingly insignificant) encounters. The best intended community building activity will have little impact if youth feel ignored or overlooked as they arrive at the door.

In regard to specific activities, it is helpful to make a distinction between ice breakers, games, recreation, and entertainment. Although any given activity may involve more than one of these dynamics, the primary focus should determine its use.

Icebreakers are intended to lessen anxiety and establish a sense of security while allowing youth to get to know each other. Unfortunately, too often they do just the opposite. Care needs to be taken so these initial interactions do not put youth in embarrassing situations. [1]"Pie-in-the-face" type dynamics serve no purpose in creating community, and in fact model inappropriate put-down humor.

Group games and *recreation* can be a great asset in creating community. Games can serve the purpose of icebreaking as well as group building. Creative variations on traditional games can reduce competition, and equalize differences in physical abilities. A blanket over a volleyball net can turn a competitive game into an entertaining endeavor. A developing tradition in our group is "crazy shots," in which youth shoot baskets in non-traditional ways and challenge others to follow suit. The results are more dependent on luck than skill, so everyone has a good time regardless of athletic ability. There is no way to "win," just lots of ways to have fun together.

Group building is also facilitated through *get-to-know-you exercises* and activities requiring *group cooperation*. Relay events, scavenger hunts, mystery solving, and group skits can bring a small group of youth together quickly. Once the youth have established safe relationships in playing together, they will be ready to share their thoughts and feelings as well. When planning get-to-know-you sharing exercises, be sure that the questions asked are appropriate for the comfort level of those participating. Initial questions should focus on likes, dislikes, and nonthreatening sharing. Such questions may include favorite foods, activities, or stories about one's last vacation. Once a sense of trust is established, youth will be open to sharing at a deeper level. At this point, questions may address times youth have felt close to God, or what they like about their families, or what worries them most in their life. [2]In any directed activity be sensitive to the response of the group. Most early adolescents will let you know clearly if you have pushed them beyond their comfort zone with both verbal comments, and nonverbal behavior.

In our "high-tech" world, I find youth respond enthusiastically to "low-tech" fun when they feel comfortable with the group. Board games, craft projects, and storytelling provide avenues for interaction which are non-threatening and fun. These non-directed times allow youth to develop friendships of their choosing. When adults join equally in the activities, the sense of community is enhanced. It is also a positive witness to the youth that one is never too old to have fun!

IMPLICATIONS FOR PROGRAMMING

When assessing or planning youth programming, it is always important to consider how you will integrate community building through intentional structured programming efforts *and* informal encounters. Here are several reflection questions related to creating community that you can use in your planning.

Does your youth ministry...

* Invite and welcome young people into the community? (Does coffee and donut hour include pop and chips for the youth?)

* Encourage participation commensurate with the comfort level of their early adolescent?

* Convey a belief that early adolescents are valued, and belong here?

* Accept the youth for who they are, and help guide them in choices about what they do?

* Affirm them as individuals who can make a difference?

* Provide a space that is safe and secure?

* Encourage and support the building of positive relationships, and provide means for resolving conflicts?

* Provide people who understand their diverse needs for fun, friendship, questioning, learning, and active participation, and who possess the skills to establish positive relationships?

* Provide a place where their role as church of today precedes the expectation that they will be "our church of tomorrow"?

What means do you use to...

* Encourage youth to discover and share themselves in a supportive environment?

* Lessen anxiety and avoid embarrassment for the youth?

* Promote opportunities to build self-esteem?

* Encourage youth to welcome and interact with new individuals?

* Assure youth of acceptance and affirmation?

* Encourage acceptance of differences as positive not negative?

* Provide guidance in choices and avenues for reconciliation?

* Celebrate the joys and struggles of growing as individuals and community?

* Ritualize experiences of entering and transitioning through our program — for welcoming, and saying good-bye?

* Identify expectations and consequences for behavior?

* Advocate for inclusion of youth as valid and valued church members?

ENDNOTES

[1] Many publications are available which include icebreaker and game resources. However, regardless of the resources, use of each activity needs to be based on the comfort level and community experience of the group. Consult the bibliography for resources.

[2] Consult the bibliography for get-to-know-you exercises. Also consider including youth in the choice of activities. They know best what will be comfortable for them to participate.

WORKS CITED

Carnegie Council on Adolescents Development. "Adolescence: Path to a Productive Life or a Diminished Future?" *Carnegie Quarterly* April 1990.

Elkind, David. *All Grown Up and No Place To Go*. Reading MA: Addison-Wesley Publishing Co., 1984.

Reynolds, Brian. "Ministry with Early Adolescents." Network Paper #36. New Rochelle: Don Bosco Multimedia, 1990.

Shaheen, David. *Growing A Junior High Ministry*. Loveland CO: Group Books, 1986.

RESOURCE BIBLIOGRAPHY: COMMUNITY BUILDING

Coleman, Lyman. *Youth Ministry Encyclopedia.* Littleton CO: Serendipity House, 1985.

Ekstrom, Reynolds, and John Roberto, eds. *Access Guides to Youth Ministry: Evangelization*. New Rochelle: Don Bosco Multimedia, 1989.

Kimball, Don. *Power and Presence - A Theology of Relationships*. San Francisco: Harper and Row, 1987.

Group Growers. Loveland, CO: Group Books, 1988.

New Games. New Games Foundation. Garden City NY: Doubleday & Company, Inc. 1976.

More New Games. New Games Foundation. Garden City NY: Doubleday & Company, Inc., 1981.

Quick Crowdbreaks and Games for Youth Groups. Loveland CO: Group Books, 1988.

Rice, Wayne. *Up Close & Personal*. Grand Rapids: Zondervan/Youth Specialties, 1990.

———. *Junior High Ministry*. Revised Edition. Grand Rapids MI: Zondervan, 1987.

Rice, Wayne, and Mike Yaconelli. *Crowdbreakers and Games*. Grand Rapids MI: Zondervan/Youth Specialties, 1988.

———. *Creative Socials and Special Events*. Grand Rapids MI: Zondervan/Youth Specialties, 1988.

———. *Great Ideas for Small Youth Groups*. Grand Rapids MI: Zondervan/Youth Specialties, 1986.

———. *Greatest Skits on Earth*. Grand Rapids MI: Zondervan/Youth Specialties, 1986.

———. *Play It! Great Games for Groups*. Grand Rapids MI: Zondervan/Youth Specialties, 1986.

———. *Holiday Ideas for Youth Groups*. Grand Rapids MI: Zondervan/Youth Specialties, 1981.

Rice, Wayne, Denny Rydberg, and Mike Yanconelli. *Fun N Games*. Grand Rapids MI: Zondervan Publishing House, 1977.

Rice, Wayne, John Roberto, and Mike Yaconelli, eds. *Creative Resources for Youth Ministry* (6-volume series). Winona MN: St. Mary's Press, 1981.

Rydberg, Denny. *Building Community in Youth Groups*. Loveland CO: Group Books, 1985.

Shaheen, David. *Growing a Junior High Ministry*. Loveland CO: Group Books, 1986.

Chapter 14

Pastoral Care with Adolescents

G. Wade Rowatt

Pastors, parents, professional counselors, youth ministers, teachers, lay volunteers, and other helping professionals are encountering adolescents in increasing numbers with more serious crises. Adolescent crises have some similarities to adult crises, but the uniqueness of the adolescent's psychosocial and faith context requires a specific understanding of the adolescent in the space age dilemma. Furthermore, an understanding of oneself in relationship to one's own adolescent issues and experiences facilitates caring with adolescents in crisis.

INTRODUCTION

The purpose of this essay is to provide readers with an understanding of adolescent crises while convincing them to participate with adolescents in their crises. In order to participate, one must examine oneself and the principles which guide one's ministry. A final purpose of the essay, developing practical approaches to caring for adolescents in crisis, provides a starting point for the reader's own creativity. The understanding and principles will be more universal; however, the practical approaches need to be custom-fitted for each context. Creativity, ingenuity, and imagination on the reader's part undoubtedly will produce new approaches for caregiving with teens.

The material for this essay grows from 25 years of attempting to work with teenagers. The author has been a high school mathematics teacher, a youth minister in a large suburban southern congregation, a pastor of a small town midwest church, a chaplain in a hospital, and a pastoral counselor. A more serious inquiry into the nature of adolescence began with a sabbatical leave that produced *Pastoral Care with Adolescents in Crisis*, a textbook for those wanting indepth study in the art of caregiving with teens. For 13 years, the author wrote an "Ann Landers" type column in a teenage magazine, *event*. More recently, a book for parents, *How to Talk with Teenagers*, has provided an opportunity to research more carefully the family dimension of adolescent crises.

In addition to professional experience and knowledge from behavioral science and ministry, the author's own personal involvement with adolescents informed this material. At various times, the author's family has cared for two adolescent foster child-type situations and has raised twins who have just completed their adolescent years.

PARTICIPATING IN ADOLESCENT CRISIS ISSUES

"Understanding adolescent crisis issues" could well be the heading of this section. However, understanding falls short of the full involvement necessary to understand. Participating in adolescent crises connotes the necessity of engaging oneself more deeply with adolescents in their world. It is a broader commitment to an "I-Thou" relationship (Martin Buber) with the adolescent world. To understand adolescents requires a commitment to know them and even beyond knowing them, to struggle with them. One must be a participant-observer in the matrix of their relationships. The detachment frequently proposed for professionals involved in crisis counseling does not work as well with adolescents. The theoretical detachment of classical psychoanalysis misses the adolescent psyche.

To understand the adolescent we must first understand the adolescent's context. Adolescence itself is a modern phenomenon. Obviously the teen years following puberty have existed since the beginning of the species. However, adolescence as a life stage begins with the Reformation and the Industrial Revolution. In biblical times young men and women were introduced directly into adulthood. Rituals that marked the rite of passage, frequently around the age of 13, placed on their shoulders the full responsibility of adulthood. Young women were given in marriage or to religious service; young men were given to be priests, warriors, shepherds, and farmers.

With the Industrial Revolution and even more now in the Electronic Age, adolescence emerges as a time of preparation for adulthood. The changes brought about in society necessitate more training and skill, academically and socially, in order to participate fully in society. As David Elkind points out in his creative volume, *All Grown Up and No Place to Go*, youth are ready for the real world long before the real world has a place for them. This need for a time to be prepared is more pronounced in industrialized countries. Third World nations and cultures closer to the rhythms of the earth still introduce their adolescents into the adult world earlier and appear to have fewer adolescent crises, i.e., fewer pregnancies out of wedlock, lower adolescent suicide rates, and lower adolescent chemical dependency rates.

The Industrial Revolution soon took the father out of the home and lessened or completely removed his influence on the adolescent's development. The Space Age has made labor a touchpad, push button, electronic experience, and now the mother has followed the father out of the home. Children and adolescents experience less support from their parents in the family system at the very time society is placing more stress upon them. Understanding the adolescent dilemma of more demands and less support underscores the critical nature of involvement on the part of the church and others who dare to care for this segment of society.

Today's Western adolescents have more free time, less supervision, and consequently are searching for real involvement. This situation adds to their consumerism, romanticism, and sometimes even casual attitude toward life.

One factor further complicating the adolescent dilemma is the image created in the media. Adolescents see from commercials, music videos, and movies an image of other adolescents in idealized, romantic worlds where love and attention invade their psyche like invaders on a video screen. Unfortunately, the real world does not substantiate this romanticized image of adolescence. In the real world, today's teenagers are more lonely, have fewer true friends, and feel less loved. They despair in the face of the discrepancies of the idealized image of the modern teen and their actual experience as a young person.

In a survey regarding pastoral care with adolescents in crisis, ten issues surfaced as crisis areas for teenagers. Questionnaires were sent to ministers, counselors, chaplains, and youth workers in each of the 50 states. Approximately 100 questionnaires were returned.

LEVELS OF NEED FOR CARE WITH ADOLESCENTS

The following chart lists in order the intensity of the crisis which adolescents experience, as ranked by these professional caregivers. (G. Wade Rowatt, Jr., *Pastoral Care with Adolescents in Crisis* 12).

Levels of Adolescents' Needs

Ranked as Greatest Need	Area of Need
1	Identity Crisis
2	Friendships and peers
3	Parent conflict
4	Drug and alcohol usage
5	Sex related problems
6	Job and vocation
7	Personal depression
8	Faith questions
9	Suicidal thoughts
10	Physical hospitalization

These may be perceived in a different order by the reader. Perhaps the context in which you minister contains elements that would intensify one area of the above concerns. Nevertheless, I believe if you are not dealing with these ten issues, then you are missing either a segment of adolescents in your community or perhaps are even closing your eyes to the needs in your group. These headings seem to be rather self-explanatory. (For specific guidance in dealing with a specific crisis you can turn to the book *Pastoral Care with Adolescents in Crises*.)

EARLY ADOLESCENT CONCERNS

While I did not survey formally the concerns of youth, I did interview teenagers from Miami to Honolulu, from Texas to Connecticut, and across the spectrum of sizes of communities, from rural communities to small towns to suburban communities and large inner cities. I conducted conversations with small groups and individual teens. Middle and late adolescents voiced concerns a bit differently from early adolescents.

Early adolescents, the group from puberty to age 14 or 15, expressed a number of anxieties. More than a few were anxious about the transition from junior/middle high to high school. There was a fear of social pressure, older adolescents, and perceived uncaring teachers.

A second concern of the beginning teen group was losing their parents and feeling less concern from their parents. Several expressed frustration over decreased time with their parents.

Social concerns emerged in a number of young teenagers. While there was an understandable idealizing of the concerns around ecology and their commitment to "save the earth," there was a surprising number concerned about nuclear war and a fear of space age destruction. While some voiced a pride in perceived military power, most were fearful for their own lives and safety.

Safety at school emerged as a concern for lower and middle class teens whose confidence in the public schools seems to be eroding quickly. They imagined being confronted by older teens with weapons or they feared being physically intimated.

LATE ADOLESCENT CONCERNS

Middle adolescents (age 15 to 17) and late adolescents (age 18 to adulthood) expressed similar concerns with varied degrees of intensity. This group's major concern seemed to be social relationships including dating and friendships. While many of them assumed that most of their peers were happily dating, they expressed frustration themselves. Surveys indicate 80% of teenagers want to be dating while fewer than 20% have a date on a regular basis. Group dating seems to be the norm for middle and late adolescents as it used to be for early adolescents.

A profound sense of isolation and loneliness pervades the psyche of many teens. They feel no one really cares. They overgeneralize the acceptance others experience and catastrophize the rejection they experience.[1]

A further concern of middle and late adolescents focused on their families. For the most part they were wanting freedom from their parents but not from their parents' economic support. Middle and late adolescents want to have their cake and eat it too. They want to make all their own decisions and finance them with their parents' support. Materialism seduces many middle class and upper middle class adolescents and not a few from the lower socioeconomic group. Adolescent crime is on the increase because of the pressure to have things. In the face of the existential anxieties of loneliness and separation from parents, accumulating electronic gadgets and gizmos offer some teens a false sense of identity.

A second older teen concern was dealing with dysfunctional parents. While many had been traumatized by the divorce of their parents, a large number felt equally traumatized by living with what I would call dysfunctional parents. The parents did not have sufficient boundaries between the parent role and the child role in the family.

A further concern of late adolescents was being pushed vocationally. This expressed itself in early and middle adolescents as being pushed to excel too soon. A number of teens who felt they were supposed to be "superkids" expressed the feeling that they had to either be at the top of their class or be ashamed. This appeared more pronounced among Asian Americans than among Afro-Americans or Euro-Americans. Others felt pushed to excel athletically, dramatically, musically, or in whatever area of concern appeared important to their parents. The late adolescents felt pushed to select a vocation or a profession. A few middle adolescents felt that they were to have their college selected and their life goal set at age 15.

Among poverty stricken adolescents, a sense of hopelessness, frustration, and in some cases rage, prevailed. While living in the land of plenty, they experience hunger and poverty. The hopelessness seemed most pronounced among young black males who are not in church. Interestingly enough, there was a high sense of self-esteem and hope among black churched adolescent males. Generally speaking, black adolescent females expressed more hope from their poverty context than did white adolescent males or females whose families experienced poverty.

It seems that to understand the contemporary adolescent one must understand the dynamics that contribute to the lessening of support systems for teenagers. Also one needs to understand the social pressures as perceived by professionals and adolescents. Finally one needs to understand the adolescent developmental context. (For further reading in understanding the adolescent developmental cycle see *Understanding Today's Youth* by Daniel O. Aleshire.)

Perhaps 30-50% of all adolescents will experience some type of crisis in the teen decade. That is, their parents will divorce, they will be hospitalized or depressed, or lonely, or they will be the victim of some tragedy.

PRINCIPLES OF CARING WITH ADOLESCENTS

Principles of caring with adolescents provide a sense of direction in the complexity of the multifaceted problems that encompass problem teenagers. Pastoral principles underscore the unique role of the minister as she or he cares for adolescents. Certainly more troubled adolescents will need the care of other professionals such as family counselors, social workers, and physicians; nevertheless, staying theologically grounded underscores the uniqueness of the minister's role. There are three areas of principles that deserve further reflection: awareness, assessment, and actions.

Our awareness of the nature of our relationships with teens contributes to a sense of mutual trust. However, our capacity as professionals must move us beyond just trust and friendship to the level of assessing accurately the nature of the crisis. After we assess the crisis and communicate with some clarity that assessment with the teen, then certain actions on our part and theirs must be undertaken for appropriate response to the crisis.

AWARENESS PRINCIPLES

Perhaps the most important awareness to take into a ministry context with a teenager is egalitarian partnership. Ministers need to be aware of the adolescent's concern to be treated as an equal. As caregivers offer first their friendship, they communicate respect for the teenager as a human being. This helps confront the "you're a little person" attitude. One needs to be cautious not to take teenagers and their problems too casually. Belittling and talking down to teens reflects the opposite of this egalitarian partnership attitude. Before teens will trust a minister privately, this attitude of partnership will need to be communicated publicly through teaching, preaching, and social situations.

The second attitude to carry into an adolescent crisis situation is commitment. The adolescent needs to feel that the minister will stand by them and be on their side regardless of where the relationship leads. Often troubled juveniles are detached from caring adults and therefore need this sense of commitment even more. A few will never have had a durable relationship with an adult, even a parent, whom they could trust. Building this bond will be an even more critical variable in crisis management.

Specific ways of expressing the attitude of "I'll stand by you" involves such things as taking initiative in negotiating contacts and appointments, maintaining an interest in their other activities, and discussing future events such as graduation with them. If the minister can participate in some of their events such as showing up for a ballgame or appearing in court with them, this further underscores an attitude of commitment.

Openness to new issues through a non-defensive posture is a third attitude necessary for ongoing care with adolescents in crisis. Such openness calls for meeting the teenager in his or her world of language and ideas. It may even call for meeting them outside of the office, in their home, at the pizza parlor or the parking lot. The context of caring for adolescents in crisis may not be the church office, sanctuary, or counseling room, but will more likely need to be a long walk, a casual conversation pacing around the room, or sharing a soft drink in a fast food place. While flexibility is important to the context of the care, it is perhaps even more important in the relationship. While a teenager may be open and willing to respond to a minister's offer of care at one time, a few days later the adolescent may need to pull back and remain detached. An attitude of openness to let the teenager's mood set the stage for the depth of the conversation strengthens the capacity to care in the midst of a crisis. Care needs to be taken that this openness does not communicate powerlessness on the part of the caregiver. There is still a time for setting limits, drawing the line, and remaining firm, but precaution must be taken not to be rigid.

An attitude of privacy must be maintained at all times. This fourth attitude is a vital principle in caring for adolescents in crisis. Remember certain information such as physical abuse and sexual abuse cannot be maintained in secrecy but must be reported to the legal authorities. Nevertheless, other information such as a broken dating relationship, being fired from a job, having a brush with legal authorities, needs to be held in the strictest of confidence.

Most ministers will find this attitude difficult in their parish setting because of the sense of responsibility to the family and parents. While each person must determine ethically what he or she will hold secret and what must be shared with family or other professionals, an attitude of respecting the boundaries of the adolescent's information must be conveyed. Ministers need to communicate clearly with adolescents information that must be shared. It is better to tell the adolescent ahead of time than to have the adolescent discover late that a confidence has been violated. For example, the minister might say, "I feel compelled to inform your parents that you are having these self-destructive thoughts. We must get you some help. I've got to refer you for professional care." Adolescents will respect professional use of confidence. However, they are understandably slow in forgiving a minister who slips in conversation and shares embarrassing information about a date or an awkward social event with other members of the congregation.

A fifth attitude for caring with adolescents is understanding. Simply put, you must know teenagers and communicate to them that you know not only their general plight but their specific problems. Teenagers are often more concerned that their point of view be understood than they are worried about getting their way. Many adolescents cry for understanding from the adult world. They feel adults have forgotten the pain and perhaps never knew the depth of frustration that they experience.

While exhibiting empathy, ministers need to be cautious not to communicate that the adolescent world was the very same for them. While we have some memories from our own adolescent experience, teenagers are put off by attempts to make one-to-one correlations between our adolescent world and theirs. They don't need us to say "It was exactly that way when I was your age" as much as they want to hear, "Tell me what it's like for you. I remember some of those struggles but I'm sure your situation is different."

A final attitude to carry into our ministry with adolescents in crisis is an attitude of sensitivity to gender issues. Boys and girls, men and women, males and females are different! While the universality of personhood calls for equality between men and women, the differences necessitate a respect for uniqueness. Men's identity formation and women's identity formation in pre-Industrial Revolution society had a clarity of roles even though it seems to have neglected equality and respect. Hard work on the part of social and political activists has brought more respect and equality, but there is a danger in losing the individuality of the sexes. Ministers need to understand that perhaps a person of the same sex will be needed to discuss some problems with teenagers in crisis. For example, as soon as possible after learning of sexual abuse or rape, a person of the same sex needs to be available to talk with the victim. In providing role models, persons of the same gender need to be available in the group. An attitude of respect for gender differences needs to reflect the equality of Scriptures like Galatians 3:28: "There is neither Jew nor Greek, bond nor free, male nor female, for you are all one in Christ Jesus." While these attitudes create an atmosphere necessary for establishing a bond with adolescents in crisis, the capacity to detach oneself and observe carefully the dynamics is necessary for an accurate assessment. Caregivers need to be simultaneously involved in the process of relating to the adolescent and removed from the process enough to assess the nature of the crisis.

ASSESSMENT PRINCIPLES

As the adolescent shares the nature of the crisis, the first assessment principle is to avoid projection. Caregivers who do not know themselves well or perhaps are unaware of their own spiritual struggles and psychosocial issues run the danger of seeing their own issues projected on to the screen of the adolescent's life drama. Such "personal issue" blindness makes assessing the adolescent's situation impossible. While delayed adolescent issues may help some youth ministers relate recreationally with the teen world, delayed adolescent struggles handicap caring adults in attempts to respond during crises. While this would be true of emergency crises such as hospitalization, family problems, or legal issues, it is perhaps more true of developmental, emerging, crises such as turning 16, dealing with a vocational decision, or handling the grief over a lost love.

A second assessment principle, using your own relationship as a guide to understanding the teen, requires a high level of self-awareness. As the teenager discusses the nature of their crisis, the caregiver develops feelings toward the teenager. Sensitive assessors know how to use these feelings as a guide to understanding how other persons will respond to this teen. For example, one might begin to be hostile or angry toward the teenager asking for help. As these angry feelings emerge, caregivers can ask what about the teenager prompts the hostility and could that same dynamic be contributing to the nature of the crisis? Manipulative teenagers might be sabotaging their own systems of help at home, school, or work. When the manipulation appears to the minister as a reason for hostilities, it can be used as a tool for assessment.

A third assessment principle focuses on understanding the developmental stage and issues of the teenager. In emergency crises, developmental issues for the teenager form a lens through which they see the emergency event. For example, if a teenager's key developmental issue is learning to date, concerns about dating may become a primary lens through which he or she views decisions around their parents divorce. One teenager chose to live with the father, whom she despised, rather than move with the mother she loved. Her key issue was that the father was staying in the community, and she had begun dating a boy at her school only two weeks before. Knowing the teenager's developmental issue provides vital information in assessing not only the cause and impact of the crisis but also in assessing the probable resolution of the crisis. Remember teens mature at different rates. Knowledge of what is developmentally normal for a given age must be coupled with the ability to hear each youth's own developmental concerns.

A fourth principle takes into account the tension between social pressure and responsibility. In assessing the crisis, the caregiver needs to sort out contextual issues from personal issues. For example, a young man who has been arrested for shoplifting may have a personal problem or may in complex ways be reflecting the injustice of his own economic plight. Social factors are a major force in adolescent behavior. Because a minister may be enmeshed in the same social context, assessing such factors can be quite difficult. If there is a pattern of types of crisis among a given adolescent group, that should be a "red flag" indicator to the minister that some larger social issue may be impacting all of them. Of course it could be personal peer pressure accounting for the universality of the crisis. For example, if a disproportionate number of teenagers are dealing with suicidal thoughts within a youth group, it could be that they have formed a suicide pact, or there could be social pressures generating a pervasive hopelessness in their society.

A fifth assessment principle involves understanding the faith issues and spiritual formation of the adolescent. Assessing the adolescent's religious history is more than looking at a litany of religious activities. Knowing faith development and spiritual formation processes enables the minister to assess the pilgrimage of each adolescent. Unresolved faith issues may precipitate a crisis. For example, a teenager may become angry at God because a sibling had an accident, and God is blamed for it. In anger at God, the teenager may begin acting out irresponsibly. (For further discussion of discussing faith issues with teens see *How to Talk with Teenagers* by G. Wade Rowatt.)

Assessing faith issues also involves looking at the stages of moral development. Many youth are doing the right things but for the wrong reasons. For example, they may be living within the boundaries of acceptable behavior only out of fear of being caught. These youth have not matured to the point of pursuing the right for the sake of love, of self, God, and others. Faith and moral development issues are an important part of assessment because of their impact on the youth's decision making process. Decisions concerning response to a particular crisis are often made out of insufficient faith development and immature moral development. (See James Fowler's *The Stages of Faith* for an expanded discussion.)

A final assessment principle involves assessing the family environment. Effective caregivers know how to assess the adequacy of a family structure and the health of family relationships. Ministers are uniquely able to offer such assessments because often they will have a relationship with the family as well as the youth. In most communities ministers still maintain the right of making home visits and on behalf of the adolescent can visit and make an assessment without infringing upon the rights of the family. Using a family genogram produces unusual insight into patterns of family behavior. (See J. C. Wynn for a discussion of the use of genograms in a religious context.)

As caregivers reflect on these assessment principles, they will uncover areas for further professional development. If, for example, one does not understand spiritual formation in adolescents or family dynamics or even developmental issues, further studies in those areas may be necessary.

Having looked at principles of awareness and assessment, we now turn our attention to some principles that inform our actions in the conversation with an adolescent in crisis. Certain behaviors on the part of the caregiver strengthen the relationship and increase the probability of successful resolution. One does not need to become a skilled psychotherapist in order to help teens in crisis. However, one needs to know when and how to refer troubled adolescents for depth counseling as needed. (See Howard Clinebell's *Basic Types of Pastoral Counseling* for specific guidelines in referral counseling.) Ministers need to develop a list of trusted referral resources. Who in your community can help teens? How do you get a youth into a program? Know your limits and know how to involve other professionals in working with your adolescents whose crises exceed these limits.

PRINCIPLES FOR CARING ACTIONS

Specific principles guide one's action while caring with adolescents during a crisis. These principles, like the principles of awareness and assessment, may vary with the context of the situation. Nevertheless, they provide a framework for reference.

Caregivers need to listen twice as much as they talk when assisting adolescents in crisis. Careful listening avoids interruptions, gives undivided attention, and frequently checks out the accuracy of understanding. The importance of listening to the adolescent's hidden message as well as the story line of the crisis cannot be overstated. Adolescents frequently do not know the issues underneath their story line. The hidden message is beyond their awareness frequently. Don't protect, but do offer insights for their consideration.

One teenager underscored the importance of this listening principle when asked to give three guidelines to adults who are helping teenagers. She said: "Listen, listen, and listen."

A second principle for action involves guiding the decision-making process during the crisis. When the crisis event is fresh and emotions are still raw, providing such guidance not only lowers anxiety but also increases the probability that another crisis will not be precipitated by unwise action. For example, one teenager driving recklessly to an emergency room to visit a parent who had been in an accident had an accident himself and was critically injured. Simple guidance or finding someone to drive the panic-stricken youth to the hospital could have perhaps have prevented further tragedy.

In guiding teenagers' decision-making, one must exercise caution not to be a shallow advice-giver. Guidance at its best draws out the issues and clarifies the alternatives, but leaves the decision-making as a responsibility for the youth. After decisions have been finalized, youth may need help in planning their implementation.

A third principle for action, being an advocate for the youth, might involve interfacing with other agencies or authority persons on the youth's behalf. Teenagers receive little respect when they confront legal, academic, or even economic systems. This might mean going to court with them or finding someone who can visit with them in the counselor's office at school or accompanying them to discuss the crisis with their parents. Youth need to feel you are present with them emotionally even when you are not physically present.

Youth feel powerless before the complexity of administrative and social systems. It is not that the systems always intend to manipulate youth, but youth may be inexperienced and unaware of how to utilize the system. A danger exists that being an advocate will open one up to being used by the youth. A high degree of self-awareness and reflection can minimize this danger for the caregiver.

A fourth principle, expressing and receiving honest emotions, permits the adolescent to ventilate negative, noxious feelings. By sharing one's own emotions, the caregiver models for the adolescent appropriate ways of emotional release. Providing a safe environment for ventilation reduces the probability of the teenager acting out dangerously at a later time.

A few caregivers err on the side of repressing the adolescent's "ranting and raving." While it is understandable that reducing anxiety and controlling the hysteria around a crisis can be important, one must also remember that adolescents need to express their feelings before thinking carefully through the alternatives. Feelings most likely needing to be ventilated will be anger, guilt, fear, disappointment, and grief. As these feelings are shared, biblical materials that parallel such emotions maybe helpful to the youth.

A final principle for action is to hold out realistic hope in the midst of the crisis. As religious caregivers, hope is grounded in our system of faith. Likewise, the adolescent's hope must grow realistically from his or her system of faith. Working within the adolescent's faith parameters is perhaps the only alternative. Teens cannot navigate life from a borrowed perspective on faith. Until they own a faith perspective they remain rather hopeless.

This principle of hope should not minimize the reality of danger but can focus on possibilities for the future. Frequently adolescents look only to the past and feel hopeless about themselves, their environment, and the future. Those who provide care for adolescents in crisis do well to refocus their attention on the future with an attitude of hope.

PRACTICAL CONSIDERATIONS IN CARING WITH YOUTH IN CRISIS

Ministers are ideal persons to respond to the needs of teens in trouble. While ministers may be overlooked by crisis trauma teams in some cases, they are uniquely equipped to deal with youth in times of crisis. *For one thing, ministers are the professionals most likely to be exposed to several generations of the family.* A minister will know and understand the parents and perhaps the grandparents and extended family in some cases. This unique viewpoint assists in diagnosing the reasons behind the crisis but also provides a unique vantage point when considering alternatives and follow up.

A second reason ministers are uniquely qualified involves their training in biblical and theological foundations. A time of crisis is a time of questioning one's foundational assumptions. Physicians, social workers, and secular counselors are ill-equipped by training to assist in reflecting upon life's basic assumptions. Because of the minister's understanding of theological, ethical, and philosophical concepts, she or he can play a unique role in turning the crisis from just another tragic event into an opportunity for growth, not only for the individual youth but also for the family system.

In the third place, crises often bring broken relationships. And ministers are agents of reconciliation. Due to the minister's awareness of the dynamics of love, sin, repentance, forgiveness, and reconciliation, he or she can respond at deeper levels when relationships are broken. As agents for justice and love, ministers model peacemaking and urge families to do the same.

A final reason for ministers' central role in crisis caregiving is their context for involvement. The church, as an ongoing community of faith, provides not only a spiritual but also emotional and sometimes physical sanctuary during the time of the crisis. Existing youth programs can be oases of security for adolescents recovering from a major crisis. Outreach programs are frequently used in preventive crisis education (such as a place to teach sex education, alcohol and drug education, and dating information). They can also be used for crisis intervention. For example, a youth group may be utilized to visit a hospitalized teenager.

GROUPS THAT CARE

Ministers can guide their congregation to provide ongoing groups that make a difference to teens in crisis. These groups may be informational, relational, or therapeutic. While no church would be expected to provide all of these services, any church can expand its program with appropriate resources.

Churches responding in the survey have indicated success in offering adolescent growth groups where eight or ten adolescents meet and discuss relevant issues as they are raised. These groups function on a non-specific agenda that might include such topics as understanding today's music, what makes parents act like they do, how to get a date, how to stop smoking, or is Jesus like the Easter Bunny and Santa Claus.

"Parents of teenagers" support groups have been successful in a number of churches. These groups usually meet for an hour on Sunday with a variety of activities. Some discuss books, other share personal incidents, a few have gone through self-guided parenting courses such as *Systematic Training for Effective Parenting or Parenting by Grace.*

Churches can provide space for existing groups. Numerous churches offer a place for Alcoholics Anonymous, for Alateen, or for Narcotics Anonymous meetings within their facilities. Other self-help groups might include Survivors of Suicide, Compassionate Friends, or a specialized group coping with any type of illness or accident.

PRACTICAL REFLECTIONS

A number of pragmatic issues were sent to this author by ministers who care for adolescents. Perhaps the most frequently mentioned issue is the necessity to have adequate referral resources available before the crisis. One minister built a referral file when she moved into a new community. She would visit and call the agencies in her community until she had confidence that she knew where to refer persons for a variety of crises. She had cases for referral that involved employment, medical care, counseling, and educational guidance. She had even made contact with the local juvenile justice system.

"Include the family as a part of the caregiving" was a recurrent suggestion from pastors. While full time youth ministers more likely focused on the adolescent, pastors saw the need to work with the family as well as the teen. A crisis with an adolescent obviously reverberates throughout the home. While a few pastors seem to neglect the teen and to focus only on the family, most strive for some balance between caring for the family and caring for the youth.

Bad thinking leads to dangerous action. Thinking errors and errors of judgment not only precipitate crises but worsen crises when they go unconfronted. Ministers who care for teenagers will need to help them not "make a mountain out of a molehill" or only see the dark side of the storm clouds. Furthermore, one does well to expose adolescents to the reality that they are not the only persons in crisis. Perhaps it will be necessary to confront their egocentric negative questioning. Some teens will ask, "Why does everything happen to me?" In reality, it doesn't. Care must be exercised not to build a wall between oneself and the teenager as one confronts these errors in thinking.

THE MINISTERIAL BLACK BAG

When physicians made home visits, they carried their medical instruments and a limited supply of medication in a black bag. That black bag served as their unique professional identity. Physicians in electronic, modern medical facilities no longer carry a black bag. Similarly, many ministers have lost their professional black bag by trusting exclusively their training in behavioral science when responding to a crisis. Ministers do well to remember the unique power of Scripture, prayer, and the community of faith in responding to adolescents in crisis.

Scriptures can be used most effectively with adolescents in crisis when the adolescents are well informed concerning the Scripture. Reminding such a teen of scriptural support can strengthen their faith, hope, and love in the time of crisis. However, scriptural stories can be read or perhaps retold in a modern setting in ways that provide strength and support for teens unaware of the Bible. Storytelling can convey scriptural truths, hold the teen's interest, and provide a rapport between the caregiver and the youth. Perhaps when the crisis is most intense, the Scripture will do little more than inform the approach of the minister and set a context for ministerial identity. However, especially in times of reflecting upon the alternatives available before the team and in times of reflecting upon what was learned from crisis, Scriptures play an important role.

Prayer with teens in crisis requires sensitivity. While ritualistic prayer will mean something to youth whose past has been enriched by such experience, youth who are unaccustomed to ritualistic prayers may be turned off, embarrassed or confused or even frightened. In praying with teens in crisis, one does well to ask permission of the teen, reflect the teen's concerns and anxieties in the prayer, and lift up appropriate areas for hope. If a teen feels uncomfortable and requests that the minister not pray, the minister can at least assure the teen that he or she will pray for them in their private time of meditation. Sometimes during this assurance, one can even be specific about the focus of the prayer. For example, one could say something like, "I want you to know I will be praying for you to be able to get a good night's rest, for you to find strength in yourself to face this difficult situation, and for doors to open for getting out of this situation."

The church as a community of faith is perhaps the most undertapped resource for facing crisis. We know that when burdens are shared, they diminish in intensity. A caring congregation provides a rich resource for dispersing the pain during a crisis. Persons can still exercise the ministry of presence by simply being with crisis victims. The church can provide individuals to stay with the family, to visit regularly, or perhaps even to open up their own homes for a period of time to members healing from the crisis.

CONCLUSION

This essay has attempted to guide the reader's reflection on participating in crisis issues with teens as it underscored principles of caring with adolescents and offered practical approaches to such care. The issues facing teens in crisis are indeed complex. But we need not despair or abdicate our responsibility of caring only to non-ministerial resources. Ministers are an important part of the crisis team in caring for youth, their families, and their friends in times of trouble. The reader will undoubtedly have rich insights to add to the perspectives offered in these pages.

ENDNOTES

1. For further information concerning cognitive distortions in adolescents, see David Burns, *Feeling Good: The New Mood Therapy*.

2. Again, see David Burns, *Feeling Good: The New Mood Therapy* for a full discussion of cognitive distortions and approaches to confronting these distortions.

WORKS CITED

Aleshire, Daniel O. *Understanding Today's Youth.* Broadman Press: Nashville TN: 1982.

Clinebell, Howard M., Jr. *Basic Types of Pastoral Care and Counseling: Resource for the Minister of Healing and Growth.* Rev. & enl. ed. Nashville TN: Abingdon Press, 1984.

Elkind, David. *All Grown Up and No Place to Go: Teenagers in Crisis.* Reading MA: Addison-Wesley Publishing Co., 1984.

Fowler, James W. *The Stages of Faith: The Psychology of Human Development and the Quest for Meaning.* New York: Harper and Row, 1981.

Ross, Richard and G. Wade Rowatt, Jr. *Ministry with Youth and Their Parents.* Nashville TN: Convention Press, 1986.

Rowatt, G. Wade, Jr. *Pastoral Care with Adolescents in Crisis.* Louisville: Westminster/John Knox Press, 1989.

Wynn, J. C. *Family Therapy in Pastoral Ministry.* San Francisco: Harper and Row, 1982.

RESOURCE BIBLIOGRAPHY: PASTORAL CARE

Arnold, William V. *Introduction to Pastoral Care.* Philadelphia: Westminster Press, 1982.

Augsburger, David W. *Pastoral Counseling Across Cultures.* Philadelphia: Westminster Press, 1986.

Clinebell, Howard M., Jr. *Basic Types of Pastoral Care and Counseling: Resource for the Minister of Healing and Growth.* Rev. & enl. ed. Nashville TN: Abingdon Press, 1984.

Egan, Gerard. *The Skilled Helper.* Monterey CA: Brooks/Cole, 1975.

Elkind, David. *All Grown Up and No Place to Go: Teenagers in Crisis.* Reading MA: Addison-Wesley Publishing Co., 1984.

Lester, Andrew D. *Pastoral Care with Children in Crisis.* Philadelphia: Westminster Press, 1985.

Olson, Keith. *Counseling Teenagers.* Loveland CO: Group Books, 1984.

Parsons, Richard D. *Adolescents in Turmoil, Parents Under Stress: A Pastoral Ministry Primer.* New York: Paulist Press, 1987.

Ross, Richard, and G. Wade Rowatt, Jr. *Ministry with Youth and Their Parents.* Nashville TN: Convention Press, 1986.

Rowatt, G. Wade. *Pastoral Care with Adolescents in Crisis.* Louisville: Westminster/John Knox Press, 1989.

Van Ornum, William, and John B. Mordock. *Crisis Counseling with Children and Adolescents*. Revised Edition. New York: Continuum, 1991.

Van Pelt, Rich. *Intensive Care — Helping Teenagers in Crisis*. Grand Rapids MI: Zondervan, 1988.

Wicks, Robert, and Richard Parsons, and Donald Capps eds. *Clinical Handbook of Pastoral Counseling*. New York: Paulist Press, 1985.

ACCESS GUIDES TO YOUTH MINISTRY

SPIRITUALITY

Edited by Sharon Reed

What is a spiritually challenging vision for youth? The contributors to this Access Guide provide a theological base to help readers answer this question. Thomas Hart, Joan Chittister, Thomas Groome and Kathleen Fischer, among others, offer foundational insights into adolescent spiritual life. Practical strategies regarding spirituality and education, justice, prayer, liturgy and spiritual direction are presented in the second part of this volume.

Paperback 210-2 $14.95

RETREATS

Edited by Reynolds R. Ekstrom

A complete resource for learning how to develop youth retreats: the nature and purposes of youth retreats, principles, guidelines, models and strategies for developing your own retreat. Everything from planning to follow-up.The best theory and practice for

- Confirmation coordinators
- retreat ministers
- DREs, campus ministers
- Search, TEC, COR teams

Paperback 152-1 $14.95

JUSTICE

Edited by Thomas Bright and John Roberto

An overview of the scriptural and theological foundations of justice, and the current global social situation. Part One offers biblical and ecclesial foundations of justice while Part Two develops essential principles for justice education, and action with youth. Part Three offers examples of doing social analysis, education and action programming with youth. Included: A resource guide to education, activities, and organizations.

Paperback 149-1 $14.95